Foreign Aid to the Gaza Strip between Trusteeship and De-development

Foreign Aid to the Gaza Strip between Trusteeship and De-development

Ahmed H. Tannira

A

ANTHEM PRESS

Anthem Press
An imprint of Wimbledon Publishing Company
www.anthempress.com

This edition first published in UK and USA 2022
by ANTHEM PRESS
75–76 Blackfriars Road, London SE1 8HA, UK
or PO Box 9779, London SW19 7ZG, UK
and
244 Madison Ave #116, New York, NY 10016, USA

First published in the UK and USA by Anthem Press in 2021

British Library Cataloguing-in-Publication Data
A catalogue record for this book is available from the British Library.

Library of Congress Control Number: 2020950327

ISBN-13: 978-1-83998-541-6 (Pbk)
ISBN-10: 1-83998-541-0 (Pbk)

This title is also available as an e-book.

I dedicate this book to my parents, my loving wife and my two wonderful children, Lama and Anas.

CONTENTS

ILLUSTRATIONS

Tables

Figures

Box

Map

ABBREVIATIONS

CSO	civil society organisation
EEAS	European External Action Services
EU	European Union
FDI	foreign direct investment
FIDA	Palestinian Democratic Union
FTA	free-trade agreement
GDP	gross domestic product
GNP	gross national product
GOI	government of Israel
HQ	headquarters
ICG	International Crisis Group
IDF	Israeli Defence Forces
INGO	international non-governmental organisation
JICA	Japan International Cooperation Agency
MOF	Palestinian Ministry of Finance
NGO	non-governmental organisation
NPA	new policy agenda
OCHA	United Nations Office for the Coordination of Humanitarian Affairs
oPt	occupied Palestinian territories
PA	Palestinian Authority
PCBS	Palestinian Central Bureau of Statistic
PECDAR	Palestinian Economic Council for Development and Reconstruction
PFLP	Palestinian Front for the Liberation of Palestine
PLC	Palestinian Legislative Council
PLO	Palestinian Liberation Organisation
PNGO	Palestinian non-governmental organisation
QSE	Quartet Special Envoy
UN	United Nations
UNCCP	United Nations Conciliation Commission for Palestine

UNCTAD	United Nations Conference on Trade and Development
UNDP	United National Development Programme
UNGA	United Nations General Assembly
UNRWA	United Nations Relief and Work Agency
USAID	United States Agency for International development
VAT	value-added tax
WB	West Bank
WFP	World Food Programme
WTO	World Trade Organization

Chapter 1

INTRODUCTION

> When foreign aid to Palestinians is analysed from a neo-colonial perspective, it may not be failing at all. With an increasingly subdued Palestinian population in the WB[1] governed by a pliant PA,[2] Gaza locked up and surrounded by an impenetrable blockade, and Palestinians in Jerusalem being squeezed out, aid may actually be a great success. (Wildeman and Tartir, 2013: 5)

Foreign aid is acknowledged as a tool to assist progress in developing countries, yet in the Palestinian case, instead of enhancing the standard and quality of life, promoting democracy and political reform, and assisting Palestinians to build their state institutions, foreign aid is argued by some to have aggravated these aspects (le More, 2005). Discussions in this book will investigate whether and how the political promotion of certain areas has created social-economic and political imbalances within society in Gaza. It also examines how these imbalances might hinder the opportunity for *marginalised groups* from advancing economically and, in many cases, how these groups might deteriorate.

As is the case in other communities, social division has always existed among Palestinians. Yet, in the context of Palestine, and Gaza in particular, these social divisions have been heavily influenced by several political events starting from the *Nakbeh*[3] in 1948, to the Six-Day War in 1967[4] to the post-Oslo era (post-1993). Palestinians were divided along lines drawn by various national and international institutions that provided economic support. Social divisions among Palestinians can be seen in the classifications of Palestinians as refugees and non-refugees, locals (*mowatineen*) and returnees (*aydeen*), and metropolitans (*mutamadenin*) and peasants (*fellahin*) (Peretz, 1977). These classifications have extended themselves from merely being an external

---

[1] West Bank.
[2] Palestinian Authority.
[3] Palestinians' dismissal from their original land in 1948 upon the establishment of the State of Israel.
[4] Israel's occupation of the WB and the Gaza Strip.

perception to mapping the population, to one where Palestinians began to self-identify into, and place themselves within, these different groups. We will look at the context within which these divisions have emerged and will investigate whether foreign aid represents an additional factor that has exacerbated de-development by widening these socio-economic divisions. We will also look at how aid has mobilised Palestinians politically and economically, and whether and how these forms of mobilisation have influenced the current Palestinian social reality. Moreover, the book will enquire whether foreign aid agencies demonstrated duality in their aid policies (Schumacher, 1989) in dealing with different sectors of Palestinians. In this context, this book will investigate the nature of this duality. It will suggest that inclusion and exclusion can exist in the use of a developmental aid agenda that focuses on higher status and income groups and a humanitarian agenda for lower income groups and marginalised areas. Accordingly, we will investigate whether this duality has promoted certain groups at the expense of others and has thus furthered and facilitated social fragmentation.

The book will investigate the extent to which aid to Palestinians has been influenced by the political context within which aid is delivered. While looking at the extent to which donors' aid policies have been influenced by the Israeli-Palestinian conflict, especially in relation to conditions tied to aid, the book will try to unpick how concepts of 'need' and 'eligibility' have been redefined in accordance with the securitisation and politicisation of aid. The securitisation and politicisation are seen in the complex vetting procedures that aid agencies use to determine the pool of their aid beneficiaries (Zanotti, 2013) by assessing beneficiaries on the basis of their political and ideological affiliation rather than their actual need. To do this, the book will analyse the different aid policies, aid eligibility criteria and conditions formulated by donors and aid agencies. This analysis will be guided by focusing on development as the imposition of governmentality (seen in the way beneficiary populations or groups become subject to various development agendas set by an individual donor or a group of donors) and how this governmentality in return extends power over local communities through aid agencies (Duffield, 2007, 2001). The analysis will show how governmentality, as Foucault (in Rabinow, 1984: 28) suggests, is 'affected through an entire series of interventions and regulatory control' and how this governmentality entails a power of discourse that mobilises subjects and makes them act accordingly.

1.1 Development Trusteeship

Through examining foreign aid within the framework of development, this book aims to enquire whether aid in the context of Palestine has established

what Michael Cowen and Robert Shenton (1996) call *trusteeship*. They argue
that trusteeship is a form of power that is enjoyed by the developer over the
objects (people) it intends to develop. In their view, aid agencies use development assistance as a fundamental instrument to facilitate their imposition of
control and governance through drawing a particular image of these objects
that later makes the act of intervention necessary (1996: 19–20). Trusteeship
also represents the power to include or exclude, especially when aid agencies
impose certain conditions or use specific criteria on the basis of political or
social background rather than economic need. Consequently, a large number
of people find themselves excluded (ibid.: 23–24). This, as a result, facilitates
the creation of what Mark Duffield (2007: 8) calls *surplus population* whose skills,
status and overall existence are 'in excess of prevailing condition and requirement'. Duffield argues that this type of trusteeship is also a dual power. Not
only does it work to include or exclude but it is also a form of power that
'aims to change behaviour and social organization according to a curriculum
decided elsewhere' (ibid.: 7). To this end, the book attempts to study the role of
aid agencies and donors in the distribution and redistribution of power within
society in Gaza.

1.2 Political Dynamics of Aid to Palestinians

The 1991 Oslo talks acknowledged that large-scale international aid would
be required to facilitate the peace process between Palestinians and Israelis
(Lasensky, 2005). Yet donors believed that it was necessary for aid to be tied
to the achievement of three important objectives: (1) supporting the establishment of a Palestinian state through the peace process, (2) endorsing economic
development in the Palestinian territories and (3) developing Palestinian civil
institutions (le More, 2008). Donors believed these interrelated methods of
aid assistance may enhance the prospects for peace (Brynen, 2005). First,
economic development was suggested so as to generate tangible benefits (i.e.
rising incomes and improved services). Second, external aid could act as a
reward for political actors (i.e. Israel and the PA), altering their incentive structure and increasing the attractiveness of cooperative behaviour. Alternatively,
withholding aid can be used to punish parties that abstain from cooperation.
Third, external resources can influence local pro-peace actors (i.e. to redirect
them to strengthen their political positions through local patronage politics,
including NGOs and civil society organizations (CSOs)) (ibid.: 129–30).

When discussing the establishment of a Palestinian state, according to
Nigel Roberts (2005), Western donors have become a third party in the Israeli-
Palestinian conflict. Donors felt the need to establish a structure that would
equally encourage and discipline the two parties and build trust between them.

Aid to Palestinians served not only Palestinians but also Israel. Palestinians needed a financial resource that could enable them to sustain the PA institutions and economy (Roberts, 2005: 18), and a stable PA was necessary to ensure Israel's security. Consequently, a major burden the PA has had to bear is that it had to operate as a guard for Israel. This policing role was seen by many Palestinians as a questionable compromise, especially political parties who opposed the Oslo Accords.

Toufic Haddad suggests that this policing role as a dynamic that has surrounded aid delivery has made Palestinian development to 'remain fundamentally determined by its vertical linkages' with Israel and Zionism, on the one hand, and international donors community, on the other. This has meant that horizontal linkages with the already fragmented parts (i.e. the public and private sectors, security establishment or civil society which is comprised mainly by leftist political parties) could not be forged. Instead, all of these would begin to be 'enfolded in this politics of vertical dependency and the liberal machination it entailed'. Accordingly, the PA would operate as 'subcontractor' to the responsibilities that Israel, as an occupying power, should bear (security and civil functions alike). These functions, according to Haddad, tend to be 'politically, ideologically, and economically costly to Israel and Zionism more broadly, and none of which were enough to fulfil Palestinian rights to expectations' (Haddad, 2016: 145).

Additionally, it encouraged donors to endure a Palestinian system that has featured 'certain opaque elements that could operate beneath any radar screen of public accountability' (Roberts, 2005: 18–19). Western donors had to turn a blind eye to democratic and human rights violations; for instance, political arrests that were based, and forbidding any criticism of the peace process, especially in the local newspapers and TV channels. Such conduct by the PA demonstrated that if there were to be conditions of any opposition to peace with Israel that needed to be co-opted, then Fatah would need to have the ability to buy the necessary support of its own party members or leaders and members of other parties. Consequently, this has led to an unprecedented and growing level of neo-patrimonial use of resources seen in the random employment of Fatah party members within the PA institutions and the disbursement of financial rewards and bonuses to maintain support to Fatah. This kind of behaviour was believed to be impossible without sufficient funds from international donors (le More, 2005: 985) and the lack of opposition of such neo-patrimonial use of donors' funds by donors themselves.

Meanwhile, the economic reality of the WB and the Gaza Strip was primarily shaped by the policy limitation of the Oslo Accords and later by the Paris Protocol[5]

---

[5] Signed in 1994, the protocol was part of the Oslo Accords, and it sets out the economic relations between the PA and Israel. The protocol established what became a *Customs Union*

that followed. Both agreements constituted a framework within which the Palestinian economic activities and economic external relations were defined. It was the vision of the Paris Protocol to create the environment necessary for the Palestinian economy to develop a basis for liberalising trade between the two parties, increasing the investment within the Palestinian public and private sectors and easing the flow of Palestinian labour in the Israeli market (Arnon and Weinblatt, 2001; Kessler, 1999). However, the application of both agreements had witnessed (1) the continuation of Israeli military law during the interim period,[6] (2) Israeli control over Palestinian key factors of production (i.e. land, labour, capital), and (3) control of Palestinian areas and external borders (Roy, 1999: 68–70). These factors constituted a cornerstone to a systemised de-development process (Roy, 2007). Shortly after each agreement, Israel began to promote among the international community that the Palestinians were not politically and economically autonomous; thus, it had the right to treat them as such when it feels that its security is jeopardised. Regardless of how much Paris Protocol was designed to satisfy Israel's economic interests and to maintain economic control over the Palestinians, the tightened closure policy[7] (as a response to the PA's failure in addressing Israel's security needs) has replaced the economic cooperation formalised in the Paris Protocol. Israel continuously imposed further restrictions on the mobility of Palestinians between the Palestinian districts, on the one hand, and has gradually banned Palestinians from accessing the Israeli labour market, on the other.

According to B'Tselem (2012), an Israeli human rights organisation, the economic relations between the two sides were based on extreme inequality in power as the PA had little room to manoeuvre due to continuing pressure from donors and the fear of further sanctions by Israel. Meanwhile, the closure policy has had drastic socio-economic effects and has hindered any progress towards achieving any form of development since 1995. In this context, donors' abstention from imposing any diplomatic pressure against Israel to stop its closure policy is believed to have encouraged it to maintain the status

---

that meant no economic borders were to exist between the two geographical territories. Consequently, the Palestinian economy was completely integrated and dependent on the Israeli economy.

[6] The interim period was supposed to be five years after the establishment of the PA in 1993, after which an independent Palestinian state was to be established.

[7] Israel has imposed various forms of mobility restrictions on the Palestinians living in the occupied Palestinian territories (oPt), and these include mobility restrictions between the WB and the Gaza Strip, within the WB/Gaza towns and villages and between the oPt and Israel. To allow such mobility, Palestinians need special permits to travel to Israel or other Palestinian districts.

quo and continue with a systematic process of de-developing Palestinians (Tartir, 2012: 4).

The case for civil society institutions was not much better. The Palestinian CSOs before Oslo were mainly dependent on funds from the Palestinian Liberations Organisation (PLO).[8] They acted as social movements that mobilised popular resistance against occupations, and hence worked under various development agendas (i.e. human rights groups and women rights groups). However, their role as grassroots organisations was significantly undermined after the establishment of the PA as funds were channelled towards establishing PA state institutions (Challand, 2008). Accordingly, civil society institutions had to seek their own means of survival through funds from Western donors mostly (Murad, 2007). Funds from international donors were characterised as being politically motivated and in many occasions have served as a means of inclusion and exclusion of organisations on the basis of their political affiliation. Therefore, the Palestinian civil society had lost much of its depth and diversity. Their work agenda was severely influenced by donors' agendas rather than reflecting the needs of the local communities (Murad, 2007: 6). Civil society had to abide by and accept various types of conditions, where many of their beneficiaries became either sanctioned or excluded according to a criteria set ahead by donors and aid agencies (Challand, 2008: 160–62).

It is, therefore, obvious from the above that the period that followed Oslo has witnessed an unprecedented level of political and economic mobilisation of Palestinians by both donors and Israel as well as a geopolitical fragmentation that has intensified after the Second Intifada (le More, 2005). It is argued that Israel has taken advantage of the international support for the peace process and the need for its cooperation in delivering aid to Palestinians (Lasensky and Grace, 2009: 4). It therefore used aid to reinforce its control over Palestinians, on the one hand, and to maximize its territorial expansion over their lands, on the other. This process of gradual 'bantustanisation' has altered East Jerusalem, the WB and the Gaza Strip into completely fragmented areas (Lasensky and Grace, 2009: 4). What remains absent in the literature discussing aid is how both political and economic mobilisation, influenced by aid structures, have impacted the restructuring and reformation of the Gaza Strip's current social reality. The Gaza Strip in this context resembles a unique

---

[8] Founded in 1964 to act as the main representative of the Palestinian people locally and internationally. Its main manifesto is to liberate Palestine through armed struggle or negotiations. The PLO comprises several Palestinian factions, including leftist factions, such as the Population Front, the Democratic Front and FIDA. Islamic factions such as Hamas and Islamic Jehad are not under the umbrella of the PLO.

case due to the political developments that the territory witnessed after the disengagement plan and later after Hamas's victory in the second Palestinian parliamentary elections in 2006. The territory's relationship with donors had a significant shift that was influenced by first its governing structures and second by its classification as a hostile territory. Therefore, this book will investigate how both the disengagement plan and Hamas's coming to power have influenced the donors' relations with the Strip, both politically and economically. As mentioned earlier, it will examine how the people of Gaza were mobilised in line with these events politically, economically and thus socially.

1.3 Theoretical Underpinnings

The Oslo agreements can be seen to have accelerated socio-economic differentiation among Palestinians. Not only has it contributed to the creation of a PA, whose first existence and current survival is dependent on foreign aid, but this dependency has also extended to impact ordinary Palestinian people. According to Ayat Hamdan (2011), the PA was first organised according to a set of power relations that have determined its scope. Instead of working towards achieving national transformation, it has become an indirect agent of external powers' desires. Hamdan (2011: 16) suggests that the first elements of these power relations are seen in the Israeli occupation as colonisation projects that are associated with Western imperialist/capitalist history. In this sense, Israel is suggested to have become a new tool to maintain the West's power in the Arab region. The second element is represented in the international system that operates through a network of aid institutions (bilateral and/or multilateral) that work with both the Palestinians and the colonial power (i.e. Israel) (ibid.: 16–17). The role of these institutions is not restricted to aid provision, but extends to influencing the relationship between Israel and the Palestinians and influencing the internal politics of both, especially the latter (ibid.). Within these dynamics emerges a third element which is seen in the Palestinian power groups, namely Palestinian individuals working in aid agencies, local NGOs and private sectors, and politicians and academics, who either directly or indirectly have affiliation with particular Western donors or international aid agencies. The Palestinian space, according to Hamdan (2011: 17), has been influenced by 'internal and local interactions that are intertwined with international relations that have formulated it and determined its reproduction'. Space in this context refers to the Palestinians' socio-economic and economic realities.

In light of the above, it would appear that a wide network of local and international aid institutions assumed responsibility and representation of the Palestinians' needs instead of assisting them to represent their own needs. Aid in the Palestinian context would seem to have functioned in similar ways to what Duffield (2011) calls a 'moral trusteeship' over the lives of those who are in need (underdeveloped). It is an 'external educative tutelage over an otherwise superfluous and possibly dangerous population that needs help in adapting to the potential that progress brings' (Duffield, 2007: 10). A liberal network of development, of which foreign aid is an integral part, comes as a substitution for 'modernity, specifically for those who are labelled as under-developed'. For Duffield, a development trusteeship is a liberal framework of control that permits the 'powers of freedom' to be learned and safely applied (ibid.: 7). The book from the development–security nexus perspective, introduced by Duffield (2007), will look at the forms of control practiced by international aid agencies and the extent to which people have become sub-ject to the rule of an institutional sovereignty dominated by local development elites that are influenced by a Western aid agenda (Challand, 2008).

By linking development to security, Duffield (2007) challenges the trad-itional notion that security without development is questionable and vice versa. He suggests that development is not solely a way of enhancing other peoples' lives, but rather an instrument to govern them. The relationship between development and security is intrinsic to liberal regimes of develop-ment (Duffield, 2011). After the Second World War, Western aid began to be perceived as a powerful tool to influence people's socio-political behaviour as well as their allegiance. Although little aid was given until the 1960s, the motive behind this was security driven and the fear that global poverty would alienate labourers and peasants, and as a result expand the pool of converts to communism. In the Gaza context, aid is proposed to have been used to modulate the people's behaviour economically and thus influence their socio-political behaviour. Aid to Palestinians, especially in the post-Oslo era, has been conditioned to achieve progress in the peace process with Israel while mostly adopting Israel's views that see political parties, groups or individuals that pursue resistance against military occupation as supporting terrorism. The entire community on an individual and institutional level had to commit to these principles to be eligible to benefit from aid. Political parties have had to revise their agendas and constitutions, institutions are forced to work according to the development agenda of their donors and abandon their local agendas and individuals must have no political affiliation with parties that are simply categorised as 'terrorists' (Challand, 2008).

According to Hans Morgenthau (1962: 302), the majority of foreign aid is given in the nature of a bribe in the name of development. For Morgenthau, this transition of services and expertise is meant to function as a price paid for political services, either rendered or to be rendered in the future. This is a bribe for both governments and their nations. While humanitarian aid is perceived as non-political and is usually given for well-defined reasons, it can still have political functions depending on the context within which it operates. In the highly politicised context of Gaza, choosing between humanitarian and developmental aid has always been controversial among aid agencies. Choosing between one form of aid and another has required intensive reconsideration of the political atmosphere, especially in relation to target beneficiaries and the implementing partners. It is the power to decide who is to benefit from development programmes and who is not, whose life should be supported or left to seek its own survival. Making this decision entails a practice of sovereignty, sovereignty over the life of those whom aid is supposed to assist and/ or neglect. This form of power was first introduced by Michel Foucault (1976) as 'biopolitics'. This is the power exercised over people's life at a collective level. This form of power according to Mitchell Dean (1999: 100) works to vindicate the act of governing people in different areas of their life (education, health, family, etc.) through its knowledge of how to sustain or invalidate life. It is again what Foucault describes as the power to decide either 'to foster life or to disallow it' (ibid.: 138).

This form of power is also vivid in the link between modernisation and aid as a materialistic means of development. Ernst Schumacher (1989) suggests that state-led aid industry bypasses people in different ways through working or focusing on one category and neglecting other(s). What emerges from this approach is what Schumacher (1989: 136) calls a 'dual economy' which leads to a dual society with 'two different patterns of living as widely separated from each other as two different worlds' (ibid.: 137). Here it does not matter whether they are rich or poor, but rather what matters is how development through aid works to redistribute power and recreate power relations within societies. According to Morgenthau (1962), this redistribution of power occurs as a result of aid being mostly associated with certain political, economic or other interests. Aid agencies tend to build alliances with groups that best serve their interests, regardless of the negative impacts the exclusion of other groups may have on the relations between those benefiting from aid and those excluded (ibid.).

It is the social and political tension that arises as a result of this 'dual economy' where a very small category of people enjoy the fruits of modernisation and development, and the rest are bypassed. Consequently, this emerging modern sector continues to grow until it absorbs the majority of economic and political resources, while other social groups struggle to survive and maintain their own resources (Schumacher, 1989: 137). It is entirely a process of societal breakdown and class reformation in which the relationship between the different societal sectors is what Schumacher (1989: 139) describes as 'mutual poisoning'. This poisoning occurs as a result of the socio-economic imbalances caused by modernisation, whereby the empowered groups destroy the basic economic structures of the weaker groups. The book will apply the 'dual society' concept to investigate whether and how aid contributed to class reformation, either through working with an already existing elite social sector or by empowering and/or abandoning other social sectors.

This process of societal breakdown and class reformation contributes to the creation of what Duffield (2007) calls 'surplus life'. It is the category of life whose original existence is a result of development practices and for whom development claims to enhance this existence. It refers to the people who do not enjoy the characteristics of modernity in its materialistic meaning and whose existence is perceived as a threat to the modern world. To manage this threat, development works to establish a form of trusteeship over this popula- tion (Cowen and Shenton, 1996: 446). To Cowen and Shenton, this form of trusteeship reflects a colonial connotation and imperialism for how it imposes certain mechanisms of control and governance. This book will attempt to argue that aid in the Gaza context reflects a dual trusteeship: a development trusteeship (Cowen and Shenton, 1996: 23) and a social trusteeship (Challand, 2008). Development trusteeship is explicit in how foreign aid programmes are designed and implemented according to donors' agendas, and those are mostly influenced by political agendas that rather respect the interest of donors to a higher level than those of beneficiaries. The social trusteeship would seem to be partially associated with and influenced by the development trusteeship. It is how development agencies tend to empower certain social sectors (elites) through granting them leadership roles within development agencies, and in turn how these elites maintain their social status and influence the work of development agencies. Furthermore, it will look at how development produces an authoritarian relationship with the society it operates within (i.e. between developers and society or donors and Palestinians), and this is represented in this trusteeship. According to Cowen and Shenton (1996: 26–27), this authori- tarian relationship is seen in how it reconstructs and reforms an entire society in accordance with the notion that certain people or groups are unable, or for some reason not qualified, to make decisions on their own; hence, others should be entrusted with this task. These are the people who are willing to accept the rules and regulations imposed by development agencies and adapt to the lifestyle of industrial countries (Gronemeyer, 1992). Consequently, it is required of these people to have 'the ability to free one from the chains of its local culture and align every culture with a universal culture that is carefully organized and modelled on Western cultures' (Hamdan, 2011: 26).

Aid has become an integral tool for the development industry. Western countries and their associate aid agencies appear to have contributed to the creation of a control system. This control system attempts to alter the wider social context of the society they work in and the web of interactions and the pattern of rewards and sanctions in which social groups operate (Castel, 1991, quoted in Duffield, 2001: 209). In this context, Kothari (2005: 427) suggests that aid entails a form of 'cultural imperialism' that is based on the intervention of different types. This assumes that those who are intervening know best the needs of those that the intervention was carried out for. According to Kothari, the relationship between colonialism and development entails an engagement with ideas generated in the West but with a global reach. In this sense, the book will attempt to see how aid agencies seem to work with aid experts and aid consultants whose knowledge and experience seem to be influenced by a rather Western/foreign agenda than being influenced by the needs of the community.

1.4 Data Collection and Sources

The complexity that encounters authors in social sciences has always been to look into issues that have already received the attentions of other researchers. There has been a significant number of researches on aid to Palestinians and the role of civil society and foreign intervention in the local Palestinian politics. Yet, every time there is an overwhelming feeling that there is still a long way to go, and what has been achieved in this very dynamic case study represents only the tip of a massive iceberg.

The book is designed to look at the three main approaches through which foreign aid is delivered to Palestinians. These approaches also represent the two aid categories: developmental and humanitarian. First, the book will look at foreign aid to the PA either directly through budget support or indirectly through institutional capacity building for the PA's civil institutions and security forces (Chapter 4). Examining this type of aid is crucial to understanding the political dynamics that surrounded aid delivery to the PA; especially, direct foreign aid to the PA was a key element of achieving and maintaining peace between Israel and Palestine. Second, the book will look at aid delivered by or via CSOs in the Gaza Strip through funding from international donors. The significance of CSOs as a case study is found in the ways in which aid contributes to reshaping the role this sector plays in the post-Oslo era and whether it has been impacted by the political agenda of the post-Oslo foreign aid. Third, the book will look at humanitarian aid delivered by the United Nations Relief and Work Agency (UNRWA). The significance of this case study is demonstrated by the way humanitarian support implicitly mobilised Palestinian refugees economically, and socially, and how this could have contributed to creating socio-economic imbalances among the socio-economic sectors in the Gaza Strip.

Since aid providers are the key stakeholders in aid delivery, representatives of bilateral and multilateral aid agencies are the first element of this case study to collect a particular set of data. This includes international as well as local staff. The inclusion of the latter is very important to explore how Palestinian citizens working within aid agencies look at aid policies with regard to conditions on aid, the internal work dynamics of aid agencies, how policies are formulated with regard to aid beneficiaries and whether it can be inferred that there are hidden policies other than those announced.

Politicians and government officials from across the Palestinian political spectrum are also key to this case study, especially representatives of the Hamas and Fatah parties. This is important in order to see their views on how aid has contributed to widening political division and thus influencing factionalism and clientelism within the Palestinian society, particularly in Gaza.

Academics and consultants who have been involved in consultancy work with aid agencies. This group of respondents is unique due to the fact that although they are seen as an outsider for aid providers and aid delivery organisations, the nature of their connection and association with both and the level of information they possess make them perform the role of insiders.

The fourth group of informants include a purposive sample of aid beneficiaries linked to the aid agencies targeted in the first group. The purposive sample was selected in a way to ensure a broad coverage of a range of beneficiary samples. It is important to explore the views of these informants in order to see what impact aid has on their lives and to what extent they were mobilised both economically and socially by aid.

The adoption of the semi-structured interview technique was chosen as it not only provides the interviewee with the opportunity to expand on a given question, topic or issue (Peabody et al., 1990: 452), but also allows the author to sample the various experiences and knowledge possessed by different respondents in ways that are meaningful to them (Stephens, 2007: 205–6). There are significant differences among the three categories of respondents regarding the interviewing technique used (aid workers, politicians and academics/aid consultants). Hence, the semi-structured interviews would give the space to respondents from each category to bring their own agenda and discussed topics according to their own knowledge and professional background. Thus, it would allow them to introduce issues they perceive as central and worthy to be highlighted (Stephens, 2007: 206).

Accordingly, each category of interviewees listed above was treated in an individualized manner when conducting the interviews, since each group of informants will potentially provide a different set of data and knowledge about the different questions that the book is posing (Manheim, Rich and Willnat, 2001: 322). In order to reduce the complexity surrounding the investigated phenomena and the interdependence of issues associated with them, the author will utilise semi-structured interviews, which will take into consideration that data gathering and analysis are located in a sensitive social and political context (Vromen, 2010: 257). Since this will involve interviewing politicians as part of this process, the elite interviewing technique will be utilised in this specific context.

1.5 Author's Positionality and Interaction with Participants

Doing fieldwork presented several dilemmas, especially if considering what Sultana (2007: 377) referred to as a 'problematic distinction' between what constitutes a 'field' versus 'home'. Home (Gaza) is where I was born and bred, and I am familiar with the historical and existing socio-economic settings that are at the core of the discussions of this book. For instance, the I come from a Palestinian refugee background, my parents grew in refugee camps and I was told stories about life in the camps and the socio-economic conditions that this particular social group had experienced over the years. Of importance here is my prior knowledge of the socio-economic advancement of the refugee community over different time periods and the familiarity with the political processes that surrounded most of these periods.

There were also further dilemmas represented in the issue being researched (i.e. foreign aid and aid agencies), which I felt very connected to and familiar with its settings due to my 11-years-plus experience working with aid agencies and international non-profit organisations in the WB and the Gaza Strip. This dilemma presented insider–outsider dynamics upon collecting data from different categories of respondents. First, I realised that I had the ability to obtain partial access to many of my target respondents, especially workers from aid agencies and those who are associated with them (i.e. academics and external consultants of aid agencies). Yet, what concerned me the most was being extra cautious to the relations and spaces that guided my data-collecting processes so that the knowledge and stories produced during these processes maintain their credibility.

Accordingly, respondents in this research placed me (as the author/ researcher) at different insider–outsider levels depending on the category of respondents they represented. For instance, I was seen as an insider to the aid worker category given my professional background and my pre-existing knowledge of the work dynamics of this sector. This, as a result, was an advantage in that it made the participants perceive me as an insider and thus open up to me. They assumed that what they offered in terms of the information and knowledge they possess was something I knew or was familiar with. Hence, participants in this category shared this knowledge in depth and detail in many instances while eliminating fear for doing so.

The case with the academics and aid agencies' consultants was somehow similar, again due to the nature of the topic researched. However, I felt it could be wrong to assume that I was an insider when dealing with this category of respondents as this would result in undermining the knowledge and experiences respondents would share. Especially, I was conscious of the differences and the professional hierarchies of some of the respondents I interviewed, especially acknowledging the scope of their experience and their access to data and knowledge. This was more obvious when I dealt with aid consultants who significantly had close ties with particular aid agencies, donors or government institutions (i.e. the US and EU donors). Distancing myself from what this category of respondents represented in terms of knowledge and area of expertise helped me undertake an in-depth investigation of issues that related to the subject of this book, thus eliminating possible subjectivities that are associated with my familiarity with the issues discussed.

Meanwhile, there was a clear hierarchy when the author interviewed politicians and government officials. The author was conscious of the way different politicians viewed me, both as a former employee of international aid organisations and as a researcher at an overseas academic institution. The way they viewed me depended to some extent on their political affiliation and representation. On some occasions, they felt I represented the 'other' in that I was different from a given political opponent but also I did not share a political ideology or identity that was similar to that of the participant. Hence, as the author, I had to emphasise and prioritise my academic identity and affiliation over my former professional affiliation in order to eliminate precautions or reservations that participants from this group maintained towards aid agencies and thus express their views and opinions as freely as possible.

Finally, the author preferred to adopt an outsider's position from this research given the multiple levels of insider–outsider dynamics discussed above. According to Lozano-Neira and Marchbank (2016), when examining outsider–within positionalities, our identities might continue to influence the topics discussed; however, this influence will be guided by the power relations between the author (investigator) and his/her participants (subjects being investigated). Hence, the author preferred to abstain from reflecting on my personal professional experience as an aid worker during the interaction with my participants or through providing personal reflection during the data analysis process.

1.6 Overview of the Book

This book is divided into seven chapters. Following the introduction, Chapter 2 begins by examining development within the context of modernity and enlightenment and how development creates a dichotomous relationship between Western developers and non-Western underdeveloped. The chapter argues this dichotomy mainly exists due to the fact that the history of development reflects a neocolonial power, hegemony and counter-hegemony (Pieterse, 2010). This chapter looks at how development suggests it can be pursued only through material advancement and capital investment, which cannot be attained without urbanisation and industrialisation. Consequently, those who are deemed underdeveloped have no choice but to seek help from the developed, who have both the knowledge and the capital (Escobar, 1997; Esteva, 1992). It raises attention towards the imbalanced power relationship between the North and the South, and shows how images of *underdeveloped* people are constructed through discourses of development. These discourses later become integral in influencing and shaping the social reality of societies. From this point, the chapter discusses how development is considered as a tool for social design and control. It discusses how the discourses generated by development agencies and developed states alike about the underdeveloped gave space for the mapping of the world's social life.

Chapter 3 introduces the idea of Gaza's de-development and control in its historical context before the Oslo Accords (1993). The first part of this chapter aims to analyse the context that the book intends to focus on. To understand why Gaza is context specific, the chapter will give an overview of the Gaza geo-strategic location through locating the district on the map historically and politically. The chapter will briefly go over major historical and political events starting from the establishment of the state of Israel, through the Israeli occupation of the district in 1967, the Oslo peace process, the disengagement plan in 2005 and Hamas rule of Gaza in 2006. It will look at how these major political events impacted the demographic and social development of the district. It will look through the different political and economic systems that the district has had across more than six decades. The second part will provide a historical overview of aid delivery to Palestinians and to Gaza in particular. It will look at the types and dynamics of aid to Gaza and the background of aid institutions that are working in the Gaza Strip. It will then move to examine how aid institutions gradually penetrated the economic and political life of Gazan society and the extent to which this involvement has impacted the overall social space. In other words, it will examine the why(s) and how(s) behind aid given to Palestinians in Gaza, with more focus on the politics of conditions tied to this aid.

Chapter 4 begins by empirically exploring the reshaping of Palestinian's political, economic and social spaces. It does so through examining the impact of the Israeli-Palestinian conflict on foreign aid delivery to the PA (thus, the Palestinian people) following the Oslo peace agreement (1993) and the extent to which the Israeli-Palestinian conflict influenced the securitisation and politicisation of this aid delivery. The chapter employs and develops the 'partner for peace' framework to understand how the Palestinian polity has been divided, especially through looking at how the Palestinian political, social and economic elite has been reconstructed and reshaped according to the workings of this framework. It also examines the structural underpinnings of Palestinian's division and the role of foreign aid in fostering these divisions. While the focus of this book is primarily directed towards Gaza, it is difficult to discuss such divisions without examining the forms and the dynamics of division that also exist among Palestinians. The chapter looks at aspects of the PA's efforts in setting up economic infrastructures that led to socio-economic injustice among Palestinians and the impact of the aid-dependent PA on ordinary Palestinians' economic sovereignty.

Chapter 5 focuses on the aspect of post-Oslo foreign aid delivered via and/or to CSOs in the Gaza Strip. It examines the ways the post-Oslo aid for peace dynamics influenced the role CSOs currently play, while drawing on their traditional role of supporting national resistance and resilience during the First Intifada and before. It looks at the ways the securitisation and politicisation of aid influenced the socio-economic promotion of these organisations as well as the social sectors they serve. Following a brief historical overview of the work of CSOs that demonstrates the development of this sector, the chapter expands on the 'globalised elite' concept through examining the characteristics of the Palestinian elite that represents CSO workers and the ways they became influenced by an international agenda than a national one that caters to needy individuals. It also looks at the relationship between these CSO elites, the emerging political elites that represent the PA and international donors, and the ways these relationships contributed to furthering different forms of control on the daily living of Palestinians living in the Gaza Strip.

Chapter 6 explores additional aspects of control and de-development which can be demonstrated in the current dynamics of humanitarian and relief operations. The chapter takes UNRWA as a principal case study as the organisation serves more than 70 per cent of Gaza's overall population (i.e. the refugee population). It analyses how humanitarian concepts and practices have been influenced by the political and economic environment that followed the establishment of the PA. The chapter seeks to see the influence of the failing peace process on transforming the role of UNRWA into making the scope of its activities rather contracted. The chapter analyses the type of operational changes the organisation has undergone as a result of the ever-deteriorating economic and political conditions in the Gaza Strip and the financial dilemma the organisation has faced post the Oslo Accords (1993). The chapter seeks to create a link between the failing peace process and the increased role of UNRWA on the daily living of refugees in Gaza. Against this background, the chapter examines the ways refugee sovereignty has been impacted as a result of donors' intervention in the work of UNRWA. By this we mean that as the population becomes more and more constrained, the safety net UNRWA provides becomes more and more critical to the survival of the Palestinians who depend on it.

Finally, Chapter 7 concludes by re-engaging with the discussions surrounding foreign aid to Palestinians and how the different players, agenda and methods of delivery have contributed to reshaping the socio-economic and political land-scape. It will also reflect on the relevance of the literature reviewed in discussing development aid to the Gaza Strip and in what ways this book could look to knowledge, especially when discussing the issue of the production and control over surplus people.

Chapter 2

PROBLEMATISING DEVELOPMENT

2.1 Introduction

This chapter provides an analytical framework for this book by offering a radical perspective on development (of which foreign aid is a key instrument) and how it turned into a tool to place the world's populations into 'developed' and 'underdeveloped' categories. The framework builds on this categorisation to show that development practices became a justification to intervene in the lives of those underdeveloped and a tool to impose mechanisms of control. The chapter focuses on the key issues underlying the development problematic: the relationship between development and modernisation, how 'development' and 'underdevelopment' have emerged as social designs that are determined by economic growth and industrialisation as materialistic indicators and finally how development has become a tool for the creation and control of 'surplus people'. Before these issues are discussed, the chapter explores how 'development' as a concept has emerged and how it has meanings, interpretations and procedures that have developed over time. The chapter will also explore how the different meanings and procedures have affected how development has been perceived by those who implement it as well as those who are supposed to benefit from it.

Through examining development as a new industry that has emerged since the Second World War, particularly through associating it with modernisation, the chapter argues that development is, as an issue, highly political in character. It has established a new form of division, a new world order that is based on scientific and economic advantages (Truman, 1949). Peoples and nations are looked at and judged in accordance with the living style they maintain and the economic powers they enjoy. The chapter will illustrate how this new world order, 'developed' and 'underdeveloped', has deliberately ignored the colonial legacies that have contributed to shaping the current resources, institutions and political settings of the so-called underdeveloped societies. This divide between 'developed' and 'underdeveloped' has also contributed to forming new power relations that are based on superiority (Willis, 2011), the superiority of the 'developer' who enjoys power that exists in both money and knowledge. Furthermore, it will be argued in the chapter that 'development' has paved the way to the emergence of a modern rather than a traditional hegemony, one that is intellectual and ideological. An illustration of this is the creation of the 'modern state idea' (Shanin, 1997) and how development offers a bureaucratic rationality of managing and controlling people.

The chapter will next discuss how 'development' has been associated with modern imperialism, as Gustavo Esteva (1992) suggests that the economisation of development has become a refined image of traditional colonisation. Development, as will be argued, has established new economic structures, meanings and procedures and has worked to bring under these structures all other social interactions among and within its target societies. The discussion will extend from linking concepts of 'modern state' and 'economic society'. The economic values embedded in the idea of 'development' in its economic growth meaning will suggest that social existence is devalued. This will be shown in how society's components (i.e. people, resources, traditions, skills) are dealt with as commodities. In this context, the chapter will explain how development has evolved from a form of trusteeship performed by the wealthy and the capitalist elite (Cowen and Shenton, 1996). The concept of trusteeship will be operationalised and applied in the entire book, especially when discussing how aid agencies, and NGOs in particular, act as trustees for the societies they work within and how development policies and programmes are influenced by this concept. From a postmodernist perspective, the chapter will look at how the 'developed' and 'underdeveloped' discourses are generated by those claiming power as 'trustees'. In doing so, the latter is portrayed as backward and barbaric. Hence, it becomes necessary and important for the developed to take steps forward to deal with this backwardness and extend a control technique under the assumption that underdevelopment is a threat to both the developed and the underdeveloped (Duffield, 2007).

The last section of the chapter is dedicated to discussing how development has become a tool for the creation of surplus people (Duffield, 2007) and wasted lives (Bauman, 2004). Extending from the social engineering of development, it will be argued that development intervention itself is a power design in the sense that it works under the assumption that it has a solution to the socio-economic problems within the underdeveloped worlds. This power design creates its own terminology to describe people, imagine its own solutions and strategies, and build relations and alliances. Consequently, it extends the mechanisms of control and governance. As will be shown, integral to this power design is the ability to create new social sectors, to separate and isolate others through the use of 'development' as a universal scale against which people, nations, states and cultures are weighed. A result of this is the emergence of 'surplus' or 'waste' people whose existence can be a threat to 'developed' life/people. Accordingly, development as a liberal problematic of security (Duffield, 2007) exerts its powers on the lives of people under the assumption of securing their biological and social interests. The social divide and the creation of 'surplus people' will be very important to illustrate how development has emerged as a regulatory control technique and how development agencies through choosing to work with certain social sectors could contribute to social reformatting (i.e. promoting certain social groups or de-promoting others).

2.2 Different Developments, Different Definitions

Development is a highly contested concept, in terms of both different meanings and interpretations it has carried over time. The present development term dates from the post–Second World War era of modern development thinking. Although the term 'development' was not necessarily in use, its practices have reflected antecedents of development policy over different eras (Pieterse, 2010: 5). Pieterse states that the latecomers to industrialisation in Central and Eastern Europe had to face basic development questions upon the Cold War with regard to the relationship between agriculture and industry. These countries were caught in two competing development strategies which were offered by Western development economics and the central planning offered mainly by the Soviet Union. Development in this context meant basically how these latecomers could catch up with industrialised countries.

Another meaning of development in the nineteenth century was uncovered by Michael Cowen and Robert Shenton (1996). Through linking development as a concept that refers to modernisation and industrialisation, they argue that development emerged to offer remedies for the shortcomings of progress, for example, poverty, environmental issues, job loss and other socio-economic maladies. Accordingly, developers felt that they had the power to invoke a form of trusteeship that aims at managing the colonial economies with a view of serving the interest of the underdeveloped population. According to Cowen and Shenton (1996: 4), in the nineteenth century, those who considered themselves to be developed undertook a trusteeship to determine a form of development for those whom they thought of as underdeveloped.

Additionally, Cowen and Shenton (1996: x–xi) argue that development emerged and prolonged as a doctrine and a practice that targets the underdeveloped populations as the opposite of developed is underdeveloped. In other words, development clearly embodies a trusteeship in the sense that it claims a responsibility over and for the dangerous populations that are in need to cope with the progress that development brings about; otherwise these surplus populations could pose a risk to the rest who are enjoying the fruits of development.

A core meaning of modern development is linked with economic growth as introduced by Walt Rostow in the 1960s. According to Rostow, the road to Western development in its capitalist form takes various stages; of importance in this context is the creation of a mass consumption society. The prerequisites to this creation included agricultural and industrial infrastructures along-side political modernisation and nation building (cited in Hettne, 1995). Meanwhile, dependency theory within development and in accordance with capital accumulation and economic growth suggested that the economic advancement of certain countries will certainly contribute to the advance-ment of others. Yet according to Ferraro (2008: 60–62), the relationship between dominant (developed) and dependent (underdeveloped) states is dynamic; thus, interactions between them tend to reinforce and intensify unequal relationships. Consequently, dominant states will continue to progress at the expense of dependent ones.

Different from the economic growth and material accumulation meaning of development, alternative development or 'other development' offered a new understanding of development in the 1990s, with more focus on human development and capacity building. Amartya Sen, a pioneer proponent of this view, suggested that the core meaning of development should be limited only to focusing on enabling people and enlarging their choices (Sen, 1999). Sen's belief was that in order to enlarge the peoples' choice and enhance their opportunities to progress economically and socially, there is a need to enhance their skills and knowledge. By that, Sen neglected factors of economic growth that usually expanded the scope of people's choices.

The neoliberal view of development in the 1980s was slightly different in the sense that the major focus was on the liberalisation of markets and prices. From the neoliberal perspective, development is seen to be hindered by governments' intervention in both market and prices; hence market deregu-lation and privatisation is seen to be essential in order to achieve economic growth. Accordingly, development agencies should shift their efforts from state development to market development. Post-development in the 1980s and the 1990s, on the other hand, suggests authoritarian engineering and a means of social control over the majority of populations in underdeveloped states (Pieterse, 2010: 7). It therefore reflects an anti-development perspective in terms of goals but not in terms of means. For post-development scholars, such as Teodor Shanin, Arturo Escobar, James Ferguson, Gustavo Esteva and others within this school of thought, development has failed and the entire development/underdevelopment discourse has been generated by colonial powers. While much of the debate within various corners of 'development' thinking is important, this research will focus on views offered by some from the post-development perspective, as well as those of Mark Duffield and Zygmunt Bauman, as they are more relevant to the arguments presented in this research. It is useful in the sense that it supports how development has emerged as a colonial inheritance, especially after the Second World War, and how the whole idea of underdeveloped states is constructed by colonial powers and according to a very material definition of development. Furthermore, the colonialist feature, embedded in development according to post-development thinking, is seen in how knowledge about people and cultures is produced by foreign experts. Accordingly, strategies and policies are designed without respecting and recognising the cultural and social differences of various contexts.

In explaining the idea of development, Teodor Shanin (1997: 65) suggests that development as a secular idea has provided a 'powerful pervasive supra-theory' that has brought every aspect of human life to its own interpretation. Shanin states that all societies are generally advancing on the scales of economic growth, politics, science and knowledge. Therefore, when speaking of development, we propose a gradual shift from a primitive lifestyle towards a more advanced one which benefits both individuals and societies. The intention beyond this is to make the whole development idea an 'ethical promise'. As indicated above, although development is loaded with various meanings, it has succeeded in establishing its own terms of reference. It has associated itself with terms like 'Industrial Revolution' and 'urban development'. It has given historical colonial legacies 'metaphysical meanings – an image of the unilinear and the necessary which was also universally right and positive in the unfolding of human history' (Shanin, 1997: 68). Accordingly, development has established a new knowledge of the world's societies (i.e. 'developed' or 'underdeveloped').

The production of development knowledge echoes a neocolonial division of labour. This is because development theories are believed to be generated in the North, while data and raw data for development activities are generally produced in the South (Pieterse, 2010: 4). Accordingly, developed societies are 'supposed to be the mirror and guide for less-developed societies' (ibid.: 4). For Pieterse (2010: 4–5), although a foremost critic of the post-development perspective, this production of knowledge has reflected a form of Western ideological hegemony, especially when looking at how each of the two Cold War rivalries, with their extremely different economic and political systems, capitalism and communism, tended to introduce their own development ideology as the most efficient and superior. Both ideologies reflected a 'top-down ethnocentric and technocratic' approach that looked at people and cultures as homogenous and can be evaluated on the scale of progress.

Accordingly, the post-development critique suggests that development is not a cultural process but rather a technical intervention that works to deliver 'badly needed goods to target population', under the justification of people's interest (Escobar, 1997: 90).

Sachs argues that development has become 'an amoeba-like concept, shapeless but ineradicable. Its contours are so blurred that it denotes nothing – while it spreads everywhere because it connotes the best of intentions' (Sachs, 1992: 4). This content-less concept continues to attract the attention of world leaders and experts, regardless of their ideological orientations. Meanwhile, development possesses the function of intervening in the name of the common good where 'right and left, elites and grassroots' fight their battle under the same banner (ibid.: 4); its intervention reflects a certain form of power. It is a form of power that those who have money tend to impose on those who do not. In other words, being rich does not mean having the power to control weather but rather to control peoples' lives through wealth (Lummis, 1992: 45–47).

Additionally, development has established itself as an apparatus that reflects a universal mission to eradicate poverty, enhance living standards and promote liberal/modern values, such as democracy and good governance, as values associated with the developed world. It is basically presented as a collective ambition that both the developed and the underdeveloped aim to achieve. James Ferguson (1994: xiv) argues that development values are presented in such a way that it has become difficult to question them. Suggesting development as a 'dominant problematic' does not mean everyone holds the same thought about it. It is therefore important to examine whether our 'ideal worlds', as suggested by governments and development agencies, reflect the same reality of what we know about them. In pursuing development activities, they tend to serve an interest other than those whom development seeks to benefit (Chambers, 1983, quoted in Ferguson, 1994: 13), accordingly putting the first last.

It can be understood from the above that development as a concept has varying meanings and interpretations supported by various approaches towards achieving it. Based on the enhancement of living standards meaning of development, the next section will discuss development in terms of modernisation and how societies and people are classified and viewed according to this understanding.

2.3 Modernisation and Development

For Ferguson (1994: 15), development as a concept refers to two different yet interrelated areas. It is used to explain the process that underpins the society's transformation towards a modern capitalist economy. To achieve this transformation, it is mandatory to enjoy the characteristics of industrial econ-omies and capitalist development and to possess the necessary forces of produc-tion. On the other hand, from the 1970s onwards, development has referred more or less to living standards and quality of life. Moreover, the implication of the concept of 'development' has referred to a social programme at the global level, equating development with 'modernisation' and linking it with poverty eradication (ibid.: 15–16). In this context, Bauman (2004) argues that the modern condition has required one to be on the move since the modern mind is born of the idea that the world should change constantly, the ever-lasting desire to remodel itself from its existing presence into something better. He views modernisation as 'a history of designing and a museum/graveyard of designs tried, used up, rejected and abandoned in the on-going war of con-quest and/or attrition waged against nature' (Bauman, 2004: 23). Thus, the perennial choice has become to either modernise or abandon existence.

Development, in the sense of modernisation, offers an intrinsic yet divided relationship between what is traditional and what is modern. This dichotomy can always be applied to the relationship between Western and non-Western society (Pieterse, 2010). Frank (1969, quoted in Pieterse, 2010: 22) suggests that the path to economic development and cultural change refers exclusively to the history of developed countries and neglects that of the underdeveloped ones. In this sense, it can be said that modernity describes specific economic and social structures that are based on Western experiences. The creation of these structures can be seen as facilitating the socio-economic divide that is later applied to the social formation of non-Western societies.

Sachs (1992) argues that this divide from a development perspective can be illustrated in how development has smashed the old way and brought people to 'deadlock' where

> the peasant who is dependent on buying seeds, yet finds no cash to do so; the mother who benefits neither from the care of her fellow women in the community nor from the assistance of a hospital; the clerk who had made it to the city, but is now laid off as a result of cost-cutting measure [...] shunned by the advanced sector and cut off from the old ways, they are expatriates in their own country; they are forced to get by in the no-man's-land between tradition and modernity. (Sachs, 1992: 3)

Accordingly, development has launched a new form of superiority and a new world order not only at the state/local level but rather at the international level. Harry Truman's (ex-president of the United States) speech in 1949 illustrates how states are categorised as developed and undeveloped according to 'sci-entific advances and industrial progress' (Truman, 1949). Development for

Truman was a new programme to embark upon for peoples' lives to advance from their 'primitive and stagnant' economic life that is perceived as threat to them as well as those who are prosperous.

Shanin (1997: 68) argues that the idea of development in the way it was presented by Truman is characterised by arrogance, due to the fact that it established that the Western development ideology was the highest measure achievement of progress. The West believed they could decide for humanity the type of future and lifestyle, following a development path that all nations should follow. Subsequently, the original idea of development has worked to reorganise societies on the scale of modernity as perceived by the West (Shanin, 1997). The Western developer, previously known as the coloniser, felt the urgency to reorder and make more sense of the world's societies and for them to be acceptable to the Western world. Kate Manzo (1991) suggests that the power of domination that is at the core of the idea of development not only threatens the indigenous societies and their authentic knowledge and lifestyle, but also works to re-inscribe these with the most violent aspects embedded in some of the development practices. In this context, Jonathan Crush (2006: 19–20) argues that development does not only seek to transform societies from primitive lifestyles to modern ones, but rather reconstructs their identity through modifying everyday practices and beliefs.

Pieterse (2010) suggests that reading theories of development is similar to reading a history of intellectual and political hegemony. He explains this hegemony is seen in how development as a practice translates contemporary relations of power; it is how knowledge and power are intertwined since both are two sides of the same coin (ibid.: 10–19). This means that those who claim they possess the knowledge for development are those who claim the power to exercise it. Therefore, Pieterse (2010: 19) thinks that 'developmentalism' is the truth from the point of view of those at the centre of power; it is 'the theorisation of its own path of development'. According to this belief, some scholars see the need to discuss development in the context of colonialism. Katie Willis (2011) argues that 'development' as a liberal value contradicts with the traditional political control of nations and land through permanent or long-term settlement by other foreign states. Instead, it poses a political control that is represented in the global power differential that is associated with dominance in different fields, such as politics, economy and social spheres. Willis suggests three reasons for situating 'development' as a colonial practice. First, Europe had created more linkages with various parts of the world in the middle of the sixteenth century. A result of European colonialism was the creation of ties and bonds with various regions and cultures. These interactions have influenced how development theories have emerged and developed over time. It is how colonisers perceived certain cultures and ways of living as backward or primitive and how they tried to enforce change through imposing certain Western values and ways of living under the name of development (Willis, 2011: 19).

The second reason for considering development as a colonial legacy is the power relations embedded in the colonial process (Willis, 2011: 19). Willis argues that the spread of Western economic and socio-political dominance over various parts of the world has illustrated the level of power enjoyed by these colonisers. In this context, development theories help to explain power inequalities between the colonisers and the colonised, in regard to differential development experiences and how colonialism brought advantageous developmental benefits to the colonising countries in the North at the expense of nations in the South. Therefore, it is argued that the autonomy of countries in the South, to plan and determine their own futures, continues to be jeopardised by the inequalities that have been created by what has come to be known as neocolonialism represented in the development agenda (Willis, 2011: 19–20). Thirdly, colonial practices differed from one continent to another, depending on the colonial power and the nature of social, economic and political systems the colonised society had. Yet what is historically obvious is that colonialism had somehow succeeded in influencing these structures from within, changing the norms in many places, and these changes continued into the post-independence period (Willis, 2011: 19–21). It is argued, therefore, that the purpose of development as a modern project is to aid capital exploitation in target countries by re-incorporating them in a world system created by historical colonisers (Ferguson, 1994: 11).

From the above context, Crush (2006: 11) argues that an essential element of development is to normalise the performance of the 'modern state' as an ultimate goal. It is an effort to make and remake both governable subjects as fundamental points of difference between modern and pre-modern states. This process of mobilising towards a modern state requires the acquirement of new skills and the adoption of new ideas about the nature of the modern world and human relations. Therefore, it entails abandoning traditional values and adopting new ones, and preferences for the deep dimension of the modernisation process requires a fundamental change in the direction to which human energies can be properly directed (Lummis, 1992: 45).

The idea of modern state creation became, accordingly, an energising mechanism for development policy as it involved modernisation theory, development strategy and economic growth. The idea as suggested by Shanin (1997: 68–69) was threefold: a general orientation device, a powerful tool of mobilisation and an ideology. Consequently, it has motivated the commitment and readiness of its admirers 'who were often prepared to sacrifice much, often life itself, to help speed up the inevitable approach of the necessary and glorious future' of the modern state they claim. For Shanin (1997) the 'modern state' is presented as the most materialistic representation and instrument of the idea of development. This is clear in the legitimation of the modern state as the 'representation of the nation', the bureaucratic rationality of how humans are to be managed and the strategies embedded in the idea of progress that are linked to the power to disburse privileges and impose new norms. This, in turn, has generated a struggle for power between different interest groups for control over the state structures and its resources, and the enforcement of certain ideologies and policies. Hence, development has become 'the main ideological raison d'être for statehood, the governability of the people and the enforcement of privileges' (ibid.: 69). Development as a modern concept was to become an ideology of disenfranchisement whose blueprints now offer unlimited space for more repressive bureaucracies at the national and international levels. The idea of development reaches an unusual level of impact through negation when it acts on behalf of science to present 'objective matters which are essentially political, thereby, taking choice away from those influenced most by such decisions' (Shanin, 1997: 70).

Another aspect that illustrates the relationship between 'development' and modernisation, especially with regard to the modern state as an important illustration of development, is that it relies on an 'endogenous approach' that adopts 'an individualistic perspective on development and social change' (Greig et al. 2007: 6). This modern state is assessed as a self-contained entity, and in order for the state to be described as modern, it has to submit to and follow the development rules that will later contribute to reconstructing its political and economic realities. As a result, Greig et al. (2007) argue that this structural perspective creates massive global inequalities that are inherent in the characteristics of development. They pose important questions as to whether the powerful actors of development maintain their dominance by undermining the non-modern/underdeveloped and whether the growth of poor countries is basically obstructed because of the strength of these powerful states. This produces a paradox whereby modernity is existent in the relation between these interconnected matters.

2.4 Economic Growth or Social Differentiation

Urbanisation and industrialisation have become necessary and inevitable routes to pursue the new modernised world. Yet those can only be pursued through material advancement represented in financial and technological infrastructure and through capital investment as the most essential elements of economic growth that lead to development (Escobar, 1997: 86). Escobar believes that the general norm has become one that makes it mandatory that poor countries secure sufficient capital that provides them with the necessary tools for development in order to follow the desired development path. The reason for this is that the important factor that influenced the formulation of the development theory was capital and other important factors associated with it, such as 'technology, population, resources, monetary, fiscal policies, industrialisation, agricultural development, commerce and trade' (ibid.). Further, cultural, education, art and other modern values are also important in this regard.

Further to this, Esteva (1992) suggests that the idea of 'developed countries' is based on a materialistic definition. It is substantiated by material possessions and how these possessions play a role that qualifies the person or the group in maintaining a certain lifestyle. Looking back again at Truman's speech, it is obvious that according to him underdevelopment is associated with poverty and backwardness, meanwhile ignoring the real factors of this backwardness and the past lootings of colonization that involved massive capital exploitation. Esteva (1992) contends that the possibility to interpret the emphasis of post-Truman developers, on the concept of economic growth, was a mistake; instead, it is a true presentation of what he truly meant. When Truman said 'no more of the old imperialism', he indirectly imagined a new form of imperialism where economisation of development was synonymous with the old colonisation. Yet he carefully managed to delink the economic sphere from the negative legacies that were associated with colonisation. This theoretical economic structure attempts to bring under it all aspects of social interaction in its target societies. Development within this frame, as a core component of this political design, appears as peaceful evolution while the reality is a mirror image of the same.

The association of development with the politics of economic growth suggests that the creation of economic society is a 'story of violence and destruction often adopting a genocidal character' (Esteva, 1992: 18). The construction of economic values that are associated with development in its economic growth meaning, development suggests that all forms of social existence are to be devalued. This devaluing means transmogrifying 'skills into lacks, commons into resources, men and women into commodified labour, tradition into burden and wisdom into burden' (ibid.: 18). As a result, these commodified labourers who represent ordinary citizens, who basically depend on the market to survive, are not the invention of the economist in a defined time but rather a historical gradual creation. This was an ongoing process of redesigning the man through the modern economic project (ibid.: 16–18). Yet the most sensitive issue that Esteva raises here is that this modern economic project did not aim to specifically forge a new pattern of human behaviour by creating the rules of the modern market. Rather, it helped by 'founding disciplines that were able to codify their observation in a form that fitted well with the ambition of emerging interest: they offered a scientific foundation to the political design of the new dominant class' (ibid.: 18). Consequently, development specialists were influenced by quantitative figures emerging from, and produced by, this complex system. Escobar (1997: 90) illustrates this idea by explaining the dynamics through which the discourse about capital accumulation was articulated. For example, the promotion of cash crops is used to generate foreign exchange rather than to secure food crops. Meanwhile, agricultural development is dependent on the use of advanced machinery and chemical substance rather than on an alternative agricultural system, ignoring any ecological considerations. Finally, the vast economic growth was at the expense of the small internal market that satisfies the needs of the great majority of people (ibid.).

According to the material definition of growth, the chronic problem underdeveloped countries face is that they are trapped in poverty. Without the assistance of developed countries, they will not be able to escape from this trap. Accordingly, through this material definition of growth, underdeveloped countries are portrayed by developed countries in a way that makes them accessible for intervention, although it is argued that development intervention, on many occasions, lacks connection to the actual economic realities of target countries (Ferguson, 1997: 227), which in turn makes these countries and their populations appear as a homogenous, indistinguishable mass (individual labourers or officials). This perception undermines the actual roots of poverty and relates it to individual behaviours, values and performances. As a result, the solution for the poverty problem can be addressed by simply changing these individuals' performances by influencing them to change into something else.

Another meaning of capital accumulation is discussed by Cowen and Shenton (1995). They argue that the main obstacles for achieving development is property ownership (different forms of property), and the solution for this disorder is to grant trusteeship to those who have the ability to benefit from this capital as a benefit for the entire society. The idea of trusteeship goes back to the first half of the nineteenth century and was first proposed by the French political movement known as Saint-Simonianism. According to Saint-Simon, evil could be overcome through placing this property in the hands of 'trustees' who are entrusted according to their ability to decide on behalf of the entire society about how its resources should be invested. Saint-Simonians thought that only banks could perform the act of trusteeship and governance through controlling production instruments and labour; hence they would make the necessary reforms to bring about development to the entire society (Cowen and Shenton, 1995: 36).

Taking economic growth as a point of departure to discuss a wider perspective for development, there is then a need to explore its impact on social transformation within societies. Going back to discussing development within the context of modernisation, Pieterse (2010) contends that modernisation is initially a project of social engineering from above and an operation of political containment. Aram Ziai (2011) states that development has two origins: first, the nineteenth-century evolutionism, which anticipated that social change occurs as a universal pattern and through different historical phases, and second, social technology, which according to Cowen and Shenton (1996) is designed to reconcile the problems created by the industrial capitalism. The second origin is what was discussed earlier in that social intervention is carried out according to expert knowledge which is thought to be owned by a group of privileged people who can act as trustees, similar to how Saint-Simonians thought about the role of banks, who can work for the common good. Ziai argues that both origins are also found in twentieth-century development theory, which itself is an illustration of 'on-going self-propelled process of social change' (Cooper and Packard, 1997, quoted in Ziai, 2011: 3). Ziai argues, therefore, that an essential part of this social change is the emergence of the idea of the 'Third World', or the underdeveloped countries, for one of the general purposes of development is to give the economic activity a real purpose for the lives of those who are deemed less developed.

In exploring how social change/engineering is embedded in the idea of development, Ziai (2011: 3–4) emphasises the importance of discussing a number of assumptions within development theory. In this context he refers to four major assumptions. First is the existential assumption that development is a conceptual frame that enables us to associate social, economic and political phenomena to a single process of development, to one organising process, and thus to interpret these phenomena as manifestations of 'development' and/ or 'underdevelopment'. Second is the normative assumption that 'development' is of such high value in itself and is a characteristic of a good society; hence, all societies should seek to attain this status. It is a process of making good change, which means society can be good only through achieving this change; hence, it is the basis upon which societies are judged. Third is the practical assumption, which suggests that development is achievable and is possible to be realised globally. Both the normative and practical assumptions constitute the overall development framework under which development institutions and governments work. Fourth is the methodological assumption, which constitutes that development is a universal measurement tool through which states or societies' development status is scaled and accordingly defined as either 'developed' or 'underdeveloped'. Ziai (2011), drawing on these assumptions, argues that since industrialisation and economic growth are core elements to achieve development, countries of the South cannot attain this status without the necessary intervention by the countries of the North. Yet to legitimise this intervention, expert knowledge on how to achieve development needs to be utilised.

Willis (2011) argues that it is a mistake to assume that the process through which the 'developed countries' became as such can be reproduced by other countries while having totally different socio-economic and political environments. Accordingly, nations and people should not be portrayed as homogenous entities that can follow the same route to development. As a result, a deconstruction process follows. The influential postmodern thinker Edward Said illustrates how the West has deconstructed the people of the East as being backward and uncivilised, for the simple fact they do not possess the same qualities as people of the West (Said, 1979). In *Orientalism*, Said indicates the way ideas and images about people are constructed by particular people at particular times, reflecting variations in power relations. Furthermore, he suggests that the construction of them (East) and us (West),apart from giving the former a particular identity, only reflects that the identity of the West is superior and of a higher status. In line with this, Jonathan Crush sees this construction of the Third World:

> As a set of ideas about the way the world works and should be ordered, understood, and governed, development should also be glimpsed if not as the creation of the Third World, then certainly as reflecting the responses, reactions and resistance of the people who are its object. Without the possibility of reaction and resistance, there is no place for the agents and victims of development to exert their explicit and implicit influence on the ways in which it is constructed, thought, planned and implemented. (Crush, 2006: 6)

This emerging discourse of the 'them' and 'us' of development creates a global dichotomy (Duffield, 2005). This dichotomy is embodied in the public and private network of development agencies and its ability to transform societies as a whole, based on opposing characteristics emerging from development discourse. It highlights the chaos and barbarity of the underdeveloped world, which encourages the developed world to take action to create regulatory techniques of control. These techniques of control aim to modulate the behaviour of the populations through controlling processes rather than disciplining individuals, Duffield suggests. Moreover, it alters the wider social context and the reward and sanction system in which the society operates. Within this control system, he argues that groups and states are presented as masses of different capacities and choices that can be fostered or discouraged by the power of development to influence and modulate the systems within which they operate (Duffield, 2005).

The discussion about the 'them' and 'us' dichotomy, and its role in social engineering and transformation, takes us to another aspect of the debate concerning how development generates its own form of discourse. This discourse creates a structure that affects and expands the bureaucratic state power (Ferguson, 1994: xiv). Ferguson suggests that through this discourse, a country's economic and social realities are portrayed as lying within the control of a neutral, unitary and effective national government, which in turn become almost immediately responsive to the blueprints generated as part of these discourses. These underdeveloped states in this context are seen as imperial instruments for exploring development plans, and those operations within the state structures perform as tools to implement social engineering and economic growth (Ferguson, 1997: 224). Furthermore, Escobar (1997) argues that the discourse of development created a space where only certain things could be said or imagined. It is the articulation of power and a space for the systematic creation of concepts, theories and practices. Yet what emerges from the creation of these concepts is what Zygmunt Bauman (2004) calls 'waste'. The discourse of development is a symbol of the knowledge factory that decides which client is good and which is a waste. It is a vision of these prospective clients, of their needs and desires, that decides who should be sent to the disposal sites (Bauman, 2004: 18)

What is decided to be a genuine development matter depends on the specific relations emerging in the middle of the development discourse. In other words, it is the relationship between what development experts say and what the international political atmosphere sees as reasonable; it is the relation between two or more forms or segments of power. In this sense it is understood that development fosters a way of perceiving social life as a technical problem or an issue to be resolved or managed by those experts or development professionals whose specialised knowledge qualifies them to undertake the task (Escobar, 1997: 90). Here, again, emerges the main purpose of development discourse: to emphasise the reason why the world should be amended (Crush, 2006: 6).

What the expert does here is to continually define and categorise problems to formulate the intervention process that resolves them (Kothari, 2005). The use of these 'technical assistance experts' is central to most development interventions. Kothari (2005: 427) states that these experts are 'taken up by prevailing ideological orthodoxies contemporaneously and ideas about professionalism, for example, have been absorbed by neo-liberal thought and operationalised in development practice'. Furthermore, by privileging certain groups of individuals and particular forms of knowledge, they articulate

a 'Eurocentrism' that is highly gendered and racialised (ibid.). In this context, Mehmet (1999: 10) describes 'Eurocentricity' as a 'European-centred
worldview' in which

> the interest or advantage of Europeans and their descendants is pursued
> at the expense of others, while justifying this worldview by paradigms or
> ethical norms that proclaim universal benefits for all. It is closely linked
> to racist theories, a subject of extensive study by social and cultural
> anthropology. (ibid.: 11)

2.5 A Design for 'Surplus People' Creation and Control

The social engineering of development extends further beyond its ability
to influence people's perception and behaviour. It extends to function as an
organising and conceptual frame and as a design (Ziai, 2011; Bauman, 2004).
Ziai (2011) suggests that it has become an organising frame because it links
diverse socio-economic phenomena to a single process. Development as a concept, according to Michael Foucault (1972: 22), allows 'to group a succession
of dispersed events, to link them to one and the same organising principle,
to subject them to the exemplary power of life [...] to discover, already at
work in each beginning, a principle of coherence and the outline of a future
unity'. According to this concept, development as associated with growth and
progress allows those enjoying power to connect random knowledge, data,
people and events and associate them with a unifying design (Pulu, 2013). It
is a design because it shows people and societies as a reflection of modernity
(Bauman, 2004). An essential part of this organising design is the creation of
abnormalities where the reform and treatment of these abnormalities become
the ultimate goal as it constitutes the legitimate reason to install the separation
fence between the developed and the underdeveloped. Escobar (1997: 88)
argues that the approaches that could possibly have had an influence in terms
of easing material constraints became associated with a form of rationality of
power and control.

  This type of discourse has given space for the mapping of the world's social
life and contributed to the creation of socio-political trusteeship over life. This
kind of mapping has also created space for thoughts (a new design for the
world); the expansion of these thoughts was deeply influenced by the same
rules introduced by the formative stages of modernisation (Escobar, 1997: 88).
Consequently, the world has been placed under a single standard of value,
according to which those who do not fit its standards are to be judged with
the most damning judgement (Lummis, 1992). Lummis argues that people of
the world have had their own living styles and standards which were based

on their local standards of judgement, yet now 'all that is [devalued] by the Western modernizer as so much waste; all the treasure trove of diverse human cultures redefined as the wretched and pitiable condition of underdevelopment' (Lummis, 1992: 45). As a result of this standardisation of the 'European modernity' as a perfect model that should be followed in pursuit of achieving development, a long legacy of 'colonialism, genocide, and transatlantic slavery' becomes neglected as the product of the very same model, and the pioneers of this model (i.e. Europeans) succeeded to emerge as 'free and masterful subject, not only through their struggle for liberty, equality and fraternity in Europe, but also through the creation of colonial empire that clashed with potentially equivalent non-Western forms of imperialism to ensure the dominance of its development model' (Danewid, 2017: 1679–80).

In the design of power over people, Crush (2006: 7) argues that development is not a 'closed system of arrogant interventionism but rather an unproblematic set of instruments and justification for the application of strategic Western power and domination'. It assumes it has the solutions for the disruption of social order within postcolonial worlds. Therefore, it is power design, a power exercised over people that originates from the terminology it uses to describe people and extend to the strategies that it generates to control and govern these people (Crush, 2006).

Development and modernisation, equally, as power designs are thoroughly illustrated in Bauman's *Wasted Lives* (2004). Bauman explains how this design goes about creating social engineering, not only at the local or national level, but rather at the global level:

> The production of 'human waste', or more corrected wasted human (the 'excessive' and 'redundant', that is the population of those who either could not or were not wished to be recognized or allowed to stay), is an inevitable outcome of modernisation, and an inseparable accompaniment of modernity. (ibid.: 5)

Integral to this social engineering is its power to create, separate and isolate. The design first goes about creating what Bauman calls 'redundant population'; then it separates this waste from the non-waste through its very use of terminology and discourse, and finally, it isolates the waste to keep its effects away:

> The disposal of human waste produced in the modernized and still 'modernizing' parts of the globe was the deepest meaning of colonization and imperialist conquests – both made possible and in fact inevitable, by the power differential continuously reproduced by the stark

inequality of 'development' [...] resulting in turn from the confinement of the modern fashion of life to a 'privileged' section of the planet. (ibid.: 6)

To better understand how waste is created, Bauman suggests that it is not the creation of waste that makes it so, but rather it is through highlighting the good product. Put slightly differently and in terms of 'discourses of modernity', those who do not fall under its rules find themselves separated and isolated; therefore, waste is created when all the superfluous, the needless and the useless are cut out, 'the beautiful, the harmonious, the pleasing, and the gratifying' become superior (Bauman, 2004: 21). Therefore, the 'waste' creation is deliberate, since those who become the 'redundant population' do not choose to be so; 'waste' is not an intrinsic or an original feature of objects. On the other hand, waste is produced when it is being assigned to waste through a human design, through which the act of separation becomes mandatory and important as it is instrumental to extracting the good from the bad and the superior from the inferior. Bauman argues that the action of waste design is never completed, so long as 'the waste is still around instead of having been swept away and deposited in a leak proof, distant location. The act of creation reaches its culmination, completion, and true fulfilment in the act of the separation and disposal of waste' (Bauman, 2004: 23).

Bauman (2004: 27) describes 'waste' referring to human waste as a 'dark, shameful secret of all production', symbolising development workers and modernity theorists as 'rubbish collectors' who happen to be the heroes of modernity who protect the good from the bad, the developed from the underdeveloped, and the modern from the non-modern. Through this, Bauman (2007) takes the debate into a completely different dimension other than the basic modern/non-modern viewpoint. These rubbish collectors have a type of security role, not in the exact manner of security as in military, but rather as modernisers, policy-makers and global social transformers of our time. Within this context, Bauman describes the processes the modernisers follow in their waste design and creation. First, developers draw the boundaries between the 'useful' and the 'waste', and, once these boundaries are drawn, they ensure proper services to 'stand guard on the line separating order from chaos' (Bauman, 2007: 28). Second, once both categories are identified, it becomes necessary that waste is cleaned for 'some human beings who do not fit into the designed form nor can be fitted into it' (ibid.: 30). Third, they create the laws and rules that make the exclusion and separation legal and permissible. Their laws are the modernisation blueprints that work to mark out those who are eligible from those who are not; they are the ones that bring 'lawlessness into being by drawing the line dividing the inside from the outside' (ibid.: 31). And finally comes the last process of all; the final produce is created or human waste is created.

Bauman's 'wasted lives' is also illustrated in Giorgio Agamben's (1998) 'bare life' as inspired by the Greek 'homo sacer' and what Mark Duffield (2007) used to illustrate the relationship between development and security in referring 'surplus life' creation. For Agamben (1998), the power embedded in modernity and development has given the privilege to some states or more precisely powerful developed states to classify order from chaos or developed life from a 'homo sacer' or a 'wasted life'. In modern politics, development becomes a power exercised over the life of human beings.

Central to Duffield's (2007) argument is the relationship between development and security, and what he means by security is not the usual meaning, but rather the liberal problematic of security with specific relations to human security. By the liberal problematic of security he means the people and all the processes that either promote or de-promote life, as he directly says: 'It is concerned with securing these biological and social processes in the name of people, right and freedom' (ibid.: 4). In this context, Duffield sees the important link between biopolitics and liberalism, on the one hand, with development, on the other, since both share the same interest, which is how to establish power of different forms over the life of human beings. Power in liberalism is embedded since it is a technology of governments that entails an explicit form of strategizing power. Meanwhile, liberalism differs from biopolitics although both contribute towards creating a distinction between developed and underdeveloped life, through acting on groups and communities in order to support and promote collective life (ibid.: 5). On the other hand, power biopolitics exists because it is a form of politics that entails the administration of the process of life across a population. This power is 'experienced as territorial or local illustrations of a particular global species-type, and when it comes to global surplus people, development constitutes those technologies and strategies' that are an 'essential expression of international bio-power' (Duffield, 2004). Drawing on Foucault's biopolitics, Duffield (2007) argues that biopolitics works to explain the problems emerging from governing people; these problems are spread and are socially, economically and politically interconnected. What liberalism does within this is to support freedom while governing people under these interconnected processes. And since the concepts of governance and freedom can sound a little paradoxical due to the power embedded in governance, Duffield argues that Foucault used biopolitics as a determinant of the classical liberal problematic of how much to govern.

Duffield also argues that both biopolitics and liberalism, as forms of power, are necessary conditions of development; regardless of the fact that they are different, they are still interconnected. They are harmonious, for if the 'biopolitics uncovers the dynamics of life at the level of population, and liberalisms seek to govern life through its freedom, then development provides a solution to the problem of governing too much or too little' (ibid.: 7). This form of power and governing is also discussed by Cower and Shenton (1996) in their concept of trusteeship. For them, trusteeship is a distinguishing and integral feature of the late twentieth-century development, yet this core doctrine of development has been widely rejected as a source of action towards development. The reason for this, they suggest, is simply that the original objectives of development in the postcolonial era are originated by those who are representatives neither of their own state nor of the Third World. Add to this, trusteeship is renounced because of the colonial connotations embedded in it and 'what implicitly reappears is the original mid-Nineteenth Century version of trusteeship untainted by imperialism' (ibid.: 446). Duffield suggests that the importance of development trusteeship to liberalism as an art of government is clear in its criticism of colonial violence. Yet trusteeship was able to tolerate the colonial legacy when 'the responsibility of trusteeship was deemed to be humanely, and hence effectively discharged'. Therefore, Duffield argues that a developmental trusteeship is a 'liberal framework of government that allows the powers of freedom to be learned and safely applied' (Duffield, 2007: 7).

Going back to understanding the creation of 'wasted lives' or 'surplus life', Duffield (2007: 9) suggests that according to developers, progress has brought socio-economic benefits and improved the lives of those targeted by development practices. However, this notion according to Duffield ignores that fact that the lives of many were ruined:

> Apart from the constant volatility from a liberal perspective the problem with capitalism was the disrupted and marginalized groups were more numerous than those from which capitalism could gain and, in so doing, improve. In other words, there was a problematic and transient 'surplus' population that required remedial attention, not only for themselves but for the stability of society as well. (Duffield 2007: 9).

Furthermore, Duffield suggests that surplus life or surplus population can be charged both politically and economically: 'the one superfluous to requirements, the other a threat to order' (Duffield, 2007: 13). Agamben (quoted in Duffield. 2007: 13) explains this by saying that these forms of exception move in and out of each other for this underdeveloped life, posing a great risk during times of emergency and trusteeship over it, which becomes necessary. The trusteeship, in this case, exists beyond morals and law. In other words, the underdeveloped life seen in and through 'bare life' becomes a devalued life, and killing it is permissible without murder being committed (ibid.: 13). Therefore, the idea of separation between developed and under-developed life, biopolitically, has been discussed as a power embedded in development that seeks to support life through intervening in the biological and social processes that constitute a human population. Brad Evans (2010) suggests that this division is crucial, not only because it offers a 'considered genealogy of the formative figures of political modernity' but rather for 'exposing the liberal will to rule'. Drawing on Duffield's 'new wars' or the 'unending modern wars', Evans suggests that these divisions created by the development project challenge the very principle of political empowerment embodied in this project:

> Understanding conflict has also moved its locus from wars between states to conflicts within and across them. Like sustainable development, households, communities and populations furnish the terrain on which such conflicts are fought. Within this continuation of total war by non-industrial means, both development and war take communities, liveli-hood systems and social networks as their point of reference. For the former they are sites of entry, protection and betterment; for the latter they are objects of attack and destruction. (Duffield, 2007, quoted in Evans, 2010: 420)

In discussing development within the human security nexus, particularly when examining the division it creates, development eventually enacts the human in biopolitical terms (de Larrinaga and Doucet, 2008). De Larrinaga and Doucet suggest that the concept of human security influences the current global governmentality existing in the development network. These forms of power invade the society as effective tools, and they assume to normalise the conduct of population. Within this context, the state and its network of agencies and institutions that enjoy this power diffuse and reach 'into the depth of social by invading a widening array of social field as a way of realising the goal of man-aging and governing the life of the population' (ibid.: 520).

Duffield further explains the reason for the importance of the separations of developed and underdeveloped biopolitically, from the viewpoint of modern development theory. He argues that this separation illustrates 'the gulf in life chances that separates insured and non-insured life' (Duffield, 2007: 18). What the insured and non-insured refer to here is the idea of self-reliance that basic-ally differentiates between developed and underdeveloped. It is the social wel-fare system and networks of socio-economic support the insured/developed life enjoys, especially during emergency context; the lack of it among the non-insured/underdeveloped is perceived as a form of security concern to the developed world:

The enlightened self-interest that connects the security of mass consumer society with bringing the world's non-insured life within an effective developmental trusteeship is based on improving the self-reliance of those involved. Since decolonization, the dangers of not doing this have regularly cast as increasing the risk of international disorder. (Duffield, 2007: 18–19).

Development in this context, as Duffield argues, is contrary to some ideas of modernisation that take material advancement, bridging the gap between the rich and the poor as its foundation. Rather, it is further concerned with establishing new forms of social structure that endorse conditions of self-reliance among the surplus population.

Furthermore, development is perceived as a liberal technology of security used to overcome the negative effects of underdeveloped people or surplus people through establishing a management system and network over this category. It is considered so because it abstains from extending the social protection it provides to the developed life to its underdeveloped counterpart (Duffield, 2007: 24). After the Second World War, establishing an effective developmental trusteeship over surplus people had become a pressing security priority for developed Western countries. Duffield explains this by saying that although decolonisation paved the road for extending technologies of development in the countries it used to rule, it is also constituted as a 'threat in terms of the new possibilities for global circulation that it made possible' (ibid.).

The main aim of this security paradigm in development is to work on modulating and changing the behaviour of surplus people from within them (Duffield, 2001). This paradigm, as Duffield argues, is not based on the accumulation of 'arms and external political alliance between states', but rather on creating a soft mechanism of penetrating societies and communities under the common good principle of bringing about development. This conceptualisation of development 'lies in the attempt fostered by sentiments that we are now all the same, to instigate a wide ranging cultural revolution that transforms societies as a whole in order to change conduct and make it consistent with the rationalities of liberal modernity' (ibid.: 313).

2.6 Conclusion

The chapter began by introducing the different meanings and interpretations that 'development' as a concept has and how this has resulted in the emergence of different 'development(s)'. The main emphasis was laid upon discussing development in the context of modernization and how 'development' has become an instrument for social reconstruction through dividing the world's people as 'developed' and 'underdeveloped'. Reflecting on Truman's speech (1949), it was argued that 'development' paved the way for a new world order after the Second World War, a world order that is based on scientific and economic advantages that former colonial powers have over the colonised countries. Accordingly, development interventions were designed under the assumption that underdeveloped countries are lacking both the resources and knowledge to get them out of the poverty trap. The development policies and strategies tend to deliberately neglect the historical colonial legacies that have contributed to shaping the current realities of the so-called underdeveloped world. In this context, 'development', introduced as a single design, deals with cultures, peoples and countries as homogenous entities that neglects that socio-economic and political problems are different. It neglects local standards, judgement, ideas of what is 'better'; for instance, Ottomanism (for some time) came across as a well-established model for progress (cultural, economic and political) and left a living legacy. Consequently, 'development' is perceived as an ideological hegemony led by the development expert who goes about drawing images and generating new knowledge about peoples and societies.

The chapter also discussed how people, cultures and resources were dealt with as commodities as part of development interventionism. It argued that 'development' has emerged as a control tool that aims to modulate and govern people's behaviour at different levels: social, economic, political and otherwise. As part of the development discourse, it was discussed that underdevelopment was associated with backwardness that is perceived as a threat to the modern world, a threat that makes intervention a necessary act and justifies any mistakes. In the pursuit of development intervention, it was discussed that a wide social sector is found neglected by developers, contributing to what Bauman (2007) referred to as 'wasted lives'. The ideas and theories presented in this chapter will accordingly be useful to understand the local development dynamics and practices in the Gaza Strip and how they relate to the global development practices. It will help to unpack the assumptions that development has emerged as a modern colonial practice that indirectly works to control people it assumes to assist without carefully considering their social, political and cultural context, especially here Gaza's uniqueness in that its occupiers deny their occupation and aid agencies tend to deal with it as an independent entity.

Chapter 3

GAZA: PERIODISING DE-DEVELOPMENT UNDER OCCUPATION

3.1 Introduction

The Gaza Strip has always been characterised by changing political and economic realities. To grasp and understand the current reality of the Gaza Strip, this chapter aims to look at the political economy of the territory over five periods since the Israeli military occupation in 1967: the First Intifada (1987–93), the Oslo Accords (1993), the Second Intifada (2000–5), the Israeli withdrawal from Gaza (2005) and finally Hamas's victory in the Palestinian parliamentary election (2006) and its taking control of the territory.[1] The political economy of each period exhibited particular characteristics that impacted the

---

[1] Under the Fourth Geneva Convention (1949), Israel has a general responsibility, as the occupying power, to ensure the full provision of public services to the population it occupies, including health, education, running and maintaining infrastructure and other essential public services that guarantee the general well-being of the occupied population. See http://www.un.org/en/genocideprevention/documents/atrocity-crimes/Doc.33_GC-IV-EN.pdf. From 1967 up to the Oslo Accords, the Israeli Civil Administration had little legal room to abrogate this responsibility, especially as it collected taxes from Palestinians in the WB and Gaza in return for these services. Israel gradually abandoned this responsibility, however, after the establishment of the PA, particularly its legal responsibility as an occupying power over the Gaza Strip following its unilateral withdrawal from the Strip in 2005. This was further confirmed after Israel declared the Strip as hostile territory following Hamas's military takeover in 2007. The Israeli government relied on the assertion that with the 'termination of the military government in the Gaza Strip, Israel has no obligation whatsoever under international law toward residents of Gaza, who should now direct all their claims and requests to the Palestinian Authority'. This came in spite of the Israeli High Court rejecting this claim and further indicated that 'the creation and continuation of an occupation does not depend on the existence of an institution administering the lives of the local population, but only to the extent of its military control in the area'.

For more, see B'Tselem. 2017. 'The Gaza Strip: Israel's Obligation under International Law'. http://www.btselem.org/gaza_strip/israels_obligations.

overall living conditions of the territory; de-development has been a common feature throughout. The chapter therefore aims to contextualise this process of de-development under occupation by examining the course of political events and their impact on shaping the economic life of Palestinians living in Gaza.

Before addressing the ways foreign (especially Western-donated) aid contributed to and consolidated a process of control and de-development similar to that under occupation, it is first important to differentiate between two important terms: de-development and underdevelopment. Each term refers to different reasons why adequate development was not achieved, thus justifying the use of one term over the other. Second, it is important to give a historical background to this process as it occurred under the occupation. This is to help us understand how donor countries post Oslo Accords (1993), particularly the United States, have not only failed to alleviate this systematic process of control and de-development, but have also indirectly contributed to this by: (a) accepting the status quo imposed by Israel and (b) adopting the Israeli security narrative in its relationship with the territory. Accordingly, the chapter will establish that Gaza's economic failure cannot be attributed to its poor economic performance or the lack of either financial or human resources, but rather to a deliberate and systematic process of economic warfare undertaken by Israel as the occupying power of the Palestinian territories in the WB and Gaza Strip. In this context, the chapter illustrates how Israeli's policy towards Gaza has always been one of 'de-development', where Israel has worked continuously to destroy Gaza's indigenous economy (Roy, 1995). Each section of this chapter will discuss the Israeli measures taken against the population in Gaza and includes the imposition of curfews during the First Intifada (1987), increased restrictions on access of Gaza labourers to the Israeli labour market, the systematic destruction of the industrial capabilities by restricting the mobility of goods and raw materials in and out of Gaza and, finally, the infrastructural damages on the agricultural sector caused mainly by the creation and expansion of buffer zones.

The chapter will begin by setting the scene of the post-Oslo Gaza Strip. Afterwards, it will chronologically demonstrate how the foreign aid agenda has taken different forms and worked within different political frameworks and in relation to the five periods indicated above. First, it will show the shift in the level of aid provision, in terms of agenda and size, towards the beginning of the Oslo Accords (1993) as compared with the First Intifada (1987) period. During the First Intifada, foreign aid came principally from the Arab countries and was channelled through the UNRWA for humanitarian and relief services. Western donors increased their intervention after the Oslo Accords in the hope that agreement would, eventually, result in ending the Israeli-Palestinian conflict. Second, the chapter will examine how these aid dynamics continued to change post Oslo, and up to the present day, and how these dynamics were influenced by internal Palestinian politics as well as the poor progress of the peace process. It will also establish how the role of CSOs had changed along the line of these changing dynamics. It will show how CSOs developed from being a major part of the popular resistance during the First Intifada to being nearly absent during the first three years of the Oslo Accords. Yet, once again the patrimonial use of aid by the PA, in addition to its poor financial and administrative experience, had motivated donor countries to reactivate the role of CSOs. Third, the chapter will examine the socio-economic realities that emerged after Israel's unilateral withdrawal from Gaza (2005). It will demonstrate the gap between what some thought an opportunity for Gaza to prosper both politically and economically, and the reality Israel's disengagement created (i.e. the introduction of further forms of control over the territory).

Fourth, this chapter will finally look at the situation in Gaza upon Hamas's seizure of power. It will first examine the environment that contributed to Hamas's political and economic growth and the extent to which policies maintained by Israel, the PA and donors contributed to Hamas's growing popularity. In this section, this chapter will illustrate how Israel's collective punishment of Gaza, through intensifying the siege and isolating Gaza from the rest of the world, contributed to a very fragile economic and humanitarian situation whose negative impact continues to grow. Finally, the chapter will address the emergence of the 'tunnel economy', a tool Hamas used to confront the internationally motivated siege and the 'tunnel economy', and how this was utilised by Hamas to reinforce its control over the Strip and to strengthen itself economically and politically.

3.2 Mapping Gaza's Post-Oslo Economy

Shortly after the eruption of the 'Second Intifada'[2] in September 2000, the US Agency for International Development (USAID) indicated if the situation in Gaza remains the same, 'there will be indications of humanitarian crisis – measured in high malnutrition rates, increased morbidity and mortality' (USAID, quoted in Roy, 2001b: 16). After more than a decade, the situation has become gloomier and more drastic in the territory. In 2012, the United Nations (UN) announced that approximately 80 per cent of the population in Gaza is dependent on different forms of aid assistance, more than 50 per

---

[2] Known as 'Al-Aqsa Intifada'. A popular uprising against the Israeli occupation in the oPt. It started when the Israeli opposition leader, Ariel Sharon, made a visit to the holy site of Al-Aqsa Mosque provoking a high level of violence between ordinary Palestinians and the Israeli Defence Forces.

cent of households are food insecure and an additional 16 per cent are vulnerable to food insecurity, and about 40 per cent population is under the poverty line (United Nations, 2012: 6). Furthermore, the report forecasted that Gaza will not be a liveable place in 2020. Between the two reports, the district has witnessed political events that have contributed to its current scene.

The Gaza Strip has always remained geopolitically significant and distinct compared to the rest of the Palestinian territories. The geographical disconnection with the rest of the Palestinian territories, its coastal borders from the West and the neighbouring Egypt from the South have made it very vulnerable to Israel's complete control. Gaza has been occupied by Israel since 1967. In 2005 Israel decided to unilaterally pull out from the territory under what is known as the 'disengagement plan'[3]; however, Israel still controls all access to the Gaza Strip. Map 3.1 shows Israeli control over land and water, as well as increased restriction of Palestinian access to fishing and the restricted access area, which reduces accessible agricultural land. Contrary to the reality that continues to exist on the ground, Israeli prime minister Ariel Sharon indicated in his plan for Gaza that this was meant to liberate the population in Gaza from Israeli control that it 'cannot hold on to Gaza forever. More than a million Palestinians live there' (Sharon, 2005). Yet, Israel technically was planning for a scenario completely different from this, one that would free it from any moral and/or legal responsibility (le More, 2005: 989) and in the meantime enable it to maintain its control over the territory.

A year after the disengagement plan was accomplished, Hamas's[4] victory against the secular Fatah party in the 2006 Palestinian Legislative Council (PLC) elections shocked both Fatah and the international community. This victory meant that Hamas formed the new Palestinian government. As a result, a financial and political boycott was instituted by the international community led by the Quartet.[5] To lift this boycott, Hamas had to fulfil the Quartet's conditions: to recognise Israel's right to exist, to recognise signed peace agreements with Israel and to condemn and abandon military resistance. Meanwhile, Hamas's failure to meet these conditions provoked internal clashes with Fatah and ended with Hamas seizing control over the Strip through military force. Israel, as a result, announced Gaza as a hostile territory and imposed a blockade on the territory. The blockade is believed to be implicitly supported by the Quartet in that it did not reject or condemn it. As a result, donors

---

[3] The withdrawal of the Israeli Army from the Gaza Strip and the dismantling of all Israeli settlements within the Gaza Strip. The plan was first proposed by Israel's prime minister, Ariel Sharon.

[4] The Islamic Resistance Movement, associated with the international Muslim Brotherhood movement first founded in Egypt.

[5] The Quartet represents the international aid community and includes the United States, the European Union, Russia and the United Nations.

had a very small window left to carry on with their aid programmes they were obliged to pursue by the Quartet's directives (Qarmout and Beland, 2012).

The geopolitical classification of Gaza as a 'hostile entity' by Israel is argued to have helped situate the territory within what the United States declared as the 'axis of evil' in the post-9/11 war against terrorism discourse. According to this declaration, the entire Gaza population has been associated with Hamas and thus with the discourse of the global war against terror (Bhungalia, 2010), a development reaffirmed by US vice president Dick Cheney. When commenting on Israel's struggle against its enemies, Cheney said, 'As we continue to work for peace, we must not and will not ignore the darkening shadows of the situation in Gaza, in Lebanon, in Syria and in Iran, and the forces that are working to derail the hopes of the world (Cheney, 2008, quoted in Bhungalia, 2010). This form of discourse accelerated a collective punishment at the international level against the entire Gaza population.

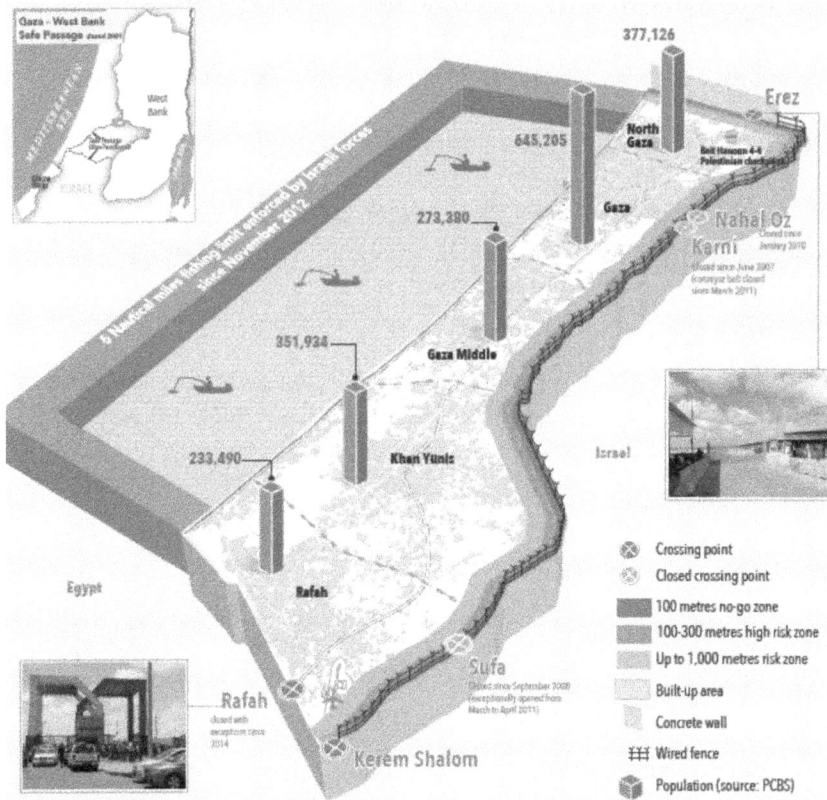

Map 3.1 Gaza closure map

(*Source:* OCHA, 2017).

Departures through Erez crossing with Israel (in thousands)

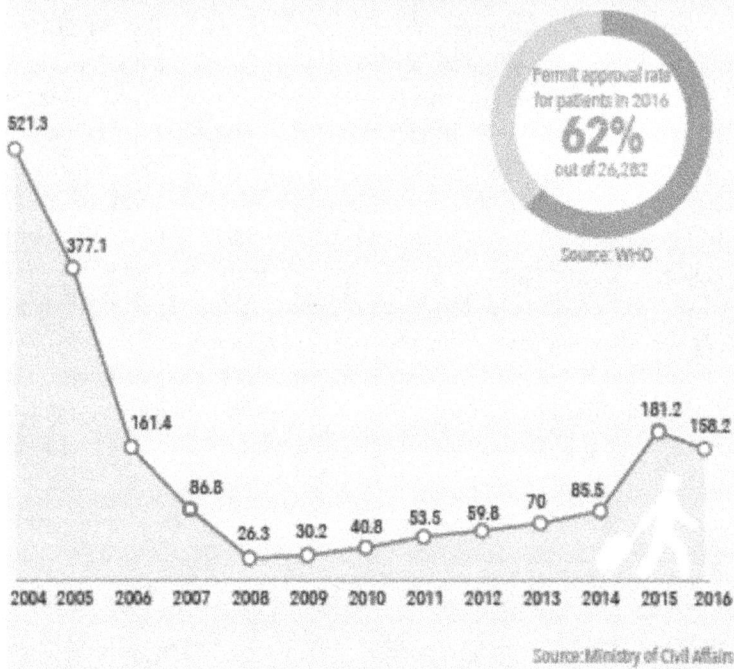

Permit approval rate
for patients in 2016
62%
out of 26,282

Source: WHO

521.3
377.1
161.4
86.8
26.3 30.2 40.8 53.5 59.8 70 85.5
181.2 158.2

2004 2005 2006 2007 2008 2009 2010 2011 2012 2013 2014 2015 2016

Source: Ministry of Civil Affairs

Departures through Rafah crossing with Egypt (in thousands)

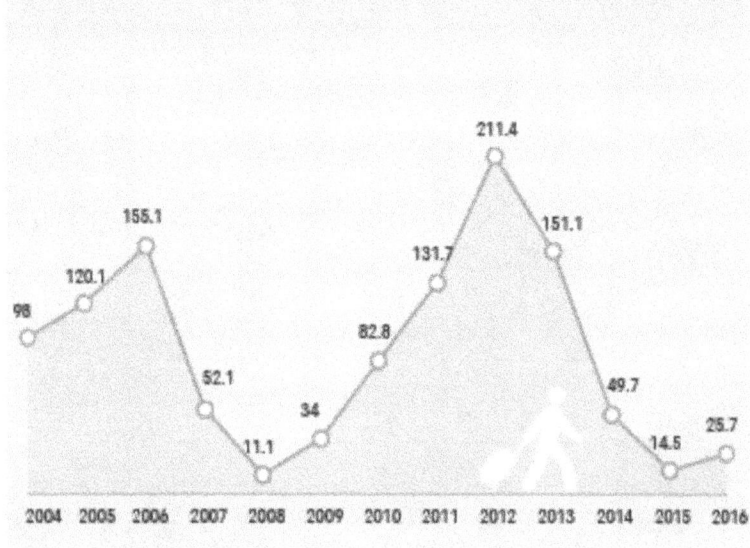

211.4
155.1
151.1
131.7
120.1
98
82.8
52.1
49.7
34
25.7
11.1
14.5

2004 2005 2006 2007 2008 2009 2010 2011 2012 2013 2014 2015 2016

Figure 3.1 Gaza citizens' mobility

(*Source:* Ministry of Civil Affairs, cited in OCHA, 2017).

The tied control over Gaza has exacerbated the humanitarian crisis. The Strip has turned into what the British prime minister David Cameron referred to as a 'giant open prison' and more like a 'prison camp' (quoted in Watt and Sherwood, 2010) with a population of over 1.7 million. Approximately 95 per cent of the industrial establishments were destroyed or were forced to close as a result of the blockade, part of which banned the entry of goods, except very basic food and medical supplies, including international aid supplies, and any kind of mobility in and out, except for very limited access to international aid agencies' workers. The blockade entirely sealed off the Gaza Strip. This, in turn, resulted in exponentially increasing the level of unemployment, with more than 120,000 losing their jobs in the private sector alone (Roy, 2011: 231). Furthermore, during this period, the economy of Gaza was characterised as a 'tunnel economy', in that it was dependent on smuggling goods and supplies through a one-way mechanism from the Gaza Strip. In fact, it benefited Egyptian traders and the Hamas government as the responsible party for regulating the work of these tunnels and collecting tax and customs. Put another way, this exacerbated the problems of Gaza's consumer economy that for decades had been unable to develop trade ties with other countries.

To avoid further deterioration in the humanitarian condition, the international community formulated a new, alternative aid strategy to deal with the growing crisis without jeopardising Israel's blockade policy. The strategy was described in the Quartet statement as one that aims to 'endorse a temporary international mechanism that is limited in scope and duration and [...] ensures direct delivery of assistance to the Palestinian people' (Quartet, 2006). Hence, it can be understood that the strategy was solely based on political reasons rather than humanitarian ones. It is argued that there was strong evidence that the motive behind this strategy was to undermine and isolate the already weak unity government led by Hamas and accelerate its failure at the local and international levels (Qarmout and Beland, 2012: 37).

3.3 Underdevelopment versus De-development

To better understand what has been happening in the Gaza Strip, or more generally in the oPt, as a result of the Israeli policy and later by donors' foreign aid activities, it is important to differentiate between the terms *underdevelopment* and *de-development*. This research suggests that the latter better applies in this context.

Underdevelopment, as associated with dependency theory, refers to deep-rooted historical processes that are embedded in the internationalisation of capitalism. Andre Gunder Frank (1966: 5) suggested that 'contemporary underdevelopment is, in large part, the historical product of past and continuing economic and other relations between the satellite underdeveloped and the now developed metropolitan countries'. It is, however, important to understand that it is the current capital system that guides and influences these relations on a global scale.

Dependency theory relays the state of nations and countries categorised as 'underdeveloped' to the unequal pattern of relations between developed and underdeveloped states. Ferraro (2008: 3) suggests that the capitalist system has imposed a 'rigid international division of labor' where dependent (underdeveloped) states provide cheap labour, natural resources and agricultural commodities, and in the meantime they serve as markets for surplus goods and technologies. Consequently, this drives the economies of dependent states to be oriented towards the outside (i.e. money, goods and services). Meanwhile, the ways these resources are allocated can only be determined according to the economic interests of the dominant states rather than the interests of the dependent states (Ferraro, 2008: 3).

Sara Roy (1987: 56) defines de-development as the 'process which undermines or weakens the ability of an economy to grow and expand by preventing it from accessing and utilising critical inputs needed to promote internal growth beyond a specific structural level'. Roy suggests that Gaza presents a unique example of how 'economic prosperity' can be attained with little economic development. However, Palestinian economic sectors have been systematically transformed by the Israeli occupation into an auxiliary of the Israeli state (Roy, 1999, 1995, 1987).

For almost five decades, the integration of Gaza's economic sectors into Israel's has made the Strip vulnerable or dependent on the Jewish state (or both) (Roy, 1999: 57). Israel has put in place policies and structures that would directly produce a severe lack of growth inside Gaza's agricultural and industrial sectors. These policies, in the first instance, are meant to ensure Gaza's full economic dependence on the Israeli state. The absence of economic development in the territory 'suggests a relationship with Israel that may in fact exceed the traditional parameters of dependency' (Roy, 1987: 57). It is one that governs very unequal economic growth of two entities, one of the occupier and that of the occupied.

3.4 The First Intifada (1987–93): An Ever-Conditioned Economy

As with the remaining districts of the oPt, the economy of the Gaza Strip suffered severe decline thanks to new Israeli policies imposed immediately after the outbreak of the First Palestinian Intifada in 1987.[6] These policies were perceived as a continuation of pre-existing and long-standing economic policies Israel had used against the Palestinians since the start of the occupation in 1967. The traditional measure used by Israel was the frequent imposition of curfews and mobility restriction cards known as 'magnetic cards'. Due to actions taken in the Gaza Strip by the Israelis at the beginning of the Intifada, curfews were imposed more often on the Gaza Strip than in the WB. According to Roy (1995: 296), this policy had an overall impact on Gaza's economy, particularly on Gaza's labourers, the majority of whom were dependent on accessing Israel's labour market. The new restrictions imposed by Israel had prevented labourers from moving freely between Gaza and Israel. Of the small population of Gaza, compared to the WB, more than 70,000 Gaza labourers worked in Israel before the Intifada. During the first three years of the Intifada, this number sharply decreased to approximately 40,000 (Bennis and Cassidy, 1990: 41). This was meant to add to the existing pressure placed upon the already low-paid Palestinians workers.

In addition, Israeli curfews as well as strikes called for by the Palestinian leadership had contributed to the precipitous decline in Gaza's economy and in particular its labour market. The local economy had experienced a long period of complete paralysis that restricted all kinds of commercial activity. In a normal day, local business could work for only four hours a day and for only four days a week. This mostly affected Gaza's middle class (Roy, 1995: 296). During the first three years of the Intifada, Gaza's gross national product (GNP) declined by 30 per cent. This decline was caused by four major factors: first, a nearly 30 per cent decline in the value of output coming from the various economic sectors minus agriculture; second, an almost 35 per cent decline in the level of trade between Israel and the oPt due to the ongoing daily clashes and curfews; third, the loss of income resulting in restrictions on labourers' movements to and from Israel; and fourth, a huge decline (estimated at 75 per cent) in the level of remittances (Roy, 2007: 43).

The deterioration in economic conditions in the first two years of the Intifada (1987–89) resulted in a severe reduction in the private income of

---

[6] The Palestinian uprising against the Israeli occupation of the Palestinian territories. The uprising started in 1987 and lasted until the signing of the Oslo Accords in 1993. The Intifada came after a series of escalating provocations by the occupation forces, but tensions reached boiling point when an Israeli military jeep struck a Palestinian vehicle, killing four Palestinians. The Palestinians believed the incident was deliberately provoked (McDowall, 1989).

Gaza's population. This seriously affected patterns of consumption, saving and investment (Roy, 2007: 44). The population in Gaza not only experienced a lack of access to luxury goods but also faced serious difficulties in securing and consuming very basic daily goods. It was estimated that standards of living among the majority of ordinary Palestinians had declined by 30 per cent. Meanwhile, this decline was followed by a significant increase in the percentage of the population in need for humanitarian aid among both refugee and non-refugee families (Roy, 2007: 44).

These measures had pushed the situation in the Gaza Strip towards total economic exhaustion. The absence of a political and economic vision, especially after the Gulf War (1990–91), decreased both individual citizens' and businesses' ability (including small and medium enterprises in agricultural and industrial sectors) to survive the economic pressures. The 'semi economic war of attrition' (UNCTAD, 1988) reflected the views of Yitzhak Rabin, the defence minister in 1989, regarding the collective sanctioning of Palestinians. This according to Rabin sought to 'strike a balance between actions that could bring terrible economic distress and a situation in which the Palestinians have nothing to lose, and measures which bind them to the Israeli administration and prevent civil disobedience' (quoted in Khalidi and Taghdisi-Rad, 2009).

Further to this, Israel had put more restrictions on the access to Palestinian products within the Israeli market, including licensing and reviewing quota regulations (Khalidi and Taghdisi-Rad, 2009). On the other hand, Israeli subcontracting in the occupied territory intensified and widened to finishing, assembling or processing Israeli raw or semi-processed raw material. According to Khalidi and Taghdisi-Rad (2009), domestic Palestinian industries faced further difficulties in maintaining supplies of raw materials from, or even through, Israel, especially in the absence of any financial or trade intermediation agreements with Israel. These measures, in return, pushed the Palestinian leadership, inside and outside Palestine (supported by the economic sector in the territories), to pursue initiatives aimed at increasing the Palestinian economic sustainability and protecting it through concerted disengagement from the Israeli economy. The new 'self-reliance' policy adopted by the Palestinians shortly after the First Intifada quickly emerged as a response to Israeli sanctions and was meant to build more cohesive infrastructure that could aid a productive economy and prevent Palestinian small businesses from relying on access to the Israeli economy (UNCTAD, 1991: 13). For example, the agricultural sector initiated what became known as a 'return to land' strategy aimed at subsidising the sector in order to maintain its dominant position (Khalidi and Taghdisi-Rad, 2009: 6).

The disengagement of the Palestinian productive sector, however, had a negative impact also as its labour-absorptive capacity was already exhausted by the Israeli economic measures. This meant that the already severe unemployment crisis continued to grow and more households faced economic hardship. Meanwhile, financial transfers coming from abroad, mainly from the PLO and Arab countries, were restricted by Israel. This was coupled with significant increases in taxes and duties and decreases in social services provided by the Israeli Civil Administration.[7] Altogether, these factors added further pressure on Palestinian society. Again, Israel had quickly realised that Palestinian efforts to separate itself from the Israeli economy, yet maintain occupation and suppress the Intifada, required a counter-economic policy to disengagement. A 'selective integration' (Khalidi and Taghdisi-Rad, 2009: 6) described the objectives of this policy as

> an unbalanced tying of the economy of the territory to that of Israel; free Israeli access to Palestinian natural and human resources; no Israeli allocation of resources to the productive sectors of the territory; and no efforts at creating conditions for the establishment of an infrastructure for employment and expansion of the local economy.

3.4.1 Impact of the Gulf War (1990–91) on Palestinian Politics and Economy

The First Intifada was just one reason that influenced the internal political and economic dynamics on the ground. Yet, it is important to highlight other regional developments, including the Gulf War of 1990–91. The war was an important underlying force that added further internal pressures on the Palestinians in the WB and Gaza (particularly the displacement of thousands of Palestinians working in Kuwait[8]). At the Palestinian level, regional political developments and the dire economic consequences of the Intifada had encouraged all parties to work for a peaceful resolution to the Israeli-Palestinian conflict. Palestinians in particular felt that the First Intifada strengthened their cause, brought more support and solidarity from the international community and they would more likely get a better deal as a result. All these developments

---

[7] It was a government body within the Israeli Defence Ministry. This body was responsible for the supervision of very basic public services for Palestinians living in territories. Staff who delivered these services were mainly Palestinians supervised by Israeli military staff.

[8] Thousands of Palestinians were expelled from Kuwait as a response from the Gulf states to the Palestinian leadership's support of the Iraqi regime under Saddam Hussein's leadership.

led Palestinians and Israelis to start the Middle East peace process in 1992 and the negotiations that led to the signing of the Oslo Accords in the same year.

Among the negative impacts of the Gulf War on the Palestinian economy was the massive and sudden loss of remittances coming from thousands of Palestinians who were working in some of the Gulf states (Rosen, 2012). The impact was felt the hardest in Gaza's economy as its private sector was smaller in comparison to the WB and income was mostly dependent on labourers. Israel had also further tightened its security measures in the Palestinian territories as it was directly affected by the regional conflict. Israel also had concerns that Palestinians might take advantage of the ongoing conflict and intensify hostilities against Israel. Longer curfews, land confiscations, settlement building and security fences were the major features of the period. According to Khalidi and Taghdisi-Rad (2009: 9), Israel's security concerns, along with the return of a large number of Palestinians from the Gulf, led Israel to intensify restrictions on Palestinians' freedom of movement, including further restrictions on labourers inside Israel. Against this backdrop, a debate emerged in Israel about the costs and benefits of maintaining reliance on Palestinian labour and the feasibility of exploring other options, that is, foreign labourers from Africa and Asia. The period following the Gulf War (1991–93) was therefore characterised by a reassessment of the economic relations between Israel and the Palestinians and the considerations of new approaches to economic interactions with the Palestinians. This was clear in what an Israeli military official declared at the time as 'there is no change in policy but there is a new approach. [...] Instead of having the workers from the territories come to factories in Israel, we want those factories to go to the territories' (UNCTAD, 1991: 15).

Following the signing of Oslo (1993), the expansion of the Erez Industrial Zone on the boundary of Gaza City with Israel, where many joint Israeli-Palestinian factories were built, reflected this approach. This was also followed by a series of relief measures, such as tax relief and the creation of credit and banking facilities. Khalidi and Taghdisi-Rad (2009: 19) relay these changes in strategy to a few factors. First, the 'self-reliance' policy called for by the Palestinian leadership, which had little impact, caused a significant decrease in trade with Israel. Israel feared that the continuation of this policy in the long run would empower the Palestinian industrial and agricultural sector. Second, peace negotiations had paved the way for further international donor involvement in development and relief projects, which would alleviate some of the pressure exercised by Israel.

Accordingly, ending the First Intifada and the reaction to the overwhelming pressure by the international community was behind the seemingly positive new Israeli policies. Official remarks by Israeli leaders had reflected, at the time, a form of interest in pushing economic development in the oPt; however, the tactics to achieve this were contradictory as these lacked coordination and coherence (Khalidi and Taghdisi-Rad, 2009). Furthermore, the Gaza Strip had suffered from the almost complete destruction of industrial and economic infrastructure. This meant that these liberalisation measures lacked any serious impact in improving economic conditions (UNCTAD, 1993). Also, a prerequisite for the newly established factories in the Erez Zone, in order for them to be licensed and authorised to work, they had to exclusively use Israeli raw materials and maintain a high level of dependence on the Israeli market for both import and export.

3.4.2 Social Services and Aid Provision prior to the PA

Toward the end of the First Intifada (1992–93), there were nearly 2 million Palestinians living in the WB and Gaza (including East Jerusalem), with nearly half of them residing in the Gaza Strip. The Gaza Strip had one of the highest natural population growth rates in the world (4 per cent per year). Gaza had always been characterised as having a young population with approximately 46 per cent of Gaza aged 14–16 years and younger (Brynen, 2000). This had an impact on the ever-growing demand for more resources (i.e. land, water and housing). At the time, it was estimated that the population density exceeded 1,900 persons per square km (almost ten times the density in the WB) (Brynen 2000: 35). Of this population, 78 per cent were refugees who lived in UNRWA refugee camps, where the physical infrastructure and social services were very basic and did not meet the daily needs of these communities. Additionally, this young population also contributed to a growing pool of labour, which this country's labour market could not accommodate, hence continually increasing the level of unemployment.

The dramatic disposition that occurred in 1949 and later in 1967 caused a significant shrinking of the land-owning and wealthy social class. Even though this class managed to successfully sustain its existence through these after the 1948 *Nakbeh* and throughout the Intifada, its power was eliminated. Speaking of the overall social strata in the Palestinian territories, the years following 1967 had witnessed a massive decline in the labour-intensive agricultural sectors, and this continued through the 1990s. Brynen argues that this population was 'proletarianised, in part through urbanisation but even more so through incorporation as unskilled and semi-skilled labourers in the agricultural or construction sectors of the Israeli economy or local Jewish settlements' (2000: 35–38). Meanwhile, the middle class had grown significantly during this period due to the expansion of postsecondary education and the increase in the number of skilled workers who used to work in the Gulf, who later returned to the Palestinian territories. This highly educated class, however, as will be illustrated later, faced problems adjusting due to the poor capacity of the local labour market, on the one hand, and the higher skills they had compared to the actual local needs, on the other.

The social services that were in place to serve the growing population in the Palestinian territories, to mitigate the continuing deterioration in the economic and humanitarian situation in Gaza in particular, came from different sources: Israel, through the Israeli Civil Administration, Jordan (mainly to the WB), voluntary organisations (mostly from Western countries) and finally local Palestinian organisations with the support from the PLO. These organisations funded services that included health, education, relief and welfare. Until the end of the First Intifada, the Israeli Civil Administration budget for the Palestinians was much bigger than that of the UNRWA, Jordan and other organisations.[9] Meanwhile, the expenditures of this administration did not grow to meet the needs of this growing population (Hunter, 1993: 19–20). UNRWA, on the other hand, was more efficient in terms of the level and quality of services it provided; however, these services were limited to Palestinian refugees only. UNRWA, for example, ran nearly 150 schools in Gaza with an enrolment rate of 90,000 refugee students, compared to 100 public schools that operated under the Civil Administration. UNRWA also provided primary health services and advanced services, which could only be obtained in public health institutions. The organisation also provided additional services that included clothes and blankets, food coupons, shelters in refugees camps and cash support when necessary (Hunter, 1993: 21)

A year after the First Intifada (i.e. 1988), the international donor community and the United Nations General Assembly called for an urgent increase in the level of assistance to the Palestinians in the oPt (Khalidi and Taghdisi-Rad, 2009: 7). The United Nations Conference on Trade and Development condemned Israel's new measures and asserted that financial assistance and relief efforts were not sufficient and that 'the international community needed to encourage Israel to allow wide-ranging economic policy reform and liberalization in the Occupied Palestinian Territory, including the right to economic policy formulation and management by the Palestinian people' (UNCTAD, 1989). This statement of Palestinians' development needs under occupation had continued to influence donor policy and was continuously endorsed by the United Nations' oPt policy reports (Khalidi and Taghdisi-Rad, 2009: 7).

---

[9] This budget mainly came from the Israeli high taxation rate of Palestinians, and there was always a huge gap between the extraction of taxes and the delivery of services.

Prior to the Oslo Accords (early 1993), most of the direct external foreign assistance to the Palestinians came from Arab countries and Western donors. The Western assistance programmes began in the 1970s and continued to grow slowly in the 1980s (Brynen, 2000: 44). According to Brynen (2000), there is little data on the level of donor contributions during this period. This was principally caused by a lack in coordination among donors and the absence of an independent and reliable Palestinian counterpart, a situation that began to change only after the signing of Oslo Accords. Early in the 1990s, data sharing between donors was promoted by the United Nations Development Programme (UNDP). As a result of this effort, the UNDP published its report on the ongoing donor activities and programmes. This report was based on a questionnaire distributed to donors and individual aid agencies. This report, however, had a significant gap as the data did not reflect financial pledges against actual disbursements; hence, the report showed a high level of duplication in donors' activities through multilateral agencies (Brynen, 2000: 45). The report also did not include any data regarding funds coming from the PLO or Arab countries and how funds were divided according to different geographical areas (i.e. WB or Gaza). Importantly, it reported a significant increase in donors' financial commitment in the early 1990s rising substantially from nearly 174 million USD to 263 million USD between 1992 and 1993. Moreover, aid from European countries was the highest among other donors, and 'education (30.3 per cent) and health (27.6 per cent) were the major areas of donor assistance, with industry (8.9 per cent) and agriculture (3.2 per cent) lagging well behind' (Brynen, 2000: 45).

According to donor disbursement strategies, when the Israeli Civil Administration was responsible for a majority of services, channelling money through Israel would have been a logical step. As Israel was an occupying power, however, and Arab countries and Palestinians would have opposed providing more resources to Israel, assistance had to be channelled through an international non-governmental organization (INGO) bypassing the services run by the Israeli Civil Administration. The number of INGOs that were operating at the time was very small (approximately two hundred)[10] and had obstacles covering different geographical areas. Israel had also required these organisations to obtain special permits and approval to implement their programmes, except those who were affiliated with the United States Agency for International Development (USAID) (Brynen, 2000: 46)

---

[10] These INGOs were mostly Christian faith-based organisations and European organilsations. A breakdown of these organisations for this period of time is not available. All of these INGOs had to seek permission from the Israeli Civil Administration at that time.

3.5 The Post-Oslo Gaza (1993–2005): The 'Singapore of the Middle East'

The newly established PA became responsible for the economic activities in the WB and Gaza. In principle, the PA was meant to be able to decide its economic policies related to taxation, trade and industry, and employment. Meanwhile and until 1999, the PA had limited control over its own territories. Although the situation in Gaza was much better compared to the WB, the PA controlled nearly eighty-five per cent of the Gaza Strip land, while it had control over only 17.2 per cent of the WB (Area A)[11] and joint control with Israel over 23.8 per cent of the land (Area B) (Farsakh, 2000). Hence, it was obvious that the PA's economic management was jeopardised from the very beginning.

Despite the elimination of many economic restrictions and the important economic improvements that followed Oslo, this period witnessed a crucial deepening and institutionalising of the dynamics of economic decline and control (Roy, 2007: 79). Israel had gradually intensified its sanctioning policies against the Palestinians by joining old sanction policies already in place with new ones. For instance, Israel had created territorial fragmentation between the WB and Gaza that disconnected the Palestinian communities, which later had negative social, political and economic impacts. Furthermore, the Oslo Accords perpetuated the closure policy in a way that made it mandatory for all categories of Palestinians, labourers and ordinary citizens to obtain special permits to move between different geographical areas. Besides the intensified Israeli bureaucratic policies and arbitrary decisions, the agreements added an additional layer of bureaucracy in issuing these permits (Carmi, 1999). On the other hand, dependency on the Israeli economy not only continued but was systematically accelerated. During the interim agreement, Israel was supposed to assist the PA to gradually build its own economic structures that could later be viable and sovereign. However, what occurred was the opposite as Israel followed a restructured form of integrating the Palestinian economy and tying it to the Israeli one. Israel wanted to strengthen and emphasise its control over the Palestinian resources during the early implementation of the Gaza–Jericho plan, which allowed it to have control over land, water and

---

[11] According to the Interim Agreement, the Palestinian territories in the WB were divided into three security areas: A, B and C. Area A is where the PA enjoys most governmental powers and control. Currently, Area A represents only 18 per cent of the WB and includes most of the Palestinian cities where the majority of Palestinian population lives. Area B comprises 22 per cent of the WB and includes rural areas in the territory. According to the agreement, Israel has continued its security control over this area and has transferred civilian matters to the PA. Area C covers 60 per cent of the WB, where Israel enjoys complete control (civilian and security). The PA is responsible only for

settlements (Roy, 2007: 81). Yet what remains a major milestone of this period was the Paris Protocol and the creation of a new customs union as part of this protocol. Until today, this protocol has been influencing the Palestinian economic life and performance and has been guiding the economic relations with Israel, with Israel having the upper hand.

It is crucial here, and before discussing the economic indicators of the Gaza Strip for this period, to understand some of the issues surrounding the Paris Protocol and the kind of impacts it had on the economic performance of the PA territories.

The PA struggled, from the very beginning, to create its national institutions in order to enforce its existence internally and externally, and whenever it did, this existence was superficial, especially in sectors like trade, banking, industry, and agriculture and land control. During the early stages of the protocol design, the Palestinians were more interested in having a free-trade agreement (FTA) according to which economic borders between Israel and the oPt would be described. On the other hand, Israel had strongly rejected the existence of any borders for both political and economic reasons. Israel had strongly rejected any economic sovereignty to the Palestinians at the time and wanted to defer the creation of a Palestinian trade policy to the final-status negotiations (Arnon and Spivak, 1998). As a result, the Government of Israel (GOI), through the creation of a quasi-customs union, effectively maintained nearly full control over the WB and Gaza external economic relations. The protocol protracted Israeli tariffs, tax rates, the imposition of restrictions on the export of certain agricultural products and the quantities to be exported, and the imposition of the Israeli value-added tax (VAT) system as Israel alleged it wanted to stop any illegal trade performed by the Palestinians.[12]

According to the protocol, Israel was also responsible for the collection of VAT and tax on behalf of the Palestinians and the amounts collected would later be transferred to the Palestinian Ministry of Finance (MOF). Although

---

educational and health services in this area; however, Israel is responsible for the construction and maintenance of the infrastructure necessary for these service. An example of Area C is East Jerusalem. B'Tselem. 2013. 'What is Area C?' http://www.btselem.org/area_c/what_is_area_c. Accessed 15 May 2018.

[12] According to the Paris Protocol on Economic Relations signed in 1994 by the GOI and the PA, a customs union was to be established to allow the Palestinian economy to merge into the Israeli one. This protocol was meant to allow the GOI to collect taxes from the Palestinians citizens on behalf of the PA. The GOI returns taxes collected on all Palestinian imports to the PA on a monthly basis. As Palestinians in the WB and Gaza heavily depend on imports of goods, revenues from taxes have represented the largest source of income to the PA for it to pay its employees' salaries and run the basic services.

the protocol assured that Palestinians would continue to have access to the Israeli labour market, it failed to give details about the nature of this access in terms of numbers and the deciding authority. In addition to this, it gave Israel the right to make its own judgement and decisions regarding the movement of Palestinian labour to its territories (Zagha and Zomlot, 2004: 120–40). Consequently, the Palestinian labourers continued to face difficulties accessing the Israeli labour market, especially labourers from Gaza, who were completely disconnected from this market upon the start of the Second Intifada in 2000. According to a European Union official, the Palestinian side had no room for manoeuvre and was forced in all rounds of negotiations to accept the Israeli condition that

> the Palestinians had to agree [to these conditions] essentially for political reasons. It was a deal, essentially to avoid having to tackle the question of territory, postponing the issue of borders until final status. The Israelis told the Palestinians: 'You shut up during the intermediary period and we let your workers work in Israel.' But it did not work, because trade and employment were undermined by the closure policy and by the prohibition of Palestinians to work in Israel. (le More, 2008: 55)

Accordingly, this quasi-customs union made the Palestinian economy fragile and unprotected against globalised trade flows and the newly liberalised Israeli economy in the 1990s (Khalidi and Taghdisi-Rad, 2009: 15). Moreover, the Palestinian economy had to pay the price of the World Trade Organisation (WTO) membership through the window of the Israeli market yet without enjoying any of the benefits from WTO trade rules. Accordingly, the agreement made it impossible to separate the economy of the Palestinian territories from that of Israel since the former has to follow the same trade agreement of the latter and use the same tax regulations and currency (Khalidi and Taghdisi-Rad 2011: 94).

3.5.1 Post-Oslo Economic Indicators

Expectations were high among the Palestinians and the international donor community that there would be rapid economic growth and that this could enhance living conditions in the WB and Gaza. This optimism was based on various reasons: first, it was thought that the PA would create a favourable environment for development through the adoption of sound economic policies; second, the financial sector would have a key role in facilitating investment in the territory; third, legal regulatory obstacles for development would be removed and the private sector would have greater opportunity to contribute to development; and finally, the local infrastructure would be improved and expanded, which in return would facilitate development (MAS and World Bank, 1999: 17). The data, however, for the first three years after the signing of the agreement (i.e. 1993–6) showed that the general standards of living in Palestine had instead seen a sharp decline (ibid.). The continuing decline of the level of Palestinian employment in Israel caused one-third drop in the remittances coming from this source, and consequently, the overall gross domestic product (GDP) declined by 10 per cent (Arnon and Weinblatt, 2001: 298). The structural changes that occurred in the relationship between the Israeli and Palestinian economies resulted in a severe economic downturn. For example, Palestinian unemployment had increased to an average of 24 per cent by 1996.

The Oslo Accords had little effect on the Israeli closure policy. In 1994, 70 per cent of Gaza labour worked in Israel prior to the Intifada. This number had fallen by 23 per cent during the first year of the agreement (Roy, 1994: 92). Gaza's already weakened economy could not compensate for these continuing losses. It was estimated that nearly 8,500 workers were employed in local industries in the Gaza Strip and almost double this number were employed in the agricultural sector (ibid.). Neither sector had the capacity to accommodate the newly unemployed labourers. Even those who could find local employment opportunities received subsistence wages in the informal sector due to the big margin between the wages of a domestic employee and their counterparts in Israel. For instance, a semi-skilled worker in Israel gained an average of 70 USD per day, while the same worker in Gaza gained 14 USD. Consequently, the decline in the level of wages coupled with the lack of access to the Israeli labour market had forced living standards to decline. The level of indebtedness among ordinary citizens as a result of this economic recession went up by 203 per cent in refugee camps such as Deil al-Balah, 350 per cent in the Jabalia camp in northern Gaza, 337 per cent in Rafah camps and 325 per cent in Khan Yunis camps.[13] These debts were necessary to cover essentials and food expenses (Roy, 2007: 97).

At the industrial level, trade between Israel and the Palestinian territories had declined by 25 per cent as imports to the Palestinian economy were cut by half by 1995, which in return had a devastating impact on local employment

---

[13] Gaza citizens relied on family and friends for personal loans in most cases and directly from the private sector or their Israeli employers. Public sector employees began to enjoy financial services offered by local banks owned by a group of rich Palestinian families inside the territories or abroad. These banks began to offer loans on a high interest rate to new PA employees who came from abroad with no family connections in the WB or Gaza.

(Table 3.1 shows the economic performance of core sectors in the Gaza Strip from 1994 to 2005). Like almost all other sectors, the industrial sector is very dependent on imports of raw materials that were either bought directly from the Israeli market or imported through Israel (Arnon and Weinblatt, 2001: 300). On the other hand, the newly established Palestinian public sector had generated additional public expenditures that caused a slight boost in the economy. This sector, however, was soon exploited for personal benefits through the imposition of restrictive measures by the PA political elite that gave access to high-ranking PA security officials to have almost full control over this sector.

Towards 1997, and following the signing of the Wye River Memorandum (1998) between Israel and the PA, the Palestinian economy saw notable growth, especially between 1998 and 1999 (UNCTAD, 2001: 3). According to UNCTAD, the GDP grew by 6 per cent, while the real per capita gross national income (GNI) grew at 3.5 per cent, increasing to 1,965 USD. This level of growth continued until the end of 2000, albeit at a lower rate. What was important, however, was that the economy was increasingly based upon a more sustainable growth rate. Unfortunately, political and security developments on the ground (upon the outbreak of the Second Intifada[14] in 2000) had devastating impacts on all economic and social sectors and had caused further structural weaknesses in the Palestinian economy that already lacked sustainable elements (see Table 3.1). According to UNCTAD (2001: 3–9), the economic implications can be summarised in the following seven points.

First, the pronounced imbalance between labour demand and labour supply, reflected in the level of unemployment, happened to rise at a critical point following the Oslo Accords. This problem accelerated over several years and was conjoined with a high proportion of labour employed in Israel and the poor absorptive capacity of the local labour market.

Second, the inability of the domestic economy to generate adequate levels of saving meant that both public and private sectors could not satisfy investment requirements. This was clear in the ever-growing gap between the national saving and investment.

Third, the poorly implemented infrastructure programmes discouraged Palestinians and international investors equally from undertaking major projects in the productive sector. UNCTAD believed that the foreign direct investment (FDI) continued to be limited during this period and that many

---

[14] This is known as Al-Aqsa Intifada. It started in September 2000, when Ariel Sharon provoked the Palestinians by his visit to Al-Aqsa Mosque in Jerusalem, the holiest site for Muslims in the city and in Palestine.

Table 3.1 Value-added tax (USD) in Gaza Strip by economic activity in key sectors (1994–2005)

Economic Activity	1994	1995	1996	1997	1998	1999	2000	2001	2002	2003	2004	2005
Agriculture	114.1	123.4	117.2	142.4	125.2	109.1	119.4	122.4	88.7	97.7	115.2	98.1
Mining, manufacturing, electricity and water	210.4	202.6	170.5	167.0	194.3	151.9	114.9	158.8	149.6	211.4	243.2	274.3
Manufacturing	163.5	157.7	132.6	114.5	137.2	100.1	40.0	71.4	49.8	106.0	103.0	140.2
Water supply; sewerage, waste management and remediation activities	21.3	15.1	10.8	7.5	8.6	6.9	6.3	7.1	6.0	6.8	8.0	8.5
Construction	134.8	109.3	128.5	99.1	109.4	132.5	95.7	118.8	63.8	74.1	86.6	111.6
Trade	125.4	127.7	110.7	124.5	144.7	135.0	119.4	119.8	140.9	148.9	141.1	210.7
Transportation	33.0	32.6	32.8	42.8	35.6	26.6	17.7	22.0	25.1	21.7	18.5	46.5
Services	271.5	306.2	314.6	384.5	418.9	419.9	420.2	421.6	408.7	414.9	424.2	450.9
Real estate activities	128.1	133.4	139.6	150.9	152.6	152.6	188.7	165.4	168.0	173.3	164.5	173.7
Education	78.5	93.8	94.6	122.8	130.6	129.5	128.6	140.0	127.3	136.6	148.4	157.3
Human health and social work activities	39.0	52.2	47.5	79.4	87.8	89.1	64.6	76.8	73.7	75.9	67.7	69.2
Public administration and defence	125.7	147.0	184.9	170.6	190.4	189.4	241.1	266.0	246.5	283.7	276.7	380.6
Households with employed persons	1.5	1.7	1.7	2.0	1.7	1.7	1.8	1.3	1.2	1.3	1.2	0.7
Customs duties	0.0	15.2	32.1	51.6	68.9	78.0	81.5	24.5	16.8	66.7	64.7	67.1
VAT on imports, net	6.9	71.9	84.7	94.4	89.8	80.3	89.8	32.5	36.0	76.9	107.1	127.0
Gross domestic product	1,026.0	1,144.7	1,182.2	1,284.9	1,379.1	1,335.5	1,317.7	1,297.7	1,185.6	1,407.2	1,493.2	1,801.9

Source: PCBS, 2016.

Palestinian expatriates withdrew their investment shortly due to the uncertain environment.

Fourth, Palestinian traders worked under extraordinary access conditions which, as a result, obstructed the expansion of trade. Moreover, frequent Israeli closures also severely affected the movement of goods.

Fifth, the closure policy was extended to include the internal closure measure, where the flow of goods and labour was restricted. Roads between cities and villages in the WB and Gaza were permanently closed. Gaza, for example, was divided into five fragments, where each 'security zone' was completely sealed off and isolated under the PA jurisdiction.

Sixth, the rate of employment had grown rapidly in this period. Approximately 300,000 Palestinians (two-fifths of the labour force) were jobless by 2001. As a result, one-third of the Palestinian population in WB and Gaza were reported to be living below the poverty line (2.10 USD per day). It was measured that the income of more than 65 per cent of households (average household of six) had fallen below 400 USD per month. Moreover, the level of indebtedness had significantly increased in the private sector, which was already experiencing a liquidity crisis (see Table 3.2). In 2001, the PA budget deficit rose 25 per cent compared to the previous year. Towards 2003, the World Bank and the Palestinian Central Bureau of Statistic (PCBS) reported that the poverty line was ranging above 60 per cent (World Bank and PCBS, 2003).

Finally, the PA's ability to meet the development needs of territories was further curtailed, thus worsening economic conditions. The social services sectors had become overburdened with more of the budget rechannelled towards emergency sectors. By the end of 2001, the PA had budgeted nearly 650 million USD to cover costs incurred from improving the social, education and health sectors in addition to securing food assistance for the poor and carrying out minor infrastructure improvements.

By 2001 and until the Israeli withdrawal in 2005,[15] known as the disengagement plan, there were more than 30 security checkpoints across the Strip (which is less than 80 kilometre in length) (Roy, 2002). Major roads in the Strip were restricted for the mobility of the Israeli military and settlers, while pedestrians and vehicles had to take alternative routes. These closures caused extreme reduction on mobility and trade between the various cities in the Gaza Strip and contributed to the creation of isolated enclaves in the areas

---

[15] Although Israel dismantled all its settlements that used to exist across the Gaza Strip, it continued to control the territory via a number of commercial and individual crossing points.

Table 3.2 Major national accounts variables (USD): Gaza Strip (1994–2005)

Variable	1994	1995	1996	1997	1998	1999	2000	2001	2002	2003	2004	2005
Gross domestic product	1,026.0	1,144.7	1,1822	1,284.9	1,379.1	1,335.5	1,317.7	1,297.7	1,185.6	1,407.2	1,493.2	1,801.9
Net factor income from abroad	103.5	132.0	118.7	143.6	208.5	240.8	163.8	60.7	58.7	78.5	58.7	78.2
Compensation of employees, net	82.5	110.1	96.0	123.8	202.6	230.3	151.6	26.2	36.6	62.8	47.1	46.1
Property income, net	21.0	21.9	22.7	19.8	5.9	10.5	12.2	34.5	22.1	15.7	11.6	32.1
Gross national income	1,129.5	1,276.7	1,300.9	1,428.5	1,587.6	1,576.3	1,481.5	1,358.4	1,244.3	1,485.7	1,551.9	1,880.1
Net current transfers from abroad	164.9	153.4	181.3	152.5	138.3	145.0	252.6	364.5	411.8	269.5	286.6	451.0
Gross national disposable income	1,294.4	1,430.1	1,482.2	1,581.0	1,725.9	1,721.3	1,734.1	1,722.9	1,656.1	1,755.2	1,838.5	2,331.1
Final consumption	1,235.9	1,355.6	1,490.3	1,575.9	1,672.2	1,641.2	1,646.0	1,539.8	1,502.6	1,713.9	1,963.6	2,183.9
Savings	58.5	74.5	−8.1	5.1	53.7	80.1	88.1	183.1	153.5	41.3	−125.1	147.2

Source: PCBS, 2016.

around Gaza City. Meanwhile, the main crossing between Gaza and Israel (Erez Crossing) was completely closed for more than 65 per cent of the time during this period (ibid.: 129). Accordingly, the number of Gazan labourers working in Israel dropped by 90 per cent (from 30,000 to 3,000) immediately in the year following the start of the Second Intifada. At the trade level, commercial crossings between Gaza and Israel were closed for over 60 per cent of the time, with limited operating capacity during the days these crossings worked, which again had a drastic impact on all sectors: industrial, trade and agricultural.

3.5.2 *International Assistance: The Buying of Peace*

The response of international donors to the signing of the Oslo Accords was immediate, as foreign aid to the PA was perceived to be a central cog for the success of the peace process. The agreement also represented one of the most substantial examples of 'peacebuilding through aid' in the post–Cold War era (Brynen, 1996: 79). With the United States being the second top contributor after the Arab League (25 per cent or 500 million USD), foreign governments pledged nearly 2.1 billion USD (Roy, 2007: 82). During the initial period (1994–97), the largest proportion of donor spending covered mainly the PA's budget and other forms of technical assistance aimed at helping the PA establish its start-up public institutions, which in turn lowered the PA's capacity to engage or implement the investment project (Fischer, Alonso-Gamo and von Allmen, 2001: 264). The situation continued for the first six years of the agreement, when the aid pledged had gradually continued to decline and the PA's economic performance was very weak.

Roy (2007: 82) suggests that the role of the post-Oslo foreign aid illustrated the policy constraints and structural parameters that surrounded the agreement. This is because donors believed that the agreement would put an end to the occupation and would instead facilitate new political frameworks for enhancing Palestinian economic growth. However, the indicators for the first three years of the agreement showed a further decline in the socio-economic conditions among Palestinians. Additionally, prospects for development and reform faded due to the failure to eliminate the real factors behind poor Palestinian economic performance (i.e. the structures of occupation remained defined and unchanged). These very factors also impacted how the aid was put to work. For instance, there was much criticism about the slow speed, not of the flow of aid, but of the implementation of aid programmes. According to Brynen (1996: 80), large aid projects had to go through lengthy processes of bureaucratic evaluation, planning and procurement in order to meet two requirements: first, the countries' disbursement audit criteria, and second, the logistical requirement and criteria imposed by the Israeli government. In addition, donors had concerns regarding the continuing financing of the PA's administrative costs and public funding as these lacked any developmental components and were a continuing burden on donor funding.

An overriding characteristic of this period was the relationship between Israel (as both an occupying power and a partner), the PA and the donor community (mainly Western governments). It was obvious that donors avoided politically confronting Israel or challenging its policies, even when the latter severely violated core elements of the signed agreements. This was motivated by the fear that being critical of Israel after investing considerable effort, time and money in a process that had received great international attention would make donors (mainly the United States and European Union) seem unsupportive of the peace process. Alternatively, much of this pressure was directed towards the Palestinians who were caught on each and every violation, even the least effective. As a result, donors and the PA could not go beyond Oslo's framework that would enable them to create reforms necessary to create structural links. Instead, in the majority of their programmes, donors had to work around the policies imposed by Israel (Roy, 2007: 82).

For instance, 'Israel's security first' policy was very much adopted by the US administration. According to Dennis Ross, the senior State Department official during the Clinton administration, aid to the Palestinians was a necessary element to maintain the peace process in which 'Israel's security will always take precedence over the Palestinian economy' (Roy, 2007: 82–83). Roy explains the US aid programme as being guided, in principle, by political considerations that mainly accepted Israel's interest and security needs that enabled it to maintain its control, rather than enabling Palestinian's structural reforms and economic growth. Moreover, the majority of aid programmes, including US aid, lacked an important feature, which is the long-term planning and the creation of a developmental framework that could pave the way for promoting economic growth.

Foreign aid provision to the Palestinians in the post-Oslo period, especially between 1994 and the outbreak of the Second Intifada (2000), was thus surrounded by tensions inherent in the donor–recipient relationship. This relationship has traditionally been tense, but this extraordinary political context added further insult to injury. Judy Barsalou (2003: 52) relays this tension to the conflicting interests and political motives for different donors involved in the assistance programme to the PA. For instance, donors, particularly Western donors, were more interested in investing their aid in infrastructure and development projects rather than covering the PA running costs or channelling aid to humanitarian relief through the United Nations' institutions. For these Western donors, it was acceptable after the onset of the Oslo period to cover the PA's recurring expenditures if it was to help build its institution and become politically and economically independent. However, political developments during the first decade of the agreement did not produce this result. Israel continued to undermine the role of the PA and tightened its control over the oPt covered by the agreement, a situation exacerbated by the corruption within the PA (Roy, 2007: 83). Yet the continuing decline in the socio-economic well-being and the increasing destitution of the Palestinian population added more pressure on donor countries to reconsider their development plan and instead gave more focus to committing more aid to cover humanitarian relief and partial recurring expenditures. The security development following the Second Intifada had made donors realise the importance of rebuilding the destroyed infrastructure and preventing the PA's institutions from falling apart (Barsalou, 2003: 53). Despite this, it remained the assumption during this period, yet the varying agendas of donors were at times politically motivated in a way to make it commonly acceptable for donors to take sides when it came to supporting different Palestinian groups or communities.

There was a tendency among donors to encourage and fund political organisations that showed interest or practically joined the 'peace train'. According to Roy (1994: 94), the behaviour of donors at the time raised two major assumptions: First, political affiliation is a condition for receiving assistance and then development by itself was utilised to influence a specific political order. Second, and based on the first assumption, donors, intentionally or otherwise, were in the early stages of fuelling already existing political tensions between different political groups and thus fuelling fragmentation.

Another side of this tension was generated by the absence of coordination between donors regarding their aid programmes and sector priorities as well as among recipients involved in aid delivery. On the one hand, given the large number of parties involved in the aid delivery, aid programmes were duplicated by different donors and most of these programmes were similar in nature, purpose and their beneficiaries. This had resulted in a huge amount of funds being wasted as well as confusion among donors caused due to reprogramming (Barsalou, 2003: 54). On the other hand, recipient agencies, especially local NGOs, had to deal with different sets of aid policies, some of which were influenced by donor countries' policies and others were influenced by international institutions' regulations. This highly bureaucratic process of aid provision was time and money consuming, thus making aid deliverables more focused on meeting donors' policies than assessing the actual needs of the Palestinians (Prusher, 1997).

Furthermore, tensions emerged from the tendency of donors to control how aid should be spent as they do this through a process of balancing priorities rather than discussing and consulting with actual beneficiaries. Barsalou (2003: 54–55) outlines the norm that sees donors generally realise that development assistance is best served when the actual recipient plays a role or assists in defining aid priorities and also participates in implementation. However, the PA's early financial mismanagement and corruption, the latter revealed in 1996, when an internal audit indicated that more than 40 per cent of the PA's budget was misused, made this more difficult (Barsalou, 2003: 54–55). Consequently, donors, particularly EU donors, had to impose tighter policies that would give powers to monitor and control PA's expenditures.

3.6 The Disengagement Plan 2005: Building Castles in the Sky

On the eve of the disengagement in 2005, nearly 1.5 million Palestinians were living in the Gaza Strip. With the annual population growth rate estimated at 3 to 5 per cent, the population was expected to hit 2 million by 2010. Of this number, 80 per cent was under 50 years of age and 50 per cent was 15 years old or younger. Until the end of the Second Intifada, Gaza had registered the highest population density in the world, with the Jabalia refugee camp in the north of the Strip registering some 74,000 people per square kilometre compared to 25,000 in Manhattan (Roy, 2005: 65).

As mentioned earlier, the population of Gaza at the outbreak of the Second Intifada had suffered from a prolonged closure, which had a deleterious impact on the socio-economic situation (Harvard, 2006).[16] According to a special report on the disengagement plan published by the World Bank (2004), Palestinians in the Gaza Strip were experiencing the worse economic decline in the modern era, one caused by continuing Israeli security measures and restrictions. It was estimated that more than 65 per cent of Gaza's population was living under the poverty line (earning less than 2 USD per capita per day) (Samhouri, 2006: 3), 26 per cent of whom lived in extreme poverty, and nearly 35 per cent of its workforce was unemployed (Harvard, 2006). According to the World Food Programme (WFP), about 42 per cent of Gaza's population was listed as suffering from food insecurity (lacking sustainable and sufficient access to nutritious food for normal growth) (Roy, 2005: 66). This percentage increase exceeded 50 per cent in vulnerable areas (i.e. refugee camps). Of the remaining population, 30 per cent was under the threat of becoming 'food vulnerable and malnourished'.

---

[16] Population projection for socio-economic development in the Gaza Strip upon the implementation of the disengagement plan conducted by the Programme on Humanitarian Policy and Conflict Research at Harvard University.

According to Harvard (2006), the population growth and size in the Gaza Strip had left the PA without an accurate set of predictions from which it could carry out any form of economic planning. The five years of continued armed confrontation during the Second Intifada (2000–5) contributed to further physical damage to industrial and agricultural infrastructure (see Table 3.3 for a summary of economic activities in the Gaza Strip during 2006–16). The estimated cost of infrastructure damage was equal to 50 per cent of the combined economic income of the Gaza Strip and the WB (6.5 billion USD). According to UNCTAD, the PA lost approximately one-fifth of its economic base over the first four years of the Second Intifada (Roy, 2005: 66). Furthermore, the PA was very weak and inefficient. It had become hugely dependent on foreign aid for its survival and continued to exhibit serious administrative failings. Signs of socio-political division and political division were starting to appear while the PA was gradually starting to lose its power in the streets of Gaza. Hamas, on the other hand, was gaining popular support as a result of the PA's continuing failure in driving the peace process and the alarming level of internal security disorder and lawlessness (Samhouri, 2006: 3).

The PA was on the verge of collapse due to, on the one hand, its failure to achieve any success in the peace process with Israel and, on the other, the deteriorating economic and security situation in the WB and Gaza Strip. Samhouri (2006: 6) suggests that Gaza, considering these harsh realities and its damaged economy, was unlikely to have a realistic opportunity to recover unless two major requirements were achieved: first, an atmosphere of political and security stability; second, securing free access to the WB, Israeli, regional and international markets. According to Samhouri (2006: 7–8), these requirements could encourage investment in the Gaza's private sector, decrease absolute dependence on foreign aid and provide local job opportunities.

3.6.1 Israel's Unilateralism in Dealing with Gaza

What did it mean for Israel to unilaterally withdraw from Gaza? What kind of implications could it have on the territory's future relations with Israel? And how could it impact its socio-economic development? Unilateral withdrawal was meant to be an Israeli plan to be independently implemented in isolation from the Palestinian involvement, rather than it being an agreement between the two stakeholders (i.e. Palestinians and Israelis). Samhouri (2006: 4) argues that while the plan offered no assurances addressing Israel's security fears, neither from the PA nor from a third party like the United States, it still allowed Israel to continue its overall control over Gaza's outer air and maritime territories. Accordingly, no change had occurred to the existing security regime (i.e. Gaza

Table 3.3 Value-added tax (USD) in Gaza Strip by economic activity in key sectors (1994–2005)

Economic Activity	2006	2007	2008	2009	2010	2011	2012	2013	2014	2015	2016
Agriculture	100.3	168.2	173.1	174.9	200.1	241.2	173.1	201.9	156.9	142.1	136.3
Mining, manufacturing, electricity and water	193.3	127.4	147.8	150.1	275.0	314.8	341.6	416.2	225.1	317.6	374.6
Manufacturing	83.1	25.2	29.2	36.6	157.0	192.1	242.8	231.8	202.5	253.4	301.9
Water supply, sewerage, waste management and remediation activities	4.4	6.1	7.5	8.4	4.8	9.2	14.4	15.3	5.3	6.3	6.9
Construction	80.6	61.7	34.2	35.1	83.0	201.0	185.2	157.2	124.9	144.1	245.5
Trade	176.9	180.7	117.2	200.7	308.6	253.2	434.5	483.1	611.0	628.5	639.7
Transportation	20.7	11.2	9.2	12.8	18.4	21.1	27.2	27.2	33.3	41.8	46.0
Services	450.7	445.3	481.0	583.9	642.0	705.7	706.5	825.4	762.2	767.6	826.1
Real estate activities	161.8	116.5	130.3	158.9	159.2	124.3	123.1	164.9	188.0	182.3	186.7
Education	166.4	179.9	218.6	238.0	245.2	259.1	285.2	321.0	302.8	316.1	334.6
Human health and social work activities	75.4	83.0	90.8	97.5	99.9	159.7	166.0	174.0	137.5	137.6	147.8
Public administration and defence	362.3	335.6	379.3	459.1	632.2	734.7	730.0	870.4	887.7	906.0	980.5
Households with employed persons	0.4	0.0	0.0	2.1	1.5	1.8	1.8	2.0	1.5	1.5	1.7
Customs duties	61.8	63.0	62.6	36.3	45.0	25.2	25.7	28.9	29.0	40.9	44.8
VAT on imports, net	83.6	109.1	86.6	75.3	62.8	29.5	33.4	53.1	53.6	109.4	120.2
Gross domestic product	1,552.3	1,515.2	1,506.9	1,748.1	2,283.1	2,547.6	2,682.6	3,092.1	2,912.1	3,134.1	3,450.4

Source: PCBS, 2016.

remained a fully occupied territory). This surrounded the implementation of the plan in an atmosphere of political and security tension, although some level of coordination was mediated by the United States at the time of the evacuation.

The disengagement plan created two conflicting predictions for the future situation in the Gaza Strip. The assumption was made that Palestinians in the Gaza Strip would be free, be able to rebuild Gaza and enjoy democratic governance. Israel, on the other hand, would at some point withdraw from the WB or at least would strengthen the Palestinian position at any final-status negotiations and would make the continuation of occupation entirely unacceptable to the international community (Roy, 2005: 65). The plan, therefore, if it was to be implemented properly, inspired ambitions that this could be a first step to ending the Israeli-Palestinian conflict. That alone put more responsibility for its success or failure on the Palestinians as the beneficiaries of this unilateral withdrawal, because the withdrawal depended on how well they would take advantage of the process by putting down the first block of their 'mini-state' (ibid.: 65–66).

A special report by the *Economist* (2005) examined Gaza's economic potential in the event that Israel's occupation was to completely end. The report suggested that Gaza has much incentive to perform well on this front. It argued that besides the territory possessing the world's second highest population density, Gaza has all the potentials to be the cornerstone when it comes to trading and tourism, especially given its location in the Mediterranean Sea, which would enable it to function as a hub for trade and travel. Second, Gaza has been performing well in agriculture, both for crops grown by local farmers and through the imported modern technology such as greenhouses. This sector could easily flourish if it had the chance to access the outside market and would potentially attract both internal and external investment. Furthermore, the high population in a relatively small geographical area could be an advantage, especially as 50 per cent of this population is of a working age and has a high level of education and skills. Finally, it was expected that 'ending the occupation in Gaza' would strongly encourage donors to invest greater amounts of aid in rebuilding its industrial and agricultural infrastructure, especially in former settlement areas, expand its already existing industrial zones and resume the building of the Gaza seaport and restore the semi-destroyed airport.

The World Bank (the key international coordination body during the disengagement process) believed that the policy-makers (i.e. PA, Israeli government or donors) should focus on stabilising Gaza economy as part of this new political process. The PA must work on creating positive changes in the daily lives of Gaza's population, where they have the ability to trade and move freely and find work. The bank also insisted that while donor money was crucial for the economic revival in the Gaza Strip, it was not the only determining factor. It was evident from 1994 up to the disengagement plan period how little foreign assistance could achieve, even during times when this assistance was doubled. What remained important, however, was the elimination of the underlying causes of economic decline and finding the best way to address these causes (World Bank, 2004: 1–3).

3.6.2 Disengagement from the Israeli Perspective and the Post-Disengagement New Realities

Finding answers to the questions above could come through posing the question what did Israel really want from the Disengagement Plan? The answer became clear in Ariel Sharon's public statement where he explained the plan as 'a blow to the Palestinians in that it will force them to give up on their aspirations [to statehood] for many years to come' (quoted in le More, 2005: 990). Regardless of Israel's claim that it was committed to the estab-lishment of a Palestinian state, its practices on the ground and the continuous creation of new geopolitical realities said otherwise. Sharon, being the master engineer of this plan, had a completely different vision of this state than that of the Palestinian or the international community's idea of a viable or a sover-eign state. According to le More (2005: 991) the pullout from Gaza contributed to a new vision of a Palestinian state that is based on transportation rather than territorial contiguity, essentially made up of a besieged Gaza and three main demographic enclaves in the WB that are separated by major settlement blocks. The US response to the plan was much closer to Israeli intentions than the Palestinian view. The Gaza pull-out was seen by George Bush as an unprecedented concession that Israel might not be able to move any further in the future. This was clear in Bush's statement: 'In light of new realities on the ground, including already existing major Israeli population centres, it is unrealistic to expect that the outcome of final-status negotiations will be a full and complete return to the armistice lines of 1949' (quoted in le More, 2005: 991). This statement reflected a major blow to the Palestinian aspiration towards national self-determination and the establishment of a state that sat entirely within the 1967 borders.

The sudden and uncoordinated withdrawal from Gaza resulted in a security vacuum within the territory and as a result the security situation witnessed a sudden deterioration, mainly caused by the firing of homemade rockets into the bordering Israeli villages and settlements. Traditionally, Israel responded to these rockets with artillery shelling, air strikes and the imposition of further restrictions on border crossings. Practically, Gaza's conditions prior to the disengagement went unchanged, with no potential efforts on the horizon to create an atmosphere for economic revival (Samhouri, 2006: 4). Driven by frustration, the then Quartet special envoy, Wolfensohn, had to shut his office and leave Gaza due to the failure to implement the US-brokered agreement on facilitating access and movements in and out of Gaza for both individuals and goods. Moreover, the grand post-development 'Greenhouse Project', which was supposed to draw benefit from former settlements and expand Gaza's agriculture sector through exports to the outside market, failed due to Israel's closure policy. Finally, the remainder of the Gaza industrial zone in Erez was razed to the ground by the Israeli military to create a buffer zone[17] to allegedly help prevent rocket attacks against Israel.

Meanwhile, the domestic Palestinian politics witnessed major developments, especially the rise of Hamas's power in the Gaza Strip. Hamas was beginning to show it was prepared to engage politically through participation in municipal elections and achieving electoral victories over Fatah (2005–6). Hence, Hamas's victory in the legislative elections (2006) (with an absolute majority) came as no surprise to Fatah itself or to Palestinians in Gaza and WB. It demonstrated the increasing level of popular support the movement enjoyed among Palestinians, on the one hand, and the opposition to Fatah for its decade-long corruption and political failure, on the other (Shiqaqi, 2006: 125).

3.7 Hamas's Control of Gaza and the Emergence of the 'Tunnel Economy' (2006–12)

Hamas's formation of a Palestinian government, following its victory in the parliamentary election in 2006, sparked a lot of debate both internally and externally. For some, this was a good opportunity for Hamas to prove it was able to maintain a political agenda that was both acceptable to Palestinians and to the international community. The expectations were that with Hamas now being responsible to the people, it would change its policy towards Israel or at least give more priority to the well-being of the nation rather than serving its party's political agenda. Meanwhile, there was an anticipation on

---

[17] Described by the United Nations as a restricted access area, the buffer zone is located inside the Palestinian border with Israel, where Palestinians are banned from entering. The zone ranges from one to three kilometres and is mostly agricultural land, which also means that many farmers lost access to farming in this area. Israel claims that this zone is necessary to maintain its security near the border by ensuring that no human-related activities occur in these areas. The restricted access area also includes the imposing of a three- to nine-mile fishing zone, which hugely affected the fishing sector in Gaza. Meanwhile, Israel maintains its control over Gaza's airspace.

the part of international policy-makers regarding how this government would act in practice. The initial response was to give the Palestinians, especially the Palestinian president Mahmoud Abbas, the time they required to get their house in order. It was hoped that Abbas, with the help of the security institution which falls under his authority, would encourage or rather force Hamas to make a shift towards politics and give up its military resistance (International Crisis Group, 2006). Consequently, Abbas had received pressure from the US administration to disarm Hamas as part of his reform agenda, yet he clearly vowed that this would result in a civil war. He instead suggested that Hamas's participation and victory in the PLC would encourage it to give up its weapons and integrate it into the mainstream (Weisman, 2006)

However, Hamas's refusal and failure to satisfy these expectations, and to abide by the international requirements of renouncing violence and recognising Israel, made the situation more complex. As a result, Israel, with an indirect endorsement from the Quartet, suspended the transfer of Palestinian tax revenue and custom duties which, in accordance with the Paris Protocol, Israel was obliged to do. These revenues constituted nearly 40 per cent of the PA's budget, which meant a real crisis for the PA's ability to provide services and pay salaries to its employees (Reuters, 2011). Furthermore, Israel intensified the sanctions on Gaza by imposing further technical measures. Some measures within those sanctions saw the tightening of Israeli control over Gaza's six land crossings that acted as the main supply routes to the Strip (Strand, 2014: 10). Karni Crossing, the main commercial crossing between Gaza and Israel, was completely closed as Israel decided to reroute supplies to the Strip through a much smaller and underdeveloped crossing, Kerem Shalom. According to a classified cable published on WikiLeaks, the decision to close Karni Crossing and its replacement with Kerem Shalom was done to minimise the flow of humanitarian supplies rather than commercial supplies, and was done in consultation with the US administration through the American ambassador in Tel Aviv (WikiLeaks, 2011b). Accordingly, the main artery between Gaza, the Israeli market and the external market was cut. The Israeli government justified these moves as necessary, as keeping open crossings with Gaza 'could weaken efforts to undermine Hamas because monitoring the crossings require constant contact with officials of the new Hamas government' (as quoted by the Israeli foreign minister Tzipi Livni, in Strand, 2014: 10). The US administration also perceived these measures as necessary without suggesting the exercise of collective punishment to the entire Gaza Strip population, but it would 'draw attention to the failures of Hamas' (WikiLeaks, 2011a).

Trude Strand (2014) looks at the legal basis the Israeli government relied upon in justifying its policy towards Gaza. He argues that the Israeli government realised that sanctioning the citizens of Gaza would be controversial and would spark anger among some of its international partners. The Israeli government, therefore, through its legal adviser, Dov Weissglass, admitted that this economic embargo in terms of international law was a 'collective punishment imposed against a country or a type of a country and which primarily harms the civilian population with the aim of coercing the government (whether recognised or not)' (Weissglass, 2007). Weissglass continued to suggest, however, referring to chapters 6 and 7 of the UN Charter, that Israel is a democratic country that abides by international law. Also, he suggests that Israel is obliged to use economic sanctions that harm civilians as this offered means to avoid the use of military power. Therefore, Israel had every right to sanction Gaza residents and regimes through ceasing the supplies of 'goods, fuel, raw materials, communication services and other infrastructure-related services, including electricity and water' (Weissglass, 2007).

The impact of the new economic sanctions was immediate. Gaza, being eligible for humanitarian supplies, had to forego its entire industrial sector, which left both the manufacturers and labourers in a muddle (see Table 3.4). According to Gisha (an Israeli NGO that focuses on the freedom of movement of Palestinians), only 114 items and commodities were allowed into the Gaza Strip. Before the measure was put in place, more than 4,000 individual items were allowed (Gisha, 2010). None of these items consisted of materials or could be used for industrial purposes. Even some humanitarian commodities, including children's toys, cocoa, chewing gum, paper and other items, were barred, as Israel considered them luxury items. Gisha further illustrated that this policy was part of Israel's traditional 'economic warfare' ploy, designed to obstruct any economic activity in Gaza and to increase the Strip's dependence on the Israeli market. For instance, Israeli authorities allowed enough of items such as margarine and butter so as to meet needs of household consumption, while banning large blocks intended for industrial usage. The same applied to the transfer of 'rubber, glue, nylon' used for the manufacture of diapers, while allowing Israeli-made diapers. As a result, more than 90 per cent of Gaza factories were forced to completely shut down and the remaining 10 per cent worked at minimum capacity (Gisha, 2010).

Additionally, exports from Gaza to the outside market saw a massive decrease. In the period between 2007 and 2010, only 259 trucks left Gaza daily, while before 2007, 70 trucks left the territory daily (ibid.). Among other sectors, the agricultural sector was the most affected as it had always been identified as a priority with respect to employment and economic prosperity (Strand, 2014: 16). This sector was characterised as being dependent on individual investment by farmers who built their business on the export of vegetables and cash crops, such as strawberries and tomatoes. Farmers

Table 3.4 Major National Accounts Variables (USD): Gaza Strip (2006–2016)

Variable	2008	2007	2008	2009	2010	2011	2012	2013	2014	2015	2010
Gross domestic product	1,552.3	1,515.2	1,506.9	1,748.1	2,283.1	2,547.6	2,682.6	3,092.1	2,912.1	3,134.1	3,450.4
Net factor income from abroad	79.0	95.6	106.2	78.8	50.8	70.0	63.8	58.8	17.2	15.8	6.5
Compensation of employees, net	43.1	44.1	51.7	61.4	43.3	65.4	52.0	52.6	9.4	8.4	9.3
Property income, net	35.9	51.5	54.5	17.4	7.5	4.6	11.8	6.2	7.8	7.4	−2.8
Gross national income	1,631.3	1,610.8	1,613.1	1,826.9	2,333.9	2,617.6	2,746.4	3,150.9	2,929.3	3,149.9	3,456.9
Net current transfers from abroad	514.0	897.3	1,277.3	859.8	801.9	446.9	711.2	485.0	575.9	585.9	581.9
Gross national disposable income	2,145.3	2,508.1	2,890.4	2,686.7	3,135.8	3,064.5	3,457.6	3,635.9	3,505.2	3,735.8	4,038.8
Final consumption	2,158.6	2,217.7	2,235.0	2,373.3	2,660.2	2,994.0	3,088.2	3,657.7	4,019.2	3,997.5	4,103.9
Savings	−13.3	290.4	655.4	313.4	475.6	70.5	369.4	−21.8	−514.0	−261.7	−65.1

Source: PCBS, 2016.

were forced to sell their products at a local market at a very cheap price due to the huge gap between the high levels of supply and the lower levels of demand.

The livelihoods of these farmers were starting to disappear as a result, and thousands of families that were dependent on this sector had to face economic hardship and destitution. Additionally, the agriculture sector faced systematic destruction because of frequent attacks on farms that are, in the main, located near boundaries, where either farmers were prevented from having access to their farms or crops were damaged by the military assault.

Official figures in 2008 showed that the Gaza economy shrank to 1.1 billion USD and contributed to only 22 per cent of Palestinian GDP. Furthermore, the economy continued to deteriorate through 2009 with very limited commercial activity. Consequently, official figures showed that more than 40 per cent of the labour force was unemployed (Figure 3.2), while other specialised reports indicated that the level of unemployment was as high as 65 per cent (Portland Trust, 2010). Following a strong decline in the early years of the Oslo era, unemployment in Gaza has increased and reached a record high of 45 per cent in the second quarter of 2014 (World Bank 2015). The highest level of damage was within Gaza's private sector. According to the Portland Trust and data from the Palestinian Bureau of Statistics, the number of people employed between 2006 and 2010 did not change, while the workforce itself had increased by over 50 per cent (Portland Trust, 2010). The impact of keeping PA employees on the pay-roll doubled to what the public sector could afford. Employment within private sector (industry and construction) also fell by more than 75 per cent. Towards the end of 2010, nearly one-third of private sector companies were operating only at very low capacity (ibid.).

Besides this programme of economic warfare, Israel conducted major military assaults between 2006 and 2012. This included Operation Summer Rain in the summer of 2006, Operation Hot Winter in 2008, Operation Cast Lead in December 2008–January 2009 and Pillar of Defence in November 2012. These assaults contributed to the widespread devastation of infrastructure and civilian assets and caused major destruction to the already paralyzed industrial and agricultural sectors (Strand, 2014: 16). Following Operation Cast Lead, the UNDP reported that more than 46 per cent of the agricultural land in Gaza was completely damaged or has become inaccessible due to the expansion of the wall near the buffer zone between Gaza and Israel (UNDP, 2010: 67). The report also indicated that more than 1,165 private sector establishments were attacked, of which 324 were completely destroyed (44 per cent of the private industrial sector) and the remaining 56 per cent were partially destroyed (ibid.: 73). The report concluded that the main damage inflicted by the military operation saw the destruction of important

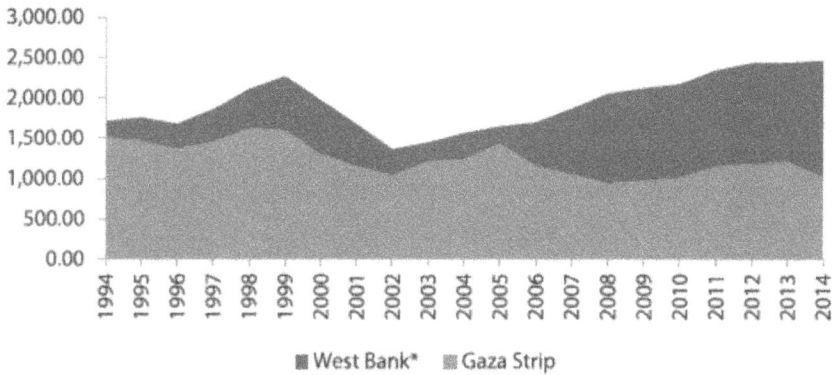

Figure 3.2 Historical overview of unemployment in the Gaza Strip.

production elements (buildings and equipment) and constituted 94 per cent of the total damage.

Within this severe destruction of all economic sectors, and access restrictions on goods and individuals, the level of poverty reached approximately 80 per cent within households (Byman, 2010: 58), 60 per cent of which cannot survive financially or can survive financially only on a day-to-day basis (UNDP, 2010: 30). The WFP, on the other hand, indicated that while the original percentage of the population classified as food insecure was 52 per cent before Operation Cast Lead, an additional 13 per cent of households became vulnerable afterwards (WFP, FAO and PCBS, 2010: 8). Consequently, the humanitarian agencies, principally UNRWA and WFP, had to double their efforts to meet the staggering level of poverty. Approximately, 1.1 million people received direct food assistance, while 750,000 refugees received food baskets from UNRWA, agency that dedicates its services to Palestinian refugees only, and nearly 350,000 people received food aid through the WFP (UNDP, 2010: 109).

3.7.1 The Emergence and Growth of the 'Tunnel Economy'

As part of its disengagement plan in 2005, Israel decided to create a new buffer zone near the Gaza border with Egypt. Some 1,500 Palestinian homes were destroyed along the borderline (Philadelphia Corridor) and within a 100 metre buffer zone between Rafah city and the border. Israel had also built a 10-metre-high metal wall to enhance security after its withdrawal. On the same day that Israel evacuated the Strip, young Palestinian men started to gradually remove the fence and infiltrated the Egyptian territory. Israelis perceived this act as a serious security threat and urged the Egyptian Mubarak regime to regain control over its borders. This chaotic situation continued for nearly two weeks until the Egyptian authorities decided to seal the borders again. As the siege intensified following the Hamas government, and the kidnap of the Israeli soldier Gilad Shalit in June 2006, access above ground was completely cut off. Alternatively, Hamas managed to gradually oversee a programme of 'industrial-scale burrowing underground' (Pelham, 2012: 9). The movement invested in and supervised the construction of more than 2,000 tunnels along the Gaza–Egypt border. It was estimated that the construction of each tunnel would cost 80,000–200,000 USD depending on its capacity and length (ibid.). What the movement managed to do in cooperation with its affiliate government was involve the various sectors of Gaza by creating partnerships with land owners, agricultural workers, local NGOs, traders, university graduates, security forces and tunnel labourers. With the relatively high cost of constructing and operating a single tunnel, yet with these tunnels being fully operational, they managed to cover the cost of their construction in a relatively short period and make high profits.

These tunnels were mostly dedicated to smuggling goods into the Gaza Strip. Over a short period, they developed to become the main trading route and driver of the Gaza economy, enabling it to overcome the crises and socio-economic pressures caused by the siege (Roy, 2012). In essence, and due to the deteriorating situation in Gaza, the tunnel economy grew to a size of more than 85 per cent of its trade and with an estimated value of approximately 1 billion USD. This also had a massive impact on the level of employment within the private sector. What the tunnel economy did more efficiently was contribute to the reconstruction of Gaza following Operation Cast Lead. Importantly, it was now possible to import construction materials through these tunnels (Pelham, 2011). There was an additional and important aspect of the tunnel trade to consider. Namely, the aim to decrease dependence on the Israeli economy and trade with Israel to the extent necessary to generate debate within the Israeli military and security community about the efficacy of continuing with the blockade of Gaza. For instance, by early 2012, an estimated 1,600 tons of cement were imported from Israel on a monthly basis, compared with the 31,000 tons smuggled through the tunnels (Roy, 2012). As stated by Nicolas Pelham (2011), 'the [tunnel] trade is fast and mercifully free of red tape. While Israel's crossings are subject to repeated closures, due to Jewish holidays or spikes in political tension, the tunnels operate 24 hours a day, seven days a week'.

As the practice continued to expand and begin to resemble formal trading, the Hamas government felt the need to regulate it in order to maximise its benefits and also ensure that revenues get directed through the government's official channels. For this purpose, the Tunnel Affairs Commission was established as a tax authority and a source for domestic revenues. At the time, the Hamas minister of national economy, Alaa Rafati, indicated that Gaza's local revenues from the tunnels constituted only a little more than 50 per cent of the Hamas government revenues (750 million USD) in 2011. Overall, the impact of the tunnel economy between 2009 and 2011 was very significant, especially in terms of private sector growth.

According to the United Nations, the average real GDP in 2010 grew by 20 per cent and continued to grow through 2011 to 23 per cent (see Figure 3.3 for the aggregate real GDP in Gaza compared to other countries in the region and the world). Meanwhile, the entire commercial life and trade activities became dominated mostly by Hamas through its network of smugglers and militants. The party was also in charge of monitoring and controlling the ins and outs of tunnels that were managed by other groups and individuals. Contrary to this, formal traders and local contractors, with whom international agencies were obliged to cooperate, were seriously weakened by the Israeli closure policies and lost their ability to compete with the underground trade (Roy, 2012).

3.7.2 Hamas Reinforces Its Control over the Strip

The way Hamas managed the tunnel economy has enabled it to not only reinforce its military and political control over the Strip but also redraw and control the economic activity of the territory. There is no doubt that Hamas managed, to a great extent, to circumvent the US-led financial restrictions and

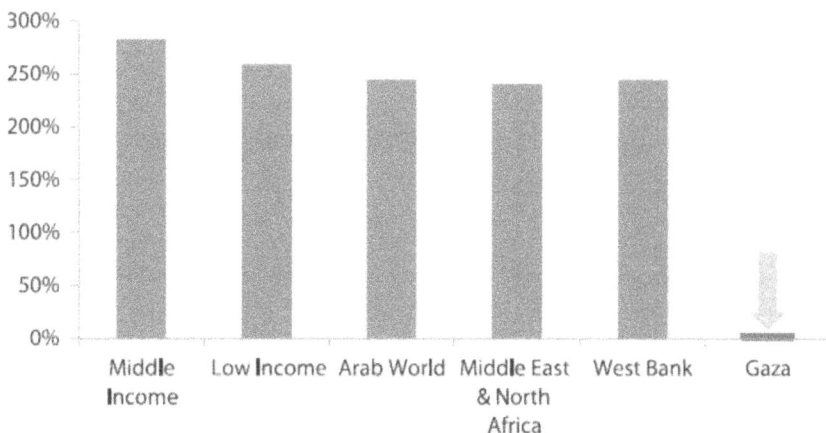

Figure 3.3 Aggregate real GDP growth in Gaza and comparator countries (1994–2013 for comparators and 1994–2014 for Gaza (World Bank, 2015)).

instead reconstruct an almost independent economic system (Roy, 2012). The flourishing Gaza economy was disturbing not only to Israel and its Western allies but also to the PA in Ramallah as the latter perceived it as a tool that would enable Hamas to extend and deepen its control over Gaza. The US administration, Israel and the PA tried to urge the Mubarak regime to exert more pressure to end the expansion of tunnels near Israel's border with Gaza. However, the political development in Egypt and the Muslim Brotherhood coming to power made this impossible and instead empowered Hamas given the common ideological heritage it shared with Egypt's Muslim Brotherhood. As Pelham (2011) argues, the 'Turnaround of an economy that Western policy-makers had connived to render a basket case has dramatically revived the political fortunes of Gaza's master, Hamas'. Subsequently, it was natural that Hamas's popularity in the Gaza Strip rose sharply. For many, especially traders and private sector business owners, Hamas saved them from starvation and from further losses to their business. Another part of Hamas's growing control over the Gaza Strip was that it created a new border control system that acted as an alternative to agreements signed with Israel. This enabled Hamas to closely monitor goods entering the Gaza Strip and thus ensure that merchants and NGOs were compliant with its policies. Hamas did, however, begin to gradually monitor the work of international agencies and NGOs as these agencies became obliged to coordinate the movement of their staff in and out of Gaza with Hamas's internal security. This outraged INGOs as coordination with the Hamas government meant breaking the no-contact policy the United States and other Western countries declared upon Hamas's victory. Although this threatened to end their activities in the Gaza Strip, they still believed that such a decision was impractical and that they would be obliged to work in Gaza when the first humanitarian crisis would occur in the future. Instead, these agencies would limit their coordination with the Hamas government through a third party, the United Nations Office for the Coordination of Humanitarian Affairs (OCHA).

The rise in Hamas's popularity has not made it immune, however, to criticism from the local population in Gaza or from other political factions operating in the Gaza Strip. This criticism emerged from Hamas's attempt to impose not only its political agenda in Gaza but also its social agenda. This was clear in some measures Hamas took in what some critics labelled 'Islamising' Gaza (Sayigh, 2010: 5). According to Sayigh (2010), this was seen in some individual government institutions' efforts to impose Islamisation guidelines, for instance, imposing a specific dress code on women, banning women from smoking in public spaces or separating boys and girls in public primary schools and inside NGOs. The other aspect of corruption is financial

(Sayigh, 2010: 6). The nature of the tunnel trade has created opportunities for corruption in an economy that is based on cash dealing. There was much debate in Gaza's streets about how senior men, by acting and controlling the tunnel trade behind the scene as silent partners (Sayigh, 2010: 6), collected massive fortunes that amounted to tens of millions of dollars in a relatively short period. Over a very short period, these top Hamas officials began to buy and control the major economic establishments in Gaza, such as hotels, factories and land.

3.8 Conclusion

To sum up, Gaza's current reality has been influenced and shaped by two conjoined factors: the continuing and deepening occupation and, with this, a systematic process of destruction of all types of infrastructure that led to the de-development of the Gaza Strip over time. Israel as an occupying power has played the major role in this de-development through its long-standing policy of closures and the ever-increasing mobility restrictions placed upon individuals, labourers and goods. Other factors have also contributed, however, whether directly or indirectly, to determining Gaza's political, economic and social life. For instance, the dismissal of tens of thousands of Gaza labourers working in the Gulf area during the 1990 Gulf War proved Gaza was never immune to regional political developments. Hopes were high that Palestinians would soon have their own independent state, of which Gaza and Jericho would be the first seeds. Not only Palestinians were optimistic, but so was also the international donor community which put in place a new foreign aid policy that was based on money for peace to encourage Palestinians to make the concessions necessary to sustain this peace. Palestinians' limited experience in handling the large number of donations, political corruption and the obstacles in reaching a final-status solution with Israel were important reasons why aid dynamics continued to change, changes that saw more pressures and conditions imposed on the weaker party, the Palestinians. It is important to mention here that the Palestinian population, particularly in Gaza, continues to be highly educated in comparison with other Arab countries, in terms of both literacy and graduates, factors necessary for a potential successful development process. At the same time, over more than six decades, Palestinians have shown great capacity and ingenuity in sustaining themselves under very difficult circumstances. It will be shown in the coming chapters how a huge sum of foreign aid had failed to create the infrastructure necessary for Palestinians to engage in a genuine development process. Instead, aid itself has become an additional burden and a means for controlling the everyday life of Palestinians, especially in Gaza, beside the occupation.

Chapter 4

AID, THE 'PARTNER FOR PEACE' AND THE RESHAPING OF PALESTINE'S POLITICAL AND SOCIO-ECONOMIC SPACES

4.1 Introduction

It is now time to look at the most important aspect of how the Israeli-Palestinian conflict, as mediated by the United States and others, has influenced aid delivery to the PA and thus the PA's structures and operations from the Oslo Accords until after Hamas took power in the Gaza Strip (2007–13).[1] Key to this, it is also important to examine the extent to which the securitisation and politicisation of foreign aid contributed to sustaining political and social divisions within Gaza and between the WB and Gaza. Although the ultimate focus of this book is directed towards Gaza, the discussion in this chapter will involve the situation in Palestine as a whole so as to properly address specific issues in Gaza.

The partner for peace framework has emerged following the Oslo peace process (1993). In the context of this chapter, this term is crucial to understand the dynamics surrounding foreign aid to the Palestinians and examine how this framework has been used to divide the Palestinian nation's polity according to their commitment to the workings of this framework. The application of the partner for peace framework assists an understanding of the terms 'securitisation' and 'politicisation' of aid in connection with the Israeli-Palestinian conflict. In this context, it is important to explore the kind of peace that was meant to be achieved, whether it is peace between the PA political and security leadership that does not include the Palestinian people or peace that is based on a security or an economic agenda. It is also important to examine the kind of partner needed to achieve this peace. Is it a political partner or a security

---

[1] Hamas continues to hold power over the Strip until the time of writing, but due to data collection purposes, this is the timeframe this book covers.

agent that caters to Israel's security agenda? Is it a partner that maintains
Israel's interest in sustaining the status quo of occupation? These questions are
key for unpicking the existing political frameworks that contribute to deciding
the legitimacy of the Palestinian partner and according to whose interests,
whether donors seek a security agent or a development agent to maintain the
flow of their aid and whether the ultimate purpose of this aid is to achieve
development or maintain Israel's security.

Defining a 'legitimate' partner for peace has also entailed complex processes
of redefining the Palestinian political elite. The complexity of this process
is embedded in how the political elite's legitimacy is defined, by whom and
according to whose interest. It is also embedded in how the roles of this political elite have changed over time and how these different roles have impacted
on internal Palestinian politics, especially following Hamas's victory in the
2006 elections. Along this line, a few questions need to be posed, that is, how
donors, using aid, have influenced the redefinition of this political elite? How
donors influenced the way political groups perceived the legitimacy of the
other? And how all these have influenced Gaza's political, social and economic divisions?

To that end, we will look at the structural underpinnings of Palestinian
divisions and how they directly impacted on Gaza's current socio-economic
reality and how foreign aid has played a role in this. This will be done by
examining the PA's efforts in creating economic infrastructure in both the
WB and Gaza and whether questions of economic infrastructure contributed
to achieving social justice and welfare among the different socio-economic
sectors. We will look at the extent to which the PA contributed to creating aid-
dependent institutions and the impact of this on the whole of Gaza's population following Hamas's victory and how both Fatah and Hamas created new
socio-economic realities in Gaza by taking full control of public institutions
and influencing the way the private sector operates.

4.2 The 'Partner for Peace Framework' and Buying the PA's Political Stability

Foreign aid to the PA, following the Oslo Accords in 1993, has been guided
mainly by the PA's ability to cooperate as a peace partner with Israel and the
international community represented by donors. Therefore, in order to understand how foreign aid influenced the PA's structures as well as the political
and social division in Gaza, there is a need to unpick the partner for peace
framework.

The term partner for peace has been used to describe the relationship
between the Israelis and Palestinians since the inauguration of the peace

process in 1993. Yet, there has been an embedded bias among the key parties in how this framework has been used to determine the characteristics of a partner for peace. Mandy Turner (2009, 2011, 2012, 2014) suggests that the partner for peace paradigm has given more power to Israel to set out the rules for its relationship with the Palestinian partner. This has also created the grounds for donors' assumptions that providing aid to the Palestinian leadership, which Israel approves as a partner, would thus facilitate and strengthen peace between the two parties (Turner, 2012: 499). Accordingly, in an interview for this book, a senior executive Fatah member suggested that the PA's mandatory commitment to this framework indirectly resulted in two essential practices, one by Israel as a primary partner and the other by the donors (mainly the US government, which has been playing the leading role in the peace process since its inception).[2] First, it has enabled Israel to justify the ill-treatment of its Palestinian partner through a spectrum of practices that include, but are not limited to, the confiscation of lands and the building of illegal settlements, the financial sanctioning through the withholding of tax revenues, the routine incursions of districts under Palestinian security control according to agreements between the two sides and various other practices.

Second, according to the senior Fatah executive, donors have used this paradigm as a conflict management tool to put more pressure (political and economic) on the Palestinians to accept the security demands made by Israel and consequently influence the PA's political and security structures.[3]

In this context, it is important to understand how the partner for peace paradigm came into effect and to analyse the uneven power relations that emerged between the PLO and Israel as a result. It is important also to analyse how the PLO's political leadership became tied to this broad and problematic framework. Khalidi and Samour (2011: 18) suggest that the PLO leadership's motive in accepting to work in accordance with this framework (while negotiating the Oslo Accords) was its long-standing desire to seek new arrangements that could potentially allow it to gradually end the Israeli occupation. Khalidi (2012) adds that the PLO's political elite consequently became involved in a new type of struggle aimed at obtaining access to rents and a place at the UN table. They were driven by the fear that they might lose their internal as well as external legitimacy if they were to be replaced by other potential Palestinian partners. Similarly, Selby (2011: 13) thinks that the primary aim of pursuing peace is not necessarily achieving it but rather sustaining the domination of

---

[2] Interview with a senior executive member in Fatah and professor of politics at Al-Azhar University in Gaza, Gaza, 3 February 2015.

[3] Ibid.

political elites as well as ensuring their legitimacy internationally. He suggests that peace processes

> are inter-elite political accommodations whose aim is often not so much 'peace' as the reconfiguration of domestic hegemony and/or international legitimacy; peace processes are reformist, conservative and far from revolutionary phenomena, and often therefore do not provide a basis for the social transformations necessary for sustainable peace.

At the time, the PLO leadership had already lost much of its credibility as a result of backing the Iraqi invasion of Kuwait (1990–91) and had found itself isolated even among Arab states who opposed the Iraqi actions. Therefore, the PLO had realised that engagement in the peace process was necessary to re-advance its status internationally and promote itself domestically as the only representative of the Palestinians.

4.2.1 Changing Internal Power Dynamics within PLO Prior to Signing Oslo Accords

According to a Palestinian technical negotiation team member at the time, the political disparities began to emerge between the PLO leadership in the oPt and the one in the diaspora. The former felt it was being sidelined and not being consulted about the details of the negotiations with Israel.[4] Feeling sidelined seemed to have inspired anger among a large majority of the PLO leadership in the WB and the Gaza Strip. In the member's words,

> They felt that they were the ones who led the Intifada and without their efforts and leadership, Israel would not have felt that need to come to the negotiations table [...] we did not know much detail of what was going on, even though we were instructed to start forming the technical teams in preparation for the technical negotiations.[5]

What happened, in fact, was that the PLO leadership in the diaspora wanted to ensure that it would become the only legitimate peace partner before Israel and the peace process sponsors, even if it came at the expense of a united leadership that operated inside the oPt. Similarly, an ex-minister in the 11th PA cabinet suggested that the PLO's leadership in the diaspora began to act

---

[4] Interview with a member of the technical negotiation team in the Orient House in Jerusalem on 10 December 2016.
[5] Ibid.

unilaterally away from the leadership in the oPt with regard to the negoti-
ations with Israel and signing agreements.[6] From that, it can be inferred that
Arafat was serious about gaining legitimacy and control upon establishing the
PA in the oPt. This was seen as the first phase of the PLO's transformation.

It was obvious from the early stages of the PA establishment that donors
and aid agencies, including the UN agencies, had put more emphasis on
the security parameters of the state-building project than building the
institutions of the potential state. These security arrangements, according
to a Hamas government official, were of course a pre-condition and integral to be recognised as a peace partner. Donors, mainly the US donors,
were accordingly keen to provide the necessary financial support to the PA
to build its security institutions and force to achieve this goal and the United
States was directly involved in supporting the PA via the former's intelligence
experts (CIA).[7]

Hamas has always perceived the PA as originally established to perform
as a client state whose viability depended primarily on external powers (i.e.
Israel and foreign donors). To the movement, these external powers had consistently demonstrated the ability to influence the former's policy-making and
the allocation of power. This allocation of power occurred when either Israel
or Western donors began to honour some of the PA's figures and leaders as
trustworthy or liable to honest peace partners. The use of aid in this instance
was essential in influencing the policy-making of the PA using various control
mechanisms. To many, ensuring the PA's economic vulnerability was fundamental to ensure its compliance with the political agenda of both the US
donor and Israel. The PA's compliance was measured by its demonstration of
the ability to ensure enough internal support among its group and leadership
for the peace agenda and suppress voices that oppose it (i.e. Hamas and other
groups). To do so, Fatah and the PA under the former's leadership had to put
in place an incentive system for those who show support and loyalty to the
peace paradigm and punish and abolish the rejectionists.[8]

Similarly, at the time Israel and Western donors perceived Arafat or Abbas
as partners for peace, they had the advantage to either embrace or eliminate
other political elites as appropriate peace partners. Plus, it could demand that
the PA adopt a similar view in this regard, accordingly creating the foundation
for political division between Palestinians.

---

[6] Interview with the an ex-minister in the PA's 11th cabinet and senior member in Fatah,
Ramallah, 4 February 2015.

[7] Ibid.

[8] Interview with a Palestinian political analyst and researcher of Palestinian politics at the
Islamic University of Gaza, Gaza, 18 February 2015.

4.2.2 Unbalanced Power Dynamics: PA, Israel and Donors

The US involvement in the region took a more serious form after brokering the Camp David Agreement (1978) between Egypt and Israel and later the military intervention in the war between Kuwait and Iraq. This has qualified it to be the most influential actor in the region. Turner (2014: 38) states that during the two or three decades before the Oslo Accords (1993), the United States offered unlimited support to Israel, whether military or direct financial support (approximately 3 billion USD of aid every year). Importantly, however, Israel has enjoyed diplomatic support from the United States in the United Nations Security Council.

The US political monopoly of the peace process has consistently been problematic for the Palestinians. It has raised important questions, not only for Palestinians but also for other key donors, and the EU in particular, who refrained from openly confronting or even criticising the United States for different reasons. Le More (2005: 997) suggests that the Americans' 'political relief' strategy of dealing with Palestinians and other donors is

> first and foremost to be explained by the dominant diplomatic role exerted by the US in the peace process, Washington's unwavering support for Israel, and the concomitant very limited diplomatic influence of other actors – whether the EU, the World Bank or the UN – on Israeli policy, the peace process or American mediation efforts. It has also been based on the naive assumption held by most non-US international actors that, given the otherwise limited ability to influence the process diplomatically, they could influence Israel through their aid to the Palestinians and also that this would buy time for further negotiations on the political front.

Le More (2005: 995) suggests that donors' relationships pertaining to the peace process reflect the familiar global power structure where 'the US decides, the World Bank leads, the EU pays, the UN feeds'. Meanwhile, the United States has never underestimated the importance of maintaining close coordination with the peace partners, yet this gives international legitimacy to its policies towards the key stakeholders, such as the PA and Israel.

All Western donors, however, have always insisted on key commitments towards achieving a viable Palestinian state, yet without jeopardising Israel's security. According to this, the EU's consultant in Gaza argued that the 'security first' framework has constituted a key factor in the entire peace process, and both the PA and donors had to abide by it during any aid delivery processes.[9]

---

[9] Interview with the EU consultant in Gaza, Gaza, 21 December 2016.

While the PA security services and intelligence agency were instituted according to this principle, donors' aid delivery was designed to make sure that the PA was doing the best it could to fulfil this commitment. A USAID representative in Gaza indicated that the US government and the Congress had developed a complicated mechanism for aid delivery to Palestinians.[10] According to the official, this mechanism is highly influenced by the Israeli-Palestinian conflict and the agency treats Israel's security demands with a high level of sensitivity. The other part relates to the US law regarding its war on terror following the 9/11 attacks and the ways this impacted on donors' relationships with the PA in general and Gaza in particular. Consequently, Western donors' aid delivery to the PA have reflected these notions in that they avoid any direct confrontation with Israel in terms of designing, planning and implementing their programmes. Meanwhile, Israel has had the capacity to strongly interfere in the day-to-day activities of donors either through facilitating their work or putting in obstacles that could result in the suspension of their operation. Israel has always done so under the claim that these programmes or aid activities could pose security threats against it.

The unbalanced power dynamics became visible in the first two years of the PA work with donors on rehabilitating and building its infrastructure. Israel's interference in the work of donors had a negative impact on PA–donor relationships and constantly caused tension between the two sides. For instance, the PA, through the Palestinian Economic Council for Development and Reconstruction (PECDAR), spent several millions of dollars of donor funding to prepare technical proposals for various industrial, agricultural, transport and water and sanitation projects. A clear example of these projects was the Gaza Water Treatment Project, which the PA and donors hoped would alleviate the existing drinking water crisis in the Gaza Strip (see Box 4.1). However, Israel's security claims resulted in the failure of the project's implementation. According to a former PECDAR official, in principle, these projects had no security implications on Israel and individual donors had to review these projects and approve them after examining the security factor.[11] Despite this, Israel's approval to facilitate the implementation of such projects was always key to donors' final approval of funding. Moreover, in many instances, Israel used vague security concerns to justify its decisions. In such instances, neither the PA nor donors had the ability to confront Israel[12] (see Box 4.1).

---

[10] Interview with the USAID representative in Gaza who supervises the implementation of projects funded by the US government, Ramallah, 20 December 2016.

[11] Interview with a former PECDAR official in Gaza, Gaza, 10 December 2016.

[12] Ibid.

Box 4.1 Gaza Water Treatment Project*

A joint project between the Palestinian Water Authority, the Land Authority, the Ministry of Foreign Affairs and the Ministry of Finance. The four partners participated in conducting a feasibility study in cooperation with Japan International Cooperation Agency (JICA), and the cost of the study alone was almost 5 million USD. The feasibility study lasted for nearly a year, and the idea of the project was to build three sewage treatment stations in the Gaza Strip. This project was very important for three reasons: (1) all rainwater in the winter season goes directly to the sea and Gaza cannot take any benefit from this resource, (2) Gaza sewage water goes to the sea and has been causing huge environmental damage to Gaza's industry as well as sea species and (3) sewage now is starting to reach the water basins and is causing a high level of contamination of drinking water.

The estimated cost of the project was not high; it was approximately 36 million USD. There was an agreement to build the largest station in between the city of Rafah and Khan Yunis; both have suffered from a severe lack of drinking water for more than two decades. Meanwhile, they have no sewage infrastructure and have been suffering from drinking water contamination due to sewage reaching water basins. Each station was potentially planned to help almost 350,000 people. The two other stations were proposed to be built near Gaza and in the northern Gaza Strip.

JICA showed unprecedented levels of enthusiasm towards the idea of the project in all phases of project preparation. Yet, the official response by the donor was that they could not carry on with the implementation of the project simply because the Israeli authorities did not approve the implementation and that these stations could have a negative impact on Israel and might pose security risks. In the end, the donor offered other alternatives, such as supplying equipment not directly to the PA but through UNDP, which again was subject to Israel's decision to allow their entry to the Gaza Strip.

* Interview with the chief technical coordinator and a senior official at the Palestinian Ministry of Foreign Affairs, Gaza, 17 December 2016.

4.3 Redefining the Political Elite

The Oslo peace process and the state-building project, of which international aid is a fundamental element, have become a new strategy to influence the Palestinian political elite and to co-opt it based on whether they qualify to be peace partners or not from the perspective of both Israel and Western donors. Israel has technically used it to classify and categorise Palestinians according to what serves its own interests and as a justification to continue its colonial practices of manipulating the Palestinian leadership and dictating the rules of the game. This included deciding what the Palestinian political leadership should look like and who should qualify to lead the PA as a legitimate partner for peace. To PLO leadership, this practice was evident in the failure of the Camp David talks in 2000 and how it motivated Israel to de-legitimise Yasser Arafat as a partner since he failed to make the political concessions desired by Israel. This was followed by various forms of pressures to influence the internal political structures within the PA in terms of how the PA should reform its security forces in a way that enhances the PA's commitment to maintaining Israel's security.

Israel consistently used the claim that 'there is not [a] genuine Palestinian partner' as a pretext for continuing activities such as confiscating more Palestinian land to expand either its settlements or its security buffer zones, halt the transfer of tax revenues, put more restrictions on the mobility of the PA political elites, increase the number of checkpoints between Palestinian cities and towns and many other unilateral measures.[13] Donors, meanwhile, have similarly used aid to exert forms of pressure on the PA's political elites. These, as will be discussed further in this chapter, influenced the latter's political attitude and identity. According to the political analyst of Palestinian politics, donors framed their policies according to what works best for Israel's security and adopted Israel's claims that the Palestinian leadership is not fulfilling security duties. This prompted them to attach a set of conditions to aid donated to the PA. Accordingly, to ensure the flow of aid, the Palestinian leadership must show their full commitment to a peace in which Israel's security interest comes first. These elites must continuously reform and reproduce themselves to maintain an identity and an ideology that fit the standards of Israel and donors.

This can be demonstrated in the way Western donors perceived Hamas's electoral victory in 2006, where these Western donors adopted Israel's political

---

[13] Ibid.

position of de-legitimising Hamas as a political power in Palestinian politics due its opposition to the Oslo peace agreement. According to the senior executive of Fatah, Israel refused proposals to integrate Hamas as a legitimate Palestinian party as this could lead to making it more politically pragmatic, thus accepting demands made by the international peace sponsor in regard to relations with Israel.[14] In contrast, Israel perceived the growing popularity of Hamas as a threat to Israel's security and emphasised that the PA under the Fatah leadership must denounce and reject Hamas as a national political partner.

Western donors' adoption of Israel's de-legitimisation strategy is believed to be a significant factor in promoting political division between Fatah and Hamas. This occurred when donors cut their financial support to the PA for months for allowing Hamas to form the new government in 2006. This practice, in particular, seemed to contradict the reform agenda of donors that followed the death of Yasser Arafat.[15] According to this agenda, the PA was to engage in good governance, democratisation and political participation reforms. A senior consultant at Tamkeen Project[16] indicated that the United States funded many projects aimed at assisting the PA and civil society organisations to promote a culture of democracy and political participation and mobilised resources and individuals for this purpose.[17] The project provided capacity-building training to relevant departments in the PA in order to ensure the results of the upcoming election would reflect the peoples' choice. Accordingly, it is obvious the US government became more concerned about the possible victory of Hamas given that Hamas achieved a significant victory in the municipal and local council elections in 2005. However, the polls the Tamkeen Project ran before the elections indicated that although Hamas would win a large number of seats in the PLC, it would not win by a majority. When the result came otherwise, USAID issued a new guidance according to which many civil society organisations that benefited from the democratisation programme lost their funding due to the inaccurate data they provided to the agency.[18]

---

[14] Interview with a senior Fatah executive in Gaza and political expert at Al-Azhar University in Gaza, Gaza, 3 February 2017.

[15] Interview with a Palestinian academic and Palestinian politics analyst, Gaza, 18 February 2017.

[16] Funded by the United States Agency for International Development, the Civil Society and Democracy Strengthening project. Tamkeen was initially a five-year project and had received a two-year extension. The initial funding was 33 million USD.

[17] Interview with a senior consultant at Tamkeen, a USAID-funded project for good governance and democratisation, Gaza, 10 December 2016.

[18] Ibid.

4.3.1 Contested Values: Donors' Tailored Democratisation and Reform

The only way to overcome this political impasse caused by Hamas coming to power was to de-legitimise the outcome of the election. The then US secretary of state, Condoleezza Rice, said that 'United States had failed to understand the depth of hostility among Palestinians toward their historical leaders. The hostility led to an election victory by the militant group Hamas that has reduced to tatters crucial assumptions underlying American policies and hopes in the Middle East' (Weisman, 2006). According to a Fatah senior executive, the US government opposed the idea of holding elections at the time. The US government warned Abbas of its outcome as Hamas was a key participant in these elections and its former strongman (Abbas) and historical party would be replaced by what the United States and its ally (i.e. Israel) consider a terrorist organisation and enemy.[19]

US war on terror, especially after the introduction of the Patriot Act that followed the 9/11 attacks, allowed Israel to use the same rhetoric against Palestinian resistance groups. Israel also prompted Western countries and the United States to adopt this principle in setting the rules for what qualifies as a Palestinian political party to be a partner that donors can work with. In doing so, Israel managed to de-legitimise Palestinian parties that adopt any form of resistance, including nonviolent resistance, thus emphasising that donors should consider Israel's security in any relationship with the Palestinians. Against this background, Turner (2014: 42) suggests that Israel succeeded in imposing a new approach underpinned by the following principle:

> Funding and working with Palestinian political elites that were regarded by Israel as being a 'partner for peace' would greatly assist them in implementing their mission of supporting the peace process. But in doing so they granted Israel the defining role in determining what constituted 'legitimate' and 'illegitimate' political practice for the PA (and Palestinians in general).

4.3.2 Designing Palestinians' Political Division

Israel placed the Israeli-Palestinian conflict within the Global War on Terror framework (2001) so that its dealings with the different Palestinian leaderships and elites (the introduction of Anti-Terrorism Certificate (2002) for this

---

[19] Interview with a former minister in the PA's 11th cabinet and senior Fatah member, Ramallah, 4 February 2017.

purpose) were structured in a particular way, namely to cater to Israel's security and political interests. Accordingly, Hamas's position at the time was that although Palestinian factions have maintained conflicting political ideologies, especially in terms of their position on the peace process, they have always maintained a common ideological approach towards Israel. To them, the disputes between Fatah and Hamas, or Hamas and Islamic Jihad, had existed as far as the early days of the First Intifada, yet all parties were united in the way they perceived Israel as an occupying power.[20]

Meanwhile, Mahmoud Abbas was initially convinced that it was important to integrate Islamist Movements like Hamas and Islamic Jihad politically and encourage their participation in the government. He was able to convince some of the European partners of this approach and to try to put pressure on the American government to accept Hamas's political participation. However, the American government had fully adopted Israel's notion that the integration of an armed resistance group could pose a serious risk not only to Israel but also to Abbas and Fatah.[21]

However, Abbas's position on Hamas's integration did not last long as the strong political criticism he faced from the American administration, and the financial and political boycott by the Israeli government which included the withholding of tax revenues, made this difficult. Abbas failed to convince Hamas to disarm its military wing Izzi Eddin Al-Qassam and accept the conditions set by the Quartet. He had no choice but to work with the American administration and sometimes with Israel to try to find a way out of this political dilemma, even if this meant toppling Hamas and regaining power over the Gaza Strip. Some of these efforts were later uncovered through former diplomats or highly classified cables or reports. From the American administration side, *Vanity Fair* reported that President George Bush and Condoleezza Rice signed a plan for Abbas to remove Hamas from the authority by channelling more money and arms to Fatah fighters to enable them to defeat Hamas militarily (Goldenberg, 2008). According to Goldenberg (2008), the United States tried to persuade key countries in the Arab region, including Egypt, Saudi Arabia, Jordan and the Arab Emirates, to train Fatah fighters, a request to which some of these countries responded (ibid.). Meanwhile, another WikiLeaks cable, published shortly after the armed confrontation between Fatah and Hamas, indicated that senior Fatah members close to Abbas had asked Israeli intelligence to target Hamas. According to

---

[20] Interview with a senior Hamas official and a senior member of the Hamas government in the Gaza Strip, Gaza, 10 May 2017.

[21] Interview with a senior Fatah executive in Gaza and political expert at Al-Azhar University in Gaza, Gaza, 3 February 2017.

the cable, Yuval Diskin, the head of Shin Bet, told the US ambassador to Israel that Fatah officials asked for Israel's help to get rid of Hamas and that the PA 'are approaching a zero-sum situation, and yet they ask us to attack Hamas. They are desperate. This is a new development. We have never seen this before' (Shaoul, 2010). Moreover, the cable showed that Abbas signed a US-Israeli plan in consultation with Jordan. The plan entailed that Abbas's security advisor, Mohammed Dahlan, would lead to an overthrow of Hamas with forces trained and armed by Washington (ibid.).

There was a strong rejection by Israel and the American administration for either a unity government that included more than 50 per cent of Fatah-affiliated ministers or a technocrat government that would report to the party holding the majority in the Palestinian Legislative Council (in this case, Hamas). This was evident in the failure to implement the Mecca Agreement[22] brokered by Saudi Arabia, which encouraged both parties to end political and military confrontation and set frameworks for power sharing, particularly within the security realm (Milton-Edwards, 2008: 1586). Despite this, the Western donor alliance had strongly insisted that Hamas should completely step aside from governing before they would resume their aid. This was evident in the report written by the United Nations coordinator for the peace process, Alvaro de Soto, in his description of the emerging situation as part of the conflict between Hamas and Fatah:

> The US clearly pushed for a confrontation between Fatah and Hamas – so much so that, a week before [the] Mecca [Agreement of February 2007], the US envoy declared twice in an envoys' meeting in Washington, how much 'I like this violence', referring to the near-civil war that was erupting in Gaza in which civilians were being killed and injured, because 'It means that other Palestinians are resisting Hamas' (quoted in Milton-Edwards, 2008: 1590).

Hamas met with Abbas on several occasions to discuss alternative options that could lead to a resolution. The PA leadership in the WB, however, was beginning to adopt the Western point of view and feel more convinced that it was impossible for Hamas to participate in any government. On the ground, the situation was beginning to deteriorate, and it was obvious that the security

---

[22] Under Saudi sponsorship, Hamas and Fatah agreed in February 2007 to end military confrontation between the two parties and form a unity government. The confrontation between the two parties had occurred as a result of the Hamas-led government asking for further powers, which Abbas-led PA rejected to grant them due to international pressure.

forces in Gaza were involved in a conspiracy against the Hamas government. There was an overwhelming feeling of insecurity among ordinary Gazan citizens, especially as there were many instances of armed confrontation between Fatah loyalists and armed Hamas members. In the words of the Hamas government official:[23]

> Hamas was under pressure to act to protect the Palestinian democracy from being kidnapped by an American or Israeli decision [...] the entire security situation in Gaza was very unpredictable and every Gazan citizen was threatened by this security chaos. [...] Hamas was forced to use power to control the situation. The PA and Fatah leadership thought this was a 'coup' while in fact it was not. The Hamas government was acting as a legitimate elected government and was trying to meet its own responsibility of maintaining order.

Accordingly, Palestinian division has now extended from being motivated by internal political disputes to being motivated by external political powers (i.e. Israel, United States and other regional powers).

4.4 The Structural Underpinnings of Division

To understand Palestinian divisions and its direct impact on Gaza, it is necessary to look beyond the role political environments played in fostering division while at the same time continuing to recognise the fundamental role these environments play in shaping the political as well as social divisions. It is important here to look at the institutional, political and economic legacy that the PLO-led PA has left after nearly 22 years of being in power. It is also important to examine whether or not and, if so, how this legacy has contributed to the improvement or deterioration of Gaza's socio-economic development and the PA's successes or failures in providing for the ordinary Palestinian citizen. Therefore, it is crucial to look at governance within the PA's institutions; this includes employment and public spending on social development and welfare, the PA's efforts in establishing an economy that is viable and less aid dependent and how the PA's governance and management of public funds and institutions, either directly or indirectly, contributed to creating socio-economic imbalances and to reshaping Gaza's socio-economic realities. In line with that, we will examine whether or not Hamas's economic policies,

---

[23] Interview with a senior Hamas official and a senior member of the Hamas government in the Gaza Strip, Gaza, 10 May 2017.

especially after the emergence of the tunnel economy, improved or deepened Gaza's socio-economic differences.

4.4.1 The PA's Governance and Social Welfare

Upon its establishment in 1994, the PA was empowered by the fact of its own creation and was perceived as the first step towards the creation of an independent state. Building state institutions was the main objective through which the PA wanted this state to materialise. The PA chairman, Yasser Arafat, wanted to take quick steps to achieve his desired goal by establishing the PA's civil ministries and bureaus and staffing them with a constantly growing number of employees. Moreover, the strategy of the PA was to open ministries of equal size in both the WB and the Gaza Strip for two reasons: Firstly, the geographical disconnection between the two territories created a need for government offices that facilitated service delivery. Secondly, the PA thought by doing this it was, in theory, forging equality between the two territories in terms of government representation, something they felt Palestinians would appreciate from their political leaders.

As introduced in Chapter 3, the public sector existed before the establishment of the PA under what was known as the Civil Administration, which was itself controlled by Israel's military governor. Although employees working within this sector comprised of Palestinian civil servants, they were still entirely controlled by the Israeli occupier. Upon signing the agreement, the PA inherited about 21,000 civil servants from the Civil Administration. Yet under the Oslo aid regime, the control over the public sector was resourced from Israel to donors (given the PA's total dependence on aid), where this control has indirectly extended to a wider and a growing sector of the Palestinian population. According to the most recent figures by the Palestinian Central Bureau of Statistics (PCBS), the number of employees working in public sector reached approximately 92,000 distributed between the WB and the Gaza Strip (53,000 in the WB and 38,000 in the Gaza Strip) (PCBS, 2015). This number does not include civil servants employed by the Hamas-led government in the Gaza Strip, which is estimated at 42,000 (Shaban, 2013) and security forces in either part of the territories (see Table 4.1).

The PA's major investment since its establishment was in public sector employment. Here, more than 56 per cent of the total expenditure by the central government (Gaza government after 2007 excluded) went on the payment of salaries for public sector employees, while only 15 per cent went towards payments for social benefits (Portland Trust, 2013). Table 4.2 indicates that while the majority of spending went towards running the PA public offices

Table 4.1 Distribution of Palestinian civil servants, 1995–2015

	1995	2005	2008	2010/2011	2015
Gaza Strip	–	32,800	31,948	29,010	28,212
WB	–	49.200	47,948	59,384	62,328
Total	21,000	82,200	97,896	88,394	90,540

Note: Figures compiled from different sources, including Palestinian Personnel Council and PCBS.

and ministries between 1995 and 2010, investment in development and the welfare programme decreased significantly year after year. Consequently, the PA seemed to have exhausted its budget by making itself develop into a large social security net for its public sector employees only. By doing so, it had tied a great portion of the Palestinian population to its own stability and future existence. What is seen as paradoxical to some is that the social security system of employment within the public sector has had absolute dependence on foreign aid whose sustainability has proved very fragile.[24] It has proven itself as a social security system that can be jeopardised by donors' political decision as well as Israel's satisfaction with the PA's performance on issues related to the latter's security. There have been many occasions when the PA experienced delays in paying salaries for its employees for weeks and sometimes for months as a result of donors suspending the direct aid that goes/went to the PA budget to pay employees' salaries or because Israel suspended the transfer of tax revenues. Consequently, both measures resulted in leaving thousands of employees and their families, especially low-paid employees, face the hardships.[25]

Tables 4.1 and 4.2 illustrate major existing gaps. First, there is a gap in the size of public institutions in the Gaza Strip compared to the WB, which is almost double the size in the latter. This is reflected in the number of public servants employed in the institutions in both territories. With this in mind, the PA's public expenditures, as shown in Table 4.2, have continuously been directed towards current expenditures and salaries. In other words, more than 60 per cent of these expenditures were channelled towards PA institutions and employees in the WB, while there has been a constant decrease in the level of spending in the Gaza Strip. Meanwhile, the PA public expenditure on social welfare that targeted members of the population that live under the poverty

---

[24] Interview with a professor of public administration and consultant for aid agencies working in the Gaza Strip, Gaza, 10 December 2016.

[25] Ibid.

Table 4.2 PA public expenditures, 1997–2010 (Numbers are in million USD)

Description	1997	1998	1999	2000	2001	2002	2003	2004	2005	2006	2007	2008	2009	2010
Total public expenditures	1,362	1,358	1,411	1,668	1,435	1,246	1,635	1,820	2,281	1,707	2,877	3,488	3,376	3,259
Current expenditures	862	838	937	1,199	1,095	994	1,240	1,528	1,994	1,426	2,567	3,273	3,190	2,984
Salaries and wages	470	467	519	622	678	642	743	870	1,001	658	1,369	1,771	1,467	1,564
Non-salaries expenditures	392	371	418	577	417	352	324	501	349	392	663	1,055	1,349	1,156
Running cost	202	181	234	294	189	154	123	206	258	156	262	293	446	493
Transfer	190	190	184	283	228	198	201	295	391	236	401	634	829	705
Welfare and development expenditure	500	520	474	469	340	252	395	292	387	281	310	215	186	275
Funded by PA treasury	0	0	0	13	22	23	36	0	0	0	0	0	139	145
Funded by foreign aid	500	520	474	456	318	229	359	0	387	281	310	215	47	131

Source: These figures were compiled from multiple sources: Nabil Abdelnabi (2012) and Palestinian Monetary Authority (PMA, 2015).

line, most of whom were concentrated in the Gaza Strip, has been extremely low and equivalent to zero in most years.

4.4.2 Absence of Economic Foundations in Gaza

From the perspective of the PA's leadership, the expansion of the public sector has become an internal tool to empower it. The Gaza public administration expert suggested that the PA has managed to enlarge the middle class, which is comprised mainly of PLO and Fatah affiliates that managed to move up the ladder of mid-rank to senior rank in public institutions.[26] Similarly, the PA has always been very cautious about public senior management within its institutions to keep them from being infiltrated by individuals that might hold political ideologies opposing or challenging those held by the PA leadership.[27] In line with that, the PA sought to maintain popularity for its political project, that is, the Oslo paradigm, among a wider number of supporters. To some, it did so by conditioning the sustainability of their employment (and thus their income) to their support of the PA and its political agenda (i.e. the peace process paradigm). Accordingly, the vetting procedure for employment in the public sector has been seen as taking informal processes that included seeking personal recommendations from well-known Fatah/PLO leaders or district leaders, security investigations into political affiliation and security investigations conducted by different security departments.[28] Hence, the Gaza public administration expert suggested that the PA had not only focused its major investment in public sector employment but also used employment as a political tool to control a wider sector of its population, making political affiliation a condition to have access to public employment and to indirectly securitise its public institution.[29]

It is clear that the PA government was operating under false economic assumptions[30] in that the PA considered that personnel salaries paid through aid money could contribute to establishing a Palestinian economy and strengthen the Palestinian market. In the case of the Gaza Strip and shortly

---

[26] Interview with a public administration consultant for aid agencies in Gaza Strip, Gaza, 10 December 2016.

[27] Interview with a professor of Palestinian party politics at the Islamic University of Gaza, Gaza, 18 February 2017.

[28] Interview with an expert in public administration and consultant for aid agencies working in the Gaza Strip, Gaza, 10 December, 2016.

[29] Ibid.

[30] Interview with a former minister in the PA's 11th cabinet and senior Fatah member, Ramallah, 4 February 2017.

after Oslo, Israel started to end its economic ties with the Strip, especially with regard to Gazan labour, allowing it access to the Israeli market. The private sector continued to be gradually targeted by Israel sanctions, closure and destruction. On top of this, very little investment was pursued by the PA to support Gaza's economy. The situation in the WB was very different as the PA gradually expanded its public sector in the WB, thus increasing the number of people employed in this sector. Israel also continued to allow WB access to its labour market. Most importantly, the private sector in the WB was empowered by both donors and Israel's economic facilitation measures (i.e. the easy flow of goods, access to Israel's labour market and mobility of traders between the WB and Israel).

In the opinion of the Gaza public administration expert, the population in Gaza has been pushed toward secure employment within the public sector. The reason is that the sector, for most people, was more secure in terms of its sustainability, job security and salaries. A great number of people employed in the private sector and former labourers in the Israeli market sought new employment in this sector after their chances of seeking employment in other sectors were beginning to recede. Meanwhile, there has been no significant investment on behalf of the PA in key economic sectors (i.e. agricultural, industrial and other sectors). The case for the WB was quite different as it had a much bigger private sector before the PA was established, one that mainly depends on capital from individuals who have far more access to Israeli market and businessmen with dual nationality. Thus, there has been less dependence on public sector employment and continued access to the Israeli labour market.[31]

With the continued deterioration of economic conditions in the Gaza Strip, especially after the Israeli disengagement in 2005, the percentage of people who became dependent on welfare services provided by local and international organisations continued to grow (until it reached more than 75 per cent, as indicated in Chapter 3). Aid beneficiaries now represent the majority of Gaza's civilians, and in many cases, some are low-paid public sector employees whose salaries are below the minimum national wage (800 NIS/200 USD). In the view of a beneficiary of one of the foreign aid programmes implemented in Gaza, ordinary Palestinians living in Gaza have been experiencing socio-economic deprivation resulting from the lack of access to secure employment in the Gaza Strip. For them, the reason is principally the politicisation of the PA's public sector:

---

[31] Interview with an expert professor of public administration and consultant for aid agencies working in the Gaza Strip, Gaza, 10 December 2016.

First of all, you have to have connections with senior Fatah or PA officials to have access to employment in the government. And even if this happens, you will be a low-paid ordinary employee with a salary that can only sustain you for a week at the most. Meanwhile, if you were a son or a daughter of senior official at one of the security forces or director general at one of the ministries, you would jump over all these obstacles. In this case, no employment exams or qualification do matter, what matters is how connected you are.[32]

In the view of Gaza youth, both Fatah and Hamas gave preference to their affiliates in Gaza in order to maintain dominance over public institutions when it came to employment in the public sector. For them, both parties have given priority to their active members for employment in the public sector,[33] while the unemployed in Gaza had limited opportunities for short-term employment, but these did not aid their economic welfare sustainably or their long-term career development. As described by a beneficiary of a graduate employment programme, there has been a new trend which is basically temporary employment through job creation programmes which are either funded or sponsored by the UNDP or other international organisations. Young graduates get job placements in government institutions, local NGOs or private sector:

Even to have a chance in one of these job creation programmes you have to have political connections […] you get employed for 3–6 months and most of the time you have no job description and you go to work to kill time with no real experience or career value. The only positive thing is you get paid 150 USD to 200 USD.[34]

4.4.3 Reshaping Gaza's Private Sector and the Middle Class

Another element of the structural division is seen in the gradual and systematic process followed by the PA and the Hamas government to intervene in the work of the private sector in Gaza. Historically, Gaza's private sector has been dominated by Gaza's middle class and through family businesses and medium-sized enterprises in different sectors, namely industry, general services, trade and agriculture. The private sector has always played a vital role in the life of Palestinians living in Gaza as they depend on it for the majority

---

[32] Interview with a job creation project beneficiary in Gaza, 2017.
[33] Ibid.
[34] Interview with a job creation project beneficiary in Khan Yunis, 2017.

of services besides the government-provided services. Furthermore, the private sector accommodated thousands of former skilled labourers from Gaza after they lost access to the Israeli labour market. As indicated in Chapter 3, this sector's existence and operations have always been at risk due to various factors, including, importantly, the Israeli closure policy. Regardless of the complexity surrounding the work of this sector, it continued to be a good source of income and employment for both the population in Gaza and the owners of the sector.

Another subsector of the middle class emerged immediately after the establishment of the PA. This component was composed of middle- and high-ranking PA officials that came from the diaspora on the eve of signing the Oslo Accords. Clearly, the connection between the two subsectors of the middle class began to develop due to the various mutual interests between the traditional middle class and the new one (middle-class PA officials). It was a classic relationship between the powers (i.e. authority) represented by the PA senior officials and the money represented by the already existing businesses' owners. From the side of the PA officials under Fatah control, a relationship with the already existing middle class would facilitate their social integration in the Gaza community and would widen their social-economic networks further than their diaspora connections.[35]

Accordingly, the traditional Gazan middle class began to feel the political and security advantages that had begun to emerge in terms of freedom of mobility between the WB and Gaza and direct connections with donor programmes and agencies and sometimes with the Israeli security institutions. At the same time, the private sector owners were looking to gain incentives from their partnership with the political elite. From their perspective, the privileges enjoyed by the PA elites were seen through the logistical facilitations that partnerships with this political elite provided. Therefore, the partnership between the private sector elite and the political elite was one based on mutual interest.

However, the meeting of these political and economic factors eventually had given the opportunity for the political elite to take further control over the private sector. The EU consultant and a former UN senior staff member suggested that this paved the way for the establishment of what has become a parallel economy in the Gaza Strip – an economy that is mainly controlled by the PA's security forces controlled by Fatah and other senior

---

[35] Interview with a senior Fatah party member who was originally from Gaza and represents the old Fatah guards that were based in Gaza during the First Intifada, Gaza, 16 December 2016.

figures working at the PA ministries.[36] For example, the PA officials realised the high monthly revenues generated by the private sector, especially the sectors that handle Gaza's main supplies (i.e. fuel, construction materials, tobacco). These supplies, most of the time, came through Israel, and the PA managed to create informal government bodies attached to or run by the security forces that became responsible for coordinating and monitoring the flow of these supplies. Private sector companies always needed Israeli clearances in order for their goods to pass through Israeli checkpoints and formal crossings.[37]

As a result, the private sector has become more dependent on the PA's senior officials to secure these clearances. In return, a large number of these officials became involved in the work of these companies through a form of partnership. Along these lines, fares and taxes that were imposed on these supplies were collected through informal processes and through individual PA officials, as discussed earlier in this chapter. The purpose for this informal process, according to the EU consultant, was to generate informal revenues to the PA elites, revenues that do not appear on reports presented to donors or other formal institutions. This was meant to give flexibility in spending in ways that needed not to be justified to donors or formal PA government institutions. According to the Palestinian Ministry of Economy, the estimated monthly amounts generated from the logistical facilitation of these supplies was approximately 50 million USD in 1997.[38] This amount had increased over time to reach up to 170 million USD a month in 2006 and did not enter the PA budgets but instead was deposited into individual accounts for some PLO and PA officials.[39] Moreover, it had entailed imposing extra overhead costs on these main supplies, and these extra costs were added to the cost of the main supplies but did not affect the work of the private sector companies or the undercover institutions and PA officials who benefited from them.[40]

Over time, the new middle class, which is comprised of middle management and senior PA officials who became involved in the private sector, managed to influence and socio-economically integrate with the traditional Gazan middle class. The Palestinian politics analyst suggested that this

---

[36] Interview with the EU consultant and former UN executive staff in Gaza, Gaza, 21 December 2016.

[37] Ibid.

[38] Interview with a former economic consultant for the PA's Ministry of Economy and the Ministry of Finance and NGO advisor, Gaza, 10 December 2016.

[39] Ibid.

[40] Ibid.

socio-economic integration extended to creating family ties, attendance at the same private education institutions and economic partnership. For example, there have been major construction and housing projects that were implemented by businessmen in the private sector. Yet, these projects also involved a number of middle management and senior PA officials. The latter's contribution to these projects was limited to facilitating the official approvals to implement these projects. In many cases, this included obtaining the necessary licenses, buying the land at competitive prices and providing other logistical support.[41]

Another aspect of the relationship between the two subsectors of the middle class involved dealing with aid agencies and donors. Most aid programmes were either implemented through international NGOs, local NGOs or directly through the government; the private sector in Gaza has always, nonetheless, been involved in the implementation of these programmes.[42] The private sector companies were usually subcontracted as part of the implementation team of some infrastructure, industrial or trade projects. The selection of these companies would also be made in the first instance through the relevant government agencies. As described by the PA policy consultant,

It was shortly after donors started to implement their infrastructure programmes when some PA officials realised the income that private sector companies were generating through subcontracting donor programmes, and therefore wanted (the PA officials) to benefit from this themselves. And in this case, they interfered in the work of the private sector in one of the two approaches: first, they made sure that specific companies won tenders or bids in return for an agreed share or percentage of the overall value of these tenders. Second, and this was the most likely scenario, they would start up new companies with already existing private sector companies, either as direct owners or shareholders or through member of their families. And again, they would facilitate that their companies win tenders in one way or another.[43]

Accordingly, the donors' selection process had focused primarily on vetting these companies or vendors from a security viewpoint; therefore, it became

---

[41] Interview with a professor of Palestinian party politics, Gaza, 18 February 2017.
[42] Interview with a former policy consultant for the PA government and aid agencies in the Gaza Strip, 11 December 2016.
[43] Ibid.

possible for these companies, especially the large or middle-sized private sector companies, to pass the vetting process due to the background of the owners or the people involved.

4.4.4 Hamas, the Tunnel Economy and the Further Reconstruction of Socio-economic Realities

In the period following the political division between Gaza and the WB in 2007, the private sector became the key sector in the Gaza Strip in terms of necessary supplies and services. This sector was once again left struggling to survive after the strict blockade was imposed on Gaza following the Hamas takeover of the Gaza Strip in 2007. More than 90 per cent of the sector was reported as paralysed (UNISPAL, 2009). The construction sector had completely stopped its operation, causing unemployment to soar, and the inflation for some goods ran to nearly 200 per cent per month between 2007 and 2009 (UNISPAL, 2009).

Additionally, there were warnings of possible lasting damage to the private sector as some manufacturers had already relocated their services and companies to Egypt, Jordan and the WB (Portland Trust, 2012). The relocation of some of the private sector was also an indirect result of the relocation of a large number of the Fatah and PLO-affiliated PA officials and their middle class associates that no longer felt safe after Hamas had control of the Strip.

As mentioned in Chapter 3, the sector revived after Gaza saw increased tunnel trade following Israel's Operation Cast Lead in 2008/2009 and the collapse of the Mubarak regime in Egypt. Gaza received its main supplies from Egypt through a network of tunnels that were controlled by the Hamas government and its affiliate militant branch Izzi Eddin Al-Qassam. The 'tunnel trade' between Gaza and Egypt was estimated at tens of millions of dollars a month, and it succeeded in creating thousands of employment opportunities.[44] The major consequence of the tunnel trade was that it created a good source of income for Hamas as a government and for the members of the party, who generally played the biggest role in operating and owning these tunnels. This income gave Hamas the opportunity to once again reconstruct Gaza's middle class and control the way the private sector operates in the Gaza Strip.

Due to the increasing economic impact the tunnel had, eventually, according to the Hamas government official, Hamas formed what became the

---

[44] Interview with a senior Hamas official and a senior member of the Hamas government in the Gaza Strip, Gaza, 10 May 2017.

Tunnels Committee, whose role was to monitor and control tunnel trade and operation. In line with this, the Hamas government applied formal taxes on goods coming through tunnels, similar to how goods coming through formal commercial crossings with Israel were handled, which meant that Hamas succeeded in generating high income for its government and party. The formal traders and factory owners struggled to operate through formal commercial crossings with Israel as the latter continued to impose high restrictions on the number of commercial items allowed into the Gaza Strip. As a result, they had no alternative except to shift their trade to the tunnels and cooperate with the new tunnel traders and owners.

The tunnel trade had created new rules of the game for Gaza's private sector. It was easy money, and Gaza was thirsty for supplies. The new traders, who were mostly Hamas affiliated and, if not, they were close to Hamas, brought almost every type of good and at a much cheaper price. The city of Rafah became the economic centre of the Gaza Strip after a few months, where loaded trucks could be seen leaving the border lines and distributing goods across the Strip. As a result, this contributed to the emergence of new businessmen and traders and to the weakening of traditional ones. Although the tunnels had solved many of Gaza's problems and had alleviated the impact of the long-lasting blockade that affected every aspect of life, yet they had serious side effects.[45]

Consequently, there were no laws in place to regulate this trade and there was no protection for consumers against prices set by the tunnel traders. This resulted in further damage to formal trade as it lost its competitive advantage in terms of prices and the ease of bringing goods into the Gaza Strip. The market also became fully controlled by those who had access to cash and by those who were mostly Hamas affiliates, who ran the highly securitised tunnel trade. Some viewed this group, who became businessmen (and some of them too young) and started to buy and run Gaza's most important businesses (properties, hotels and other important sectors), as the most dominant economic power in the Strip.[46] Under this new reality, it was very difficult to say the tunnel trade had a genuine impact on ordinary Gazans' economic welfare, and if it did, we knew it was going to be temporary and would not last long.

Consequently, Palestinians living in Gaza experienced another form of socio-economic division following Hamas's rise to power. This socio-economic division was similar to the previous experience of Fatah's control of Gaza

---

[45] Interview with an economic analyst and NGO consultant in the Gaza Strip, Gaza, 10 January 2017.

[46] Ibid.

between 1994 and 2005. This new division was influenced by the fact that affiliates of political parties in power have greater access to and privileges over financial resources. The socio-economic divisions occurred during periods when Palestinians living in the Gaza Strip experienced economic hardship resulting from decreasing employment opportunities and a long-lasting blockade, thus increasing the level of poverty.

4.5 Conclusion: Multiple Interpretations

It is useful to make sense of the various arguments and evidence presented above. The issue here is not just about presenting one view on how foreign aid has had a significant contribution on reshaping the social and economic landscape in Palestine, and more specifically in Gaza. Rather, it is about understanding the actual dynamics and workings of aid and how the different Palestinian segments and groups have interacted with these dynamics.

4.5.1 The Political Hegemony of Aid and Development

The chapter has discussed how the partner for peace paradigm has emerged as part of the peace process between Israel and the Palestinians. The paradigm is built upon the notion that Palestinians must deliver security and peace to Israel as a condition for receiving the aid necessary to rebuild and fix problems that a six-decade-long legacy of occupation has caused. Defining the Palestinian partner was thus a task Israel has undertaken based on what it saw as meeting a set of criteria, either at the individual leadership level (individuals) or at the group leadership level (parties). The Palestinian leadership has always been expected to make security and political compromises as demanded by Israel to maintain their political legitimacy as partners for peace. Consequently, donors have also found themselves committed, or often rather obliged, to follow this route since it was easier to apply pressure on the weaker Palestinian partner compared to Israel. The entire Palestinian political system had to undergo a process of reformation and reconstruction according to criteria set by the Oslo Accords' security for peace and the security for aid principles. Accordingly, the PA leadership had to play two main roles: as a security and peace agent and as a development agent. The main beneficiary of the first role is, of course, Israel. Without fulfilling the duties of the first role, the PA is deemed to have failed in fulfilling the duties pertaining to the second role, whose main beneficiaries are the Palestinian people. This suggests that Palestinians' development is conditioned upon fulfilling roles that are not directly related to the actual process of development but rather guided by the unbalanced power relations between the donors and Israel, on the one hand, and Palestinians, on the other.

The examples outlined above show how donors have addressed Gaza's needs for specific development projects. They also show how that development was not, in fact, the ultimate goal but rather reflected a political hegemony historically embedded in the development industry, as suggested by Pieterse (2010), discussed in Chapter 2. This hegemony is seen in how aid delivery as a practice reflects contemporary relations of power between those who give and those who receive. This is reinforced when aid is attached to a political or security agenda that does not directly relate to the development agenda. In this sense, developmentalism becomes a value or a view guided by those who enjoy the power rather than those who are in need of it. It is also evident in the paradox between *development* as a liberal value that emerged with the intention of assisting those in need and the hegemony and control embedded in the practices of those in charge of it. Contrary to this, development represented by aid offers new forms of political control of nations that are represented in the global power differentials linked with power and political interests and gains.

4.5.2 Ambiguous Development

Another important aspect that is associated with development under occupation, a process that is highly securitised and politicised, is that there has been no clear plan over the past two decades as to the kind of development that is needed or a clear strategy on how to achieve it. Under Arafat's leadership the PA had sought to build structures and institutions necessary to proceed with establishing an independent Palestinian state and had technically received sufficient funds from donors to run PA ministries, public institutions and other state-related projects. Arafat saw these as important symbols, and he was trying to create facts on the ground that, from his point of view, would make state establishment inevitable. Meanwhile, there was not enough attention from donors to understand the real foundations of what the PA was trying to establish and how money was being used. Issues of transparency, accountability and good governance have continued to affect the PA's performance and have impacted its ability to achieve socio-economic justice. Furthermore, donors' attention was substantially directed to issues related to security within the PA territories and security with Israel. This was illustrated in some examples (e.g. the Gaza Water Treatment Project and the Tamkeen Project) and how donors have tied their aid agenda in development projects to what Israel will or will not accept. Over time, donors have gradually become aware of Israel's preferences to issues related to Palestine's development and thus designed their aid agenda accordingly.

In the main, donors were unwilling to challenge Israel's security rhetoric or use their diplomatic channels to persuade Israel, as illustrated in the Water Treatment Project, to allow the implementation of high-impact development projects in Gaza or in the Palestinian territories in general. The other aspect of development that donors had shown more interest in, even when they called for a genuine process of reform in post-Arafat PA, was one that focused mainly on reforming PA security forces and tackling internal security issues. This again was evident in the aid agenda that followed Hamas seizing power in the Gaza Strip and the way donors strictly revised their development aid agenda in Gaza with the exception of humanitarian aid. Therefore, the aid agenda was further securitised, and all the development aid was shifted towards the WB with further reforms that targeted the PA's security forces. The aim, as shown here, was to prevent what occurred in Gaza from happening in the WB and to indirectly warn WB citizens of the expected consequences (i.e. political and economic sanctions that not only target the government institutions but also have impact on the people).

As suggested by the post-development scholars, these practices reflect what was described in Chapter 2 as anti-development practices. These anti-development perspectives are seen in terms of goals set and the means employed to achieve them. The highly securitised and politicised aid (linked to resolving the Israeli-Palestinian conflict and the position that donors take in this conflict) reflects again an authoritarian development. This authoritarian development mirrors what James Ferguson (1994) and Cowen and Shenton (1995) called a postcolonial legacy embedded in the development industry that emerged after the Second World War. These authoritarian elements are also seen in how development as a design denies nations' political and socio-economic sovereignty and presents itself as a superior power over people's lives. Denying Gaza's development as a political strategy to influence people's political attitudes, and interfering in the domestic national politics, reflects what was suggested by Willis (2011: 19), discussed in Chapter 2, as the spread of Western economic and socio-political dominance in various parts of the world done under the name of developing the underdeveloped. It is a power that former colonisers continue to maintain, and it reflects the same power inequalities between the coloniser and the colonised and the developed and the underdeveloped. In the case of Palestinians, more specifically in the case of Gaza after the victory of Hamas, these inequalities were very evident in the fact that Palestinians' political preferences were sidelined, and their democratic choices were not respected. Donor money played a major role in this context when it was used to influence the internal Palestinian politics, giving rise to the current political split.

4.5.3 New Structures of Control

Furthermore, building on the idea of development as modernisation, based on economic growth and how societies and nations are judged based on their standards of living, the idea emerges that the development industry works to promote certain social, economic or political groups. This idea is based on on material qualifications that play a role in promoting individuals and groups on the basis of the material possessions they enjoy. When referring to these possessions, Gustavo Esteva (1992: 18) suggests that they range from political to economic and social powers enjoyed by these individuals or groups. For development to operate and succeed within underdeveloped societies trapped in 'poverty and backwardness', it has become necessary for the development agents, donors or aid agencies, to empower and promote these individuals and groups. Therefore, they have become the tools through which development agents need to instigate control over the societies they claim to develop or assist. This can be described as 'the old imperialism', as referred to by Esteva (1992: 18), which, as indicated in Chapter 2, suggests a new form of imperialism where the economisation of development replaces old forms of colonisation. Esteva (1992: 18) emphasises that social and economic interactions in the target societies should be brought under the new economic structures promoted by donors.

To conclude, this chapter has provided evidence as to how economic structures represented by aid agencies and donors have influenced the way the PA has operated. This includes how its structure has developed over time in relation to the security agenda imposed by Israel and the economic agenda imposed by donors and aid agencies. More importantly, however, it has shown all too clearly how aid agencies themselves were guided by the Oslo 'security first' paradigm. The promotion of Palestinian political figures or groups was closely associated with this influence and contributed to the way the PA's performance and national allegiance were perceived by the people. What is clearly evident is the impact of the securitisation and politicisation of aid on the political dynamics in the Gaza Strip and how these two factors impacted the political division between Hamas and Fatah once the former came to power. The divide between the security role of the PA, as suggested by the Oslo Accords, and its role as the representative of the Palestinian people can be seen as one result of foreign aid dynamics that are heavily influenced by the Israeli-Palestinian conflict. It also demonstrates how much the PA has been capable in defining, leading and implementing its own national agenda (political or otherwise) as a result of Oslo aid dynamics.

Chapter 5

GAZA'S CIVIL SOCIETY AND NGOS: THE PROFESSIONALISATION OF SECURITY AND THE POLITICISATION OF SOCIETY

5.1 Introduction

After the previous examination of foreign aid delivery to institutions within the PA and the kind of structural imbalances the norms of delivery have created since the Oslo Accords (1993), the task now resides in the analysis of the impact of such phenomena within the CSOs, particularly to what extent has the post-Oslo aid agenda contributed to reconstructing the role Palestinian NGOs play as compared to the pre-Oslo era and how has the securitisation and politicisation of aid influenced the socio-economic advancement of both NGOs and aid beneficiaries? In this chapter, we are not looking at CSOs and NGOs as development actors, but rather investigating the aspects embedded in these questions will help us to understand two things: the kind of civil society that donors sought to empower and maintain in the Gaza Strip and whether this sector contributes to Gaza's development and humanitarian relief or rather to practicing further governmentality over its population. It will also help us understand how the sector's key stakeholders, both institutions and individuals, are influenced by the aid dynamics imposed by donors and the extent to which they play a role in deepening the impact of the securitised aid agenda.

The chapter is based on a dozen interviews with CSO workers and aid consultants, in addition to government and political parties representatives. Accordingly, the analysis of the relationship between CSOs and donors, on the one hand, and CSOs and the local society, on the other, is articulated in four sections.

The first section will provide a historical overview of the work of the CSOs in Palestine and more specifically in Gaza. It will discuss the political dynamics that impacted the work of this sector in three major periods: the First Intifada (prior to the establishment of the PA), the post-Oslo civil society and the Second Intifada onwards. The second section will examine the concept of 'globalised elite' introduced by Sari Hanafi and Linda Tabar (2002, 2004). Yet, it falls short of illustrating how this elite developed over time, of describing its current relationships with the governing authorities, donors and the society and how these relationships impacted the current structures of the civil society. Accordingly, the section begins by providing a general definition of 'globalised elite' and develops this term by looking at how NGOs became influenced by the new policy agenda (NPA) for economic liberalisation and political democratisation introduced in the 1990s (Edwards, 1994).[1] It will also examine how these dynamics facilitated the imposition of direct and indirect control over the daily lives of Palestinians living in Gaza. This is combined with an examination of how these forms of control relate to the Foucauldian 'biopolitics' as a concept associated with liberal modernity that perceived biological life (Foucault, 1976: 138) (individuals) as both a subject and an object of governance (Chapter 2). The third section will examine how the civil society sector and NGOs can be agents for socio-economic promotion and demotion, while investigating how preferential ties with donors can enable NGOs to advance financially, institutionally or otherwise. The fourth section will examine how the securitised aid agenda has influenced the work of the NGO sector in Gaza.

5.2 Brief History of the NGO Sector in Gaza

In order to understand the current realities of the NGO sector in Palestine, and more specifically in Gaza, there is a need to look at the historical context within which this vital sector emerged and developed, particularly in the period between the First Intifada in 1987, the establishment of the PA in 1994 and the period that followed the Second Intifada in 2000 and Hamas's election victory in 2006. This historical overview will help us understand the changes that occurred in the work of this sector and the political, social and economic dynamics that contributed to these changes in general. It will also assist an analysis of the organisational and political frameworks that guided the work of this sector in each period.

---

[1] The new policy agenda of the 1990s was introduced to elements of neoliberal economic liberalisation policies and 'good governance' and suggested that the development NGOs would act as an efficient alternative to state governments to promote democracy. It was to define and introduce a new relationship between the state and non-governmental organisations, where an 'enabling state' would be democratic, accountable and safeguarding to human rights. Meanwhile, the concern was that NGOs' involvement would be seen as taking part in implementing the condition to govern aid transfers to governments thus reshaping the traditional role of these NGOs (Robinson, 1993: 1).

5.2.1 Prior to the Establishment of the PA

Regardless of the barriers that met the work of the NGO sector in the oPt, particularly in the Gaza Strip, this sector managed to remain existence. Until the establishment of the PA in 1994, there were almost 114 organisations in Gaza (both registered and non-registered) compared to 700 organisations working in the WB (Roy, 2001a: 232). These organisations were mostly registered as charities that provided a spectrum of services: health, medical, social welfare and education. Due to the heightened oppression during the last two years of the Intifada, more than 50 per cent of these organisations were established in 1992–94 in response to deteriorating economic and political conditions (Roy, 2001a: 232). The small number of organisations is due to the fact that the Israeli Civil Administration made it difficult for Palestinian NGOs to form and maintain an organisational structure. In order to register and conduct activities, NGOs had to follow Israeli military order 686, which stated that NGOs must have no links with nationalist movements (Schulz, 2013: 247). Accordingly, political parties were completely banned from public life. In order to overcome this obstacle, political parties (mainly PLO-affiliated parties) conducted their activities under the umbrella of local associations (Alashqar, 2015: 2). Subsequently, popular committees (women, health, agriculture, etc.) and trade unions were formed. At the beginning, these committees were mainly linked to leftist parties (i.e. Communist Party, Popular Front and Democratic Front). However, the dominant PLO party, Fatah, took the lead by replicating its own model of social, economic and political mobilisation (Challand, 2008: 60–62).

The role played by this sector during this era enabled it to form a solid popular support and legitimacy among Palestinians both in the WB and in Gaza. During this time, secular NGOs (PLO affiliated) and religious charitable organisations (affiliated to Hamas and Muslim Brotherhood) were committed to providing services to different socio-economic sectors in Gaza. The ongoing occupation prompted a gradual development of a civil society that was able to respond to the political needs of its communities (Merz, 2013: 139). Besides, the NGO sector succeeded to some extent to address the shortage in institutional development under the Israeli Civil Administration. The reason for this, according to Benoit Challand (2008: 61), is that unlike CSOs in some southern countries (that were fairly a new construct with recent links with their population), Palestinian civil society is unique due to its long history of activism and professional and political links. In this context, Sara Roy (2001a: 232) relayed the emergence of civil society in the Gaza Strip in their current form for two reasons. The first was to provide services to the community and to substitute the absence of a national body that caters to the people of Gaza. Second, some of the Gaza's NGOs were quasi-governmental in the sense they were performing as municipal, village and legislative councils that regulated life in the Strip.

For instance, the popular committees, which were considered as frontline during the First Intifada (1987–93), succeeded in mobilising many grassroots organisations and enhancing their organisational structures. Their role not only provided a framework for the uprising in Gaza but also 'influenced its source of direction, cohesion and continuity' (Merz, 2013: 139). In addition to their involvement in social work and the provision of a range of activities that catered for orphans, the blind and people with physical disabilities, charitable organisations also offered refuge to Gazans fleeing Israeli prosecution, thus enhancing the resilience of the community (Roy, 2001a: 232). Of importance also is the fact that associational life in Gaza, during the late 1980s and early 1990s, was characterised by the partisan nature of civil society and the growing competition between political parties (i.e. the secular and Islamist factions). This partisanship, however, had a positive impact on the institutionalisation of grassroots organisations and their professionalisation. Parties were looking forward to creating and strengthening links with the communities they were serving. In order to do this, it was important for them to have solid organisational structures and good knowledge of community needs. This, as a result, motivated donors to create links with these organisations due to the latter's informed knowledge of the society's needs (Merz, 2013: 139).

Finally, the work of civil society was highly influenced by the socio-economic developments in the Gaza Strip. These developments were mainly influenced by the political realities that existed across different periods of time (i.e. the Ottoman rule, the Egyptian rule, the Israeli Civil Administration and finally the Palestinian national movement in the exile). The socio-economic developments influenced the work of the NGO sector. Meanwhile, these periods also reflected changes that occurred within the socio-economic hierarchy in Gaza, a hierarchy represented by traditional land-owning families and the new professional, educated urban middle class that represented those working in this sector (Challand, 2008: 62).

5.2.2 Post-PA Civil Society

Shortly after the arrival of the PA, the civil society sector saw the need to face this new reality and transform its role from that of a political agitator to one more professional in order to maintain its role in the Palestinian society. The new struggle began in Gaza, where the PA was established. Palestinian NGOs were involved in a reconstruction phase in terms of how they operate and provide services that had a degree of professionalism. According to Nancy Sadiq (2012), it was not a simple task to shift from a mass political action model to one engaged in a process of institution building as civil institutions do elsewhere. Consequently, the period where Palestinian NGOs were considered independent activists was coming to an end, and these organisations became dominated by an increasing level of professionalisation and international recognition from, in the main, Western donors. These two characteristics became prerequisites to their eligibility for financial support from donors, particularly Western donors, whose intervention following the Oslo Accords had increased significantly. Thus, their ability to continue with service delivery and organisational expansion was very much dependent on their eligibility for this financial support (Sadiq, 2012). As will be discussed later, however, this transformation resulted in many of the mass-mobilisation-based organisations to develop into socio-economic elitist organisations. These organisations can be categorised according to the field of their specialty, such as youth and community development, faith and dialogue, children and women, peace activism, agricultural relief and medical relief. It is important to indicate that within this broad camp of organisations existed international faith-based organisations that have had connections with local NGOs. Although these and their local NGO partners often had some impact on the ground, their presence was somewhat minimal. With this said, the discussion in this chapter will mainly be focused on Palestinian NGOs that attract the largest amount of funding, thus shaping the current reality of this sector.

Against this backdrop, the PA was struggling to establish political and institutional legitimacy and the political leadership was anticipating that the traditional Palestinian civil society, whose existence preceded the PA's, would come under its umbrella and professionally contribute to it. Contrary to this, the civil society sector perceived its contribution to fostering associational life as one independent of the newly established PA. To be able to do this, NGOs sought to strengthen their ties with donors and international organisations with whom they already had a connection prior to the PA. As a result, more than 30 per cent of these organisations became dependent on financial aid by the mid-1990s (Merz, 2013: 140). As usual, this dependence produced a side effect in the form of these organisations' agendas and activities becoming heavily influenced by an international funding agenda. Due to the high impact of Israeli economic measures imposed on Gaza during the First Intifada, compared to other Palestinian districts, Western donors wanted to ensure that Gazans would begin to feel some advancement in their daily lives as a result of the Oslo Accords. Meanwhile, a new type of programme emerged that aimed at changing people's perceptions and attitudes towards Oslo agreements and peace with Israel. These programmes were mainly undertaken by NGOs. According to Merz (2013: 140), this new trend had an important impact on the work of this sector as it reflected a gradual neutralisation of a politically active sector and its disconnect from popular support and mass mobilisation. This neutralisation and disconnect will be demonstrated more throughout this chapter.

The creation of the PA produced what seemed to be a radical divide between the Palestinian grassroots organisations and the national movement (Alashqar, 2015: 2). In the context of the above, this separation led to the emergence of new realities at the political and social level, especially a conflict over funding agendas and power between the NGO sector and the Fatah-led PA. Another aspect of this conflict was how some political parties began to use their party affiliation with the civil society sector to enhance their popular support and to widen their political power base in order to form an opposition front to the PA. This was mainly explicit among NGOs with Islamist and/or leftist connections. These organisations had their own particular donors, and they began to use their funding in programmes that enhanced their popular support and expanded criticism of and opposition to the pre-Oslo PA and the peace process alike.

Challand (2008: 63) associates these conflicts concerning powers and political dominance to the blurry relationship between the body of the PA as a government structure and the PLO as a group of political parties that mainly operated in exile and had some sort of affiliation with NGOs working in the oPt. This made it difficult to understand the strategies adopted by the PA leadership about the type of relationship it sought to have with the civil society sector. It was not clear, however, whether the PA wanted to take over this sector and blend it within its newly established body, or take advantage of its knowledge and expertise in developing its PA institutions, or both. Glenn Robinson (quoted in Brown, 2003: 139) explains that the 'regime did not trust its own society because it had so few connections with it'. While the PA leadership believed that they were putting the foundation of a Palestinian state, the NGO leadership preferred to focus their effort on strengthening the civil society sector and work with donors to achieve this goal. The NGO leadership began to invest in a favourable relationship with the emerging PA in order to achieve its goals, both at the institutional level and at an individual one. Over time, the relationship between the PA and the NGO leadership became, as described by Brown (2003: 143), more corporate in nature, according to which explicit oppositional missions have gradually disappeared and turned more toward mutual interest. This corporate relationship will be discussed further in the coming sections.

5.2.3 The Second Intifada and Onwards

Slightly before the eruption of the Second Intifada in September 2000, the United Nations' special coordinator in Gaza released a report showing the amount of money that human rights and democratisation-focused NGOs had received since the establishment of the PA. The report estimated the amount at more than 100 million USD, yet it did not supply a breakdown of the funds that were distributed directly to PA institutions and Palestinian NGOs. The report provoked stormy debates within the PA institutions, particularly the Ministry of Justice, which received only 4 million USD from the total of 100 million USD (Hammami, 2000: 18). This led to a legal battle between the NGO sector and the PA. The latter wanted to centralise all sources of funding through its relevant ministries, reform the laws that regulate NGOs formation, and financially and administratively monitor the work of the sector. According to the new law that was enacted by the Palestinian Legislative Council (Charitable Associations and Community Organisations Law),[2] NGOs have to report to the Ministry of Interior, which has the right to refuse or accept the registration and the licensing of any NGO. In the meantime, Arafat emphasised the role Mukhabarat (intelligence) should also assume over this sector (Challand, 2008: 65). The new civil society law was the beginning of the internal securitisation of the work of Palestinian NGOs and had paved the way for further securitisation in the future from both the PA and Western donors.

As indicated in Chapter 3, the situation for the PA became critical immediately after the eruption of the Second Intifada due to the systematic destruction of its institutional and economic infrastructures. Pressure on the PA from donors for reforms and good governance had increased. This pressure prompted the PA to start cooperating with the NGOs for their role in implementing reform and good governance programmes. In Gaza, however, the PA began to depend on these organisations to provide emergency and relief services to many sectors due to the deteriorating economic conditions (Challand, 2008: 65).

To briefly characterise the work of CSOs during this period, four major characteristics need to be discussed. First, unlike with the First Intifada, the sector lacked a unified leadership and a national reference. Although, as Tabar and Hanafi (2005) argue, Palestinian NGOs had enough awareness of the

---

[2] Counterterrorism regulations have affected different national contexts, not only in oPt. Yet due to the sensitivity of the situation in the Middle East, particularly in the oPt, the impact of such regulation has been much wider. Bloodgood, E. and Tremblay-Boire, J. 2010. 'NGOs responses to counterterrorism regulations after September 11th'. *International Journal Not-for-Profit Law* 12, no. 4.

socio-economic needs of the Strip, they still failed in developing a synergy with the political factions and the national and Islamic committees compared to how they did in the past. Tabar and Hanafi (2005: 205–6) suggest that, at the time, these organisations utilised their connection with and the recognition of international donors and aid agencies; their contribution was minimal when it came to 'harnessing the society's energies during a period of national struggle'. Thus, they did not have a significant impact on the direction of the uprising. The reason for this failure was that there were growing limitations (political and operational) imposed by the donors on how much freedom these organisations had in coordinating with the different types of national committees.

The second characteristic is demonstrated in the period that followed the Second Intifada and the unusual disconnect that emerged, both in Gaza and in the WB, between the recently professionalised and elitist NGOs and popular movements. The only exceptions here are the organisations that had an Islamist background (i.e. NGOs that were directly affiliated with Hamas or Islamic Jihad). This disconnect had a significant impact on weakening NGOs' collective action in countering the economic measures taken by the Israeli occupier. Additionally, their neutral political position, and the denouncing of armed struggle, put them in a difficult position in the face of popular sentiment and de-legitimised them in the eyes of both people and political parties (Merz, 2013: 141). The reason for this was that NGO leaders became confused between the political and the national when formulating their work agendas. Accordingly, they abstained from committing to the Palestinian national cause when refusing to engage in political activities that were similar to their actions during the First Intifada (Hanafi and Tabar, 2004). For instance, NGO leaders, even at the individual level, began to distance themselves from any political affiliation with any political parties (even those opposing armed resistance), to the extent that they avoided appearing in photographs in public events with any political figures.

Third, at the economic level, the performance of many NGOs demonstrated their serious lack of awareness of the context where they operate. The reason for this, as suggested by Hanafi and Tabar (2004), is that NGO leaders usually descend from urban, educated middle classes, while the majority of those living in economic hardship are affected by hostilities and reside in remote areas and refugee camps. Thus, Hanafi and Tabar see a disconnect between the NGO leadership and the communities they propose to serve (ibid.). According to them, the current reality of the civil society exemplifies the relationship between those who benefit from the post-Oslo aid regime, both the PA political elite and the NGO elite, and those who not only saw no gains but rather saw the post-Oslo economic and political reality exacerbate their economic hardship.

Fourth, the militarisation of the Second Intifada weakened the role of this sector and contributed to the re-emergence of military and the factional sector as dominant and authoritative components within the secular and Islamic movements (Roy, 2013: 191). Furthermore, the internal division that followed Hamas's electoral victory in 2006, and then takeover of Gaza in 2007, had directly affected the work of the civil society sector. This is due to both Fatah and Hamas using their authority to take retaliatory measures against each of their aligned NGOs (Roy, 2013: 215). For instance, in Gaza, Hamas began to closely monitor the work of NGOs that were affiliated with Fatah or those that have strong links with international institutions. Also, in the WB, the PA closed the majority of Hamas-affiliated organisations.

5.3 The Palestinian New 'Globalised Elite'

Building on the historical background of the civil society, this section aims to look at how the changes in the work of this sector over time contributed to the emergence of what is called a 'globalised elite', as suggested by Hanafi and Tabar (2002, 2004). The term has been generally applied to the emerging elite within the civil society sector in the WB and Gaza Strip as a result of the significant increase of foreign aid to this sector. This elite is represented by the educated middle class, aid workers and development practitioners that began to play a bigger role in Palestinian society. Hanafi and Tabar's contribution to the term 'globalised elite' is significant in that they associate their argument with the New Policy Agenda (NPA) for the development industry and aid delivery that emerged following the end of the Cold War. Integral to this policy is the 'good governance' agenda, which was introduced earlier in this chapter and for whose implementation the civil society and NGOs played a key role (Robinson, 1993). Although the NPA has remained centred around neoliberal and democratic beliefs, its implementation differed from one development actor to another (Moore, 2006).

According to Stephen Biggs and Arthur Neame (1994), this policy agenda has led to the emergence of a new organisational model for local NGOs, and it reconstructed the way these organisations work in association with the funding model or donors' policies. In other words, Biggs and Neame (1994) suggest that development, as a process, is perceived as a predictable one with different possible tangible outcomes (inputs equal outputs) regardless of the context-related factors where it operates. What this implies is that NGOs begin to view themselves as the solution for the problems development is meant to find given the expected inputs and outputs donors and aid agencies provideIn other words, NGOs become fully engaged with the input–output frameworks which are entirely informed by donors' global or political agenda.

Consequently, NGOs gradually become detached from the local context to which they belong. Moreover, the NPA,[3] according to Hulme and Edwards (1995), takes NGOs to a new level, making them more important players at the international level. However, they argue that NGOs become dominated by the goals and the mission of the new agenda, and they lose the links with their own original and local population they are meant to serve. Accordingly, Hanafi and Tabar (2002: 2) argue that the structural changes occurring in the development field have 'deep-rooted implications that affect NGOs international organizational practices, and therefore their external mode of actions in a manner, which is not easily addressed'. Among these organisational changes is the growth of an elite that is highly influenced by and associated with the NPA that influenced the work structures of NGOs and funding agencies alike. This elite is not necessarily comprised of leaders of national Palestinian NGOs, but rather Palestinian staff of international NGOs and the United Nations and other international agencies. Their work is deeply interlinked, and they influence each other equally through determining the type and nature of work agenda on the ground.

5.3.1 Problematizing 'Globalised Elite'

According to Hanafi and Tabar (2002: 2), the Palestinian globalised elite that emerged after the establishment of the PA in 1994 is defined as a 'local social formation which is informed by and/or closely aligned with global debates and agenda'. This formation takes place in a 'broader process of structuring of knowledge, practices [...] among Palestinian NGOs in relation to their increased entry into development cooperation'. While Hanafi and Tabar (2002, 2004, 2005) introduce the term 'globalised elite' to refer to this emerging social sector, they refer to it as 'new', which indirectly indicates that an 'old' one existed and was replaced. Accordingly, the argument in this section will be initially based on this assumption (i.e. the development of Palestinian globalised elite and how it progressed from old to new). It is important to

---

[3] Following the Cold War, it was difficult to convince taxpayers of the value of development aid, driven by the ideological differences between the South and North (quoted in Fowler, 1998). What the new policy agenda sought to achieve was emphasise 'self-interest' as a concept over the 'moral obligation' in that taxpayers should be 'convinced that their money would be well-spent and that aid was effective and efficient' (de Feyter, 2011: 34). Accordingly, the NPA was based on the neoliberal ideology that 'markets and private initiative are [...] the most efficient mechanism for achieving economic growth and providing most services to most people' (Edwards and Hulme, 1995, quoted in de Feyter, 2011: 34).

problematize the term in order to contribute to a better understanding of the characteristics of this social group.

The increased level of development funding directed towards CSOs following Oslo, compared to the decrease in funds available from Arab sources, caused a new form of hierarchy among Palestinian NGOs and a heightened level of competition (Hanafi and Tabar, 2005: 26). Both the new hierarchy and the competition resulted in the new NGO elite overturning the old one. This included charitable and societal organisations that struggled to survive. According to a civil society academic specialist, new discourses have emerged in relation to Palestinian NGOs' involvement in development cooperation, particularly those working in the Gaza Strip due to their more active role they play in the Strip sector as compared to in the WB.[4] These discourses reflect dichotomous relationships similar to those between 'developed' and 'underdeveloped', 'us' and 'them', and 'civilised' and 'uncivilised' that have been associated with development discourses. According to the interviewed specialist, however, what is more significant about these dichotomies in the Palestinian context is that these are associated with what seem identical elements. For instance, WB and Gaza, Fatah and Hamas, secular and Islamic, and independent or party NGOs. Similarly, Hanafi and Tabar (2005: 26–27) suggest that these dichotomies 'do not reflect the beliefs of the NGO actors per se, but rather actors that move within categorisations and manipulate them according to the context'. These actors include donors and international aid agencies. According to a former USAID official and manager of an international NGO, these dichotomies are best illustrated when NGOs suggest that their agendas are informed by national interests while, in fact, they are fundamentally guided by the Western donor agenda.[5]

For two or three years after the PA establishment, the civil society and NGO sector in Gaza witnessed a significant level of fragmentation. One aspect of this fragmentation is that although these organisations were claiming to address the needs of the Gaza Strip based on a national agenda set out by the PA or other national institutions, they were, in fact, competing among each other to survive.[6]

---

[4] Interview with a local academic and civil society expert who looks at the work of CSOs in Gaza, Gaza, 3 February 2017.

[5] Interview with a former local USAID official who supervise the implementation of the agency's projects in Gaza and currently is a manager of an international NGO in Gaza, Gaza, 2 February 2017.

[6] Interview with a former aid consultant and aid worker at one of the biggest civil society building projects in the Gaza Strip. The project was funded mainly by USAID and lasted for eight years, Gaza, 14 December 2016.

Moreover, success in obtaining funding from foreign donors, or through international agencies, was important to prove their credibility. This competition reflected the lack of unity they maintained in the past and the sense of pluralism in serving the Gazan community. This situation had become worse over time, especially when the relationship between Western donors and the PA deteriorated due to financial misconduct. On the one hand, more money was shifted to the civil society sector, and on the other hand, the level of competition had increased.[7]

Following claims of corruption against the PA (1996–98), NGOs began to play a bigger role. A few of them succeeded in securing their sustainable sources of funding directly via donors or indirectly through their partner international NGOs. The latter felt the equal need to create partnerships with well-established local NGOs in order to implement their programmes. The case with smaller NGOs was slightly different. They were mostly ready to accept what was offered to them, and they operated according to the motto 'if you do not take it, others will do'. This, as a result, had a significant impact on the services and programmes implemented in Gaza and their actual relevance to the local context and community's expectation.[8]

This trend influenced the growth of the 'globalised elite in that it impacted the organisational structures and the internal dynamics and bylaws of these organisations'. NGOs in Gaza conducted their needs assessment on the basis that they would reflect the needs of Gaza and its population. Yet, in fact, these needs assessments were mostly tailored to meet the requirements of donors, the regional aid policy for a particular donor country or the donor's requirement to comply with Israel's security agenda.[9]

5.3.2 Characterising the New 'Globalised Elite'

To expand this understanding of the new Palestinian elite, a number of general characteristics associated with it are raised, specifically those characteristics mostly associated with Gaza's elite due its socio-economic and political peculiarity. It can be seen in widened geographical and political disconnect between Gaza and the WB, and the growing socio-economic gap between the two sides of the territory, especially after Israel's disengagement from Gaza in 2005 and

---

[7] Ibid.

[8] Interview with a senior staff at the Palestinian NGO (PNGO) network, Gaza, 12 February 2017. PNGO works closely as an institutional umbrella for local NGOs in the oPt with governmental institutions, donors and international aid agencies.

[9] Interview with an NGO consult and academic expert in development projects and international aid in Gaza, Gaza, 10 December 2016.

Hamas taking control of the Strip in 2007. Accordingly, these major events further contributed to the growth and expansion of new social sectors. These characteristics can be summarised in the following five points.

First, Hamas is informed by global agendas and operates according to development frameworks set out by international organisations. A major feature of this group is that it is comprised mainly of individuals who work at or are linked directly to international organisations such as the World Bank, WFP, IMF, USAID and the EU. Although this group fully belongs to the local community, it demonstrates a 'global or an international vision that has minimal relevance to the Gaza context and they are empowered by the institutional spaces their affiliate organisations managed to overtake within Gaza'.[10] In the words of the former USAID project officer, there is a difference between being globalised and being global. Being globalised only indicates the external influence on the internal elements, while being global is more comprehensive as the influence is two-way. Put another way, the globalised elite's influence is only limited to influencing the local development agenda informed by the frameworks of global agendas and not the opposite. He describes this situation as

> very uncomfortable sometimes to sit in these cluster meetings with other staff from international NGOs and begin to discuss development agenda and ways to implement some of their components, and when you make a simple comparison of the local needs and problems, you easily predict massive gaps and great shortcomings that could occur when these agendas are implemented in a form of programmes.[11]

Second, it is a highly politicised elite in that it is influenced by the political agenda of either donors or their international partner organisations. A significant number of the NGOs that were established after the PA in 1994 became part of the aid regime that promoted the Oslo peace process. These organisations were either PLO affiliated, thus endorsing the same peace, or NGOs that sought foreign aid from donors whose aid to the Palestinians was or has been integral to the 'aid for peace' agenda. This is simply because 'the work of these NGOs in the past two decades was not necessarily focused on promoting peace, but it can be simply described as politically biased since Gaza's development was not the main purpose for their work'.[12] For instance, some of

---

[10] Interview with an academic who works as an advisor/consultant to NGOs working in Gaza and a lecturer at the Islamic University of Gaza, Gaza, 11 December 2016.

[11] Ibid.

[12] Ibid.

these organisations were involved in normalisation programmes that involved youth peace groups from both sides. Such programmes were part of the dichotomies that resulted from the implementation of some aid programmes and at the same time 'youth are encouraged to support peace while they are lacking it in their own community, and they hear about developments while they witness a systematic destruction of their economic infrastructures'.[13] Many of these organisations were engaged in the promotion of a democratisation programme that was meant to promote political participation and pluralism. Meanwhile, the majority of donor countries tied their aid with progress in the peace process, which many political sectors in Palestinian society opposed and thus limited their actual political participation.

Third, it is a *clientalised* elite but not in the sense that it is one that is constructed on the basis of favouritism or tribalism. This is also simply one small part of it. *Clientalised* here sees NGO workers and professionals in the Gaza Strip beset by a lack of diversity. It is a homogenous group of individuals who maintain almost the same professional, social, economic and political background and discourses. Plus, 'they represent a closed socio-economic group of middle class, educated people that speak fluent English and have their connections with the PA officials, donors, and political parties'.[14] This clientalised feature seems to be well known in this section of Gaza and is clear in the responses of aid beneficiaries interviewed as part of this book.

Fourth, it is a de facto elite. Because its expansion is highly linked to the absence of government structures that would normally be responsible for the service delivery NGOs perform at the moment. The reason for that is the absence of a unity government in Gaza and the political split between Fatah and Hamas increased the influence of the NGO elite on Gazans' daily lives.[15] The absence of a unified authority in the Gaza Strip, the ongoing boycott of both donors and the PA in Ramallah against Hamas, and the continued Israeli blockade on the territory have equally contributed to furthering the role this sector plays in service provision in the Gaza Strip. Shortly after the establishment of the PA, the work of this sector was surrounded with much controversy either because of the amount of funds or because of the new agenda it

---

[13] Interview with an NGO consultant and academic expert in development projects and international aid in Gaza, Gaza, 10 December 2016.

[14] Ibid.

[15] Interview with the consultant for the European External Action Services (EEAS) in Gaza Strip, Gaza, 21 March 2017. EEAS is part of the European Commission and it continues to monitor projects funded by the European Union. Unlike the US government, the European Union has strongly encouraged Palestinians to end the division between the WB and Gaza and sometimes vowed to use financial sanctions to push for Palestinian unity.

became involved in. As indicated earlier in the chapter, there were moments of direct confrontations with this sector; however, these confrontations failed to influence the way this sector planned or carried its activities. This is due to donors' political and financial backing even at the expense of the PA.

This de facto role also put this elite in an awkward position before the authorities in Gaza. The sector's involvement in almost every aspect of the lives of Gazans and the increased level of funding made the Hamas government feel that NGOs were conspiring with donor countries to damage this government's popularity. Consequently, Hamas put restrictions on the work of NGOs and limited the level of freedom they used to enjoy while at the same recognising it could not block them fully due to the huge service delivery gap this may cause in Gaza.

Finally, building on the above, the NGO and civil society sector can also be characterised as a non-sovereign elite. Looking at how this sector progressed over the past two decades, the NGO sector shifted from being affiliated to and dependent on Palestinian political parties to being fully dependent on donors' money and, with this, their agenda. The only exception to this is the Hamas-affiliated NGOs that continue to operate under direct guidance from the party and via funding that Hamas secures from its political allies in some Gulf countries (i.e. Qatar and Iran).[16]

5.4 Agents of Socio-economic Promotion and Demotion

In relation to the new Palestinian globalised elite discussed in the earlier section, this section aims to examine how the work of NGOs in the Gaza Strip has turned them into agents of socio-economic promotion or demotion. It will also look at the processes through which socio-economic promotion and demotion occur at different levels and develop as a tool for biopolitical control according to which NGOs perform as agents of control over the lives of the population in Gaza. The first level is evident in how some NGOs contributed to serving specific sectors within Gaza's population due to the nature of some programmes tailored by these NGOs. This, as a result, makes these small sectors the target beneficiaries of these programmes. The second level is identified in how donors' funding contributed to increasing the growth and organisational legitimacy of some NGOs (promotion) over others (demotion). This would occur through one party being marginalised, due to either political affiliation or socio-economic representation that these NGOs represent in terms of their leaders or the communities/groups they represent. As will be illustrated

---

[16] Interview with the ex-minister of economy at the Palestinian Unity Government (March–July 2007), Gaza, 10 March 2017.

in this section, sustainable funding for these organisations, which is linked to their ability to meet the criteria set by donors, contributed to the growth of these organisations and to fostering their legitimacy when attempting to reach out to communities in need.

5.4.1 Preferential Ties with Donors

Benoit Challand (2008) suggests that civil society and NGOs can, in fact, work to promote socio-economic exclusion in the societies they operate within. This is particularly true if this exclusion is based on the transformation of class structure. By class, Challand (2008: 168) refers to the group of individuals who 'share, along fictitious horizontal lines, common properties in terms of access to the means of production or broad economic and market capacities and whose positions are antagonistic to other groups'. Through examining the work of NGOs, this subsection will demonstrate how NGO leadership took advantage of connections with international donor agencies in such a way that made them privileged in their local context. When speaking of NGO leadership, we refer to the group of local aid workers and individual consultants who work either directly or indirectly with international donors. As will be demonstrated, their role enables them to establish close ties with these agencies and increase the way both parties influence each other when it comes to setting agendas for the local aid programmes. A member of the Palestinian NGO Network (PNGO) suggested that there is a second group which is represented in the traditional professional elites who usually come from business families or have strong ties with the political elite, as shown in Chapter 4. According to the PNGO member, the big NGOs in Gaza and/ or international NGOs are usually staffed and run by these groups of pro-fessional elites.[17] He stated that some of these NGO workers play a dual role. First, they have senior positions in key international or local NGOs. Second, workers, or members of their families, run their own smaller NGOs or in some instances they are members of the board of directors in these NGOs. What happens is that they take advantage of both positions to ease funding in both directions, as stated by the network.[18]

The clientalised approach, under which these NGO workers operate, allowed them to be service providers and beneficiaries at the same time, which, as a result, improved their position vis-á-vis donors and funding agencies. These NGO professionals tend to obtain dual knowledge of both

---

[17] Interview with a member of the Palestinian NGO (PNGO) network, Gaza, February 2012.

[18] Ibid.

the international organisations they represent, whether as direct employees or as consultants. At the same time, they also have enough knowledge of the local NGO structures and operations. Hence, this knowledge has facilitated significant growth of particular types of local NGOs over the past two decades compared to others. Furthermore, the influence of NGOs extended to the type of programmes donors wanted to engage in, which usually serve the smaller social sector and networks these NGO professionals represent. Surprisingly, some of the programmes USAID decided to implement in Gaza reached out and impacted a very small sector. These programmes usually did not reflect the general needs of the population in Gaza at all. For example, USAID had two special programmes, one to cover the tuition fees for private school students in Gaza and the other to cover tuition fees for university students attending one local university. Both beneficiaries did not represent the needy sector in the Strip but rather a well-off sector. The official indicated that private schools are usually attended by children of the middle-class businessmen, NGO staff and political elite, and they are usually able to self-fund their children's education.[19]

This funding mechanism indicated the nature and level of feedback local NGO professionals provide to the donors and how they influence the direction of donor funding. It does, however, also show how donors have a mutual interest in providing for and empowering this social sector in the Gaza Strip. Similarly, Alijla (2014) argues that the NGO sector endorses the expansion of a 'well-off middle class' in the Gaza Strip that struggles to maintain its socioeconomic status within Gazan society. It also seeks to maintain its professional status among donors and international organisations. Challand (2008: 187) explains this behaviour by suggesting that what matters is not the political instrumentalisation of networking only, but rather 'the prevalent factor is that of enhancing one's political position within the field of NGOs'.

Another dimension of how preferential ties with donors impact the work of NGOs in Gaza, and in particular the relationships between local NGOs in the Gaza Strip, is raised by a former Tamkeen Project senior civil society specialist.[20] The Tamkeen Project, as indicated in the previous chapter, has its purpose directed towards building and empowering civil society in the Gaza Strip, especially in areas of good governance and democracy. These dynamics are not based on cooperating with each other in what is supposed to be for the general benefit of the sector and thus ensuring further outreach to the society.

---

[19] Interview with a USAID representative for Gaza Programmes, Ramallah, 20 December 2016.

[20] Interview with a former senior civil society specialist at Tamkeen Project, Gaza, 8 December 2016.

Rather, this cooperation is based on the superiority of bigger NGOs, which usually have strong ties with the donors over the smaller ones, regardless of the fact that the latter, in many cases, have better awareness of the needs of the communities they represent more than the former.[21]

There are two essential determinants that are associated with how these dynamics are formed. First, the level of flexibility smaller NGOs demonstrate is their willingness to be controlled and to engage with programmes and activities as suggested by the bigger NGOs and donors. In some cases, these programmes are not relevant to the community the small NGOs serve or do not have any developmental aspects. Instead, they sometimes contradict with the traditional values of the small rural communities where these NGOs operate. For example, there were instances when the small NGOs were subcontracted to run gender equality programmes, a subject matter that remains quite sensitive in some small traditional communities.

Another example is the youth forums where youth from both genders were asked to participate in group discussions and activities, something considered very unusual and a 'taboo' for the overwhelming majority of small communities in Gaza.[22] The second determinant is based on the ideological and political background of small NGOs. The reason for this is twofold: (a) The bigger local NGOs in Palestine, in general, are represented by the traditional left parties who were active mostly during the late 1970s and during the First Intifada (1987–93). These were privileged over other NGOs due to their ability to build institutional infrastructures and systems over the past 20 years. This, in fact, enabled them to take the lead compared to other CSOs when the boom of aid occurred following the Oslo Accords in 1993. Their relationship with the newly established NGOs and other NGOs from different ideological backgrounds had always been characterised as a bias as they continued to favour leftist NGOs over others. (b) At the same time, bigger NGOs often have a contractual obligation to identify their subcontracted smaller NGOs on the basis of their political background. It is the responsibility of our main local partner NGOs to search for and find their subcontractors (local NGOs) before they decide to work with them. The Tamkeen official describes this process as follows:

> In this instance, we help them to make the right decision. They must collect biodata about the board of directors of these NGOs and the senior management. After that, we pass on this information to USAID or the responsible agencies of the donor government for a lengthy

---

[21] Ibid.
[22] Ibid.

vetting process. If the results came out clean, then it would be safe for us and for the main contracting NGOs to carry on with the activities.[23]

In this context, Nabulsi (2005: 123) suggests that funds channelled after Oslo by foreign donors towards civil society actors did not merely have the purpose of promoting social and economic development. The purpose was also to create a strong institutional base that would work alongside the PA to promote the peace process and sometimes engage in dialogue with Israeli partners through the implementation of inter-community negotiations. Therefore, this required the elimination of Palestinian partners that opposed this paradigm. These processes, according to Nabulsi (2005: 123), undermined the democratic and associational structures of the civil society as it affected the wider sector, including trade union platforms and community associations that represent the grassroots organisations. In doing so, the academic and former consultant of NGOs in Gaza thought that Western donors, and American ones in particular, and the leading local NGOs' practices in Gaza after Hamas's victory contributed to an unprecedented level of de-democratisation in this sector.

5.4.2 The De-democratisation of Civil Society in Gaza

There are several issues that can be discussed in relation to the role civil society organisations play as agents for socio-economic advancement and the process of de-democratisation associated with their work following the establishment of PA. The first issue is that donors lost their direct connection with the actual needs of Gaza's population. Most donors' and aid agencies' agendas were sometimes based on anticipation rather than actual needs assessments, particularly following Hamas's electoral victory (2006) and their taking control of the Strip (2007). What happened in fact is that each donor depended on a number of individual consultants to conduct assessments in Gaza in different areas of need so as to determine need. Donors in most cases 'did not engage in depth with the results of these needs assessments to validate their credibility. In some instances, donors contracted international consultants to conduct these assessments'.[24] These international consultants might have good knowledge and background of the Gaza Strip, but it is not at all realistic that they would be able to identify the pressing needs of the communities in need or diagnose the core issues that donors and aid agencies should pay attention to, especially when their consultants' visits to the Strip were usually limited to a few days and the rest of this assessment was done remotely. This, as a result, contributed to

---

[23] Ibid.
[24] Interview with a consultant for the EEAS in Gaza, 21 December 2016.

undermining the role of a large part of the NGO sector that once represented the population in Gaza and spoke on its behalf. Instead, small NGOs were replaced with a very limited number of big NGOs or consultants.

In the context of the first issue, the second issue relates to the fact that development or humanitarian needs assessment for Gaza is no longer purely decided by Gaza's civil society. The decision-making mechanism following Hamas's electoral victory in 2006 reflects an unequal relationship between CSOs in both the WB and Gaza. What this means is that more administrative and financial powers are assigned to the WB branches of NGOs over those based in Gaza. When donor countries imposed various financial and administrative restrictions on the work of aid agencies in Gaza, the majority of these agencies relocated their international staff and key local staff to the WB. Furthermore, they imposed travel restrictions on their staff to the Gaza Strip, which, as a result, emphasised the disconnect between the NGO sector in Gaza and its counterpart in the WB. Additionally, it increased the gap between Gaza's needs and the central decision-making process. This disconnect continued to grow, especially when Hamas began to tighten its policies against this sector as a response to the latter's no-contact policy referred to in the introductory chapter. Consequently, it has weakened the NGOs in Gaza and has minimised their key role in determining the Strip's developmental and humanitarian needs.

The third issue concerns how the civil society sector has been perceived as a growing business and an area of investment that generates profit for those involved in it. Accordingly, NGOs have become a 'good business' in Palestine in general, and in Gaza in particular, as described by CSO expert in Gaza.[25] The reason for this is that the increasing poverty in the district and the absent economic infrastructures have prompted a large scope of humanitarian aid and other types of aid to be directed to Gaza. This as a result has created good opportunities for the NGO sector to grow and has inspirited many professionals and NGO workers to come together and establish their own NGOs.

Profitability here does not mean to achieve revenues in the real sense but rather to benefit from the high administrative and overhead costs these organisations charge when subcontracted to deliver aid with international aid agencies. These administrative costs usually go to paying high salaries for NGO workers and consultants and for renting good-quality air-conditioned offices, which in many cases, exceed one-third of the overall amount budgeted to deliver the service.

---

[25] Interview with a local academic and civil society expert who looks after the work of CSOs in Gaza, Gaza, 3 February 2017.

5.5 Between Securitisation and the Creation of Aid-Dependence Culture

This section will discuss how the change in funding dynamics that existed before the establishment of the PA (1994), compared to the dynamics that emerged in the post-Oslo aid regime (1994 to present), resulted, to some extent, in securitising the work of this sector. It will also focus on how the deteriorated political and economic situation, especially in relation to the absence of any progress in the peace process with Israel and the rise of Hamas, increased the role NGOs play in the Gaza Strip and its impact on the daily lives of people in Gaza. It will also look at the impact of securitising the work of NGOs on lowering the efficiency of aid programmes and the emergence of an aid-dependence culture.

5.5.1 The Burdens of the New Reporting Duties

As indicated earlier in the chapter, NGOs following the PA establishment were categorised according to their role in supporting the peace process between Israel and Palestine. All funds and programmes for NGOs were planned accordingly. To ensure conformity with this role, NGOs had to increase the level of reporting they originally had to do as part of their contractual agreements. Normally, reporting included information about the type of activities, progress reports and programme-related statistics. Yet over time, the type of information that became required as part of this reporting had significantly increased, and

> we gradually began to expand the scope of detail from factsheets, outputs and impact data to focus more on collecting information about general situation in Gaza and the political atmosphere [...] to our understanding this was necessary for planning and we, as aid workers, had no concerns as to how this information would be used by donors or aid agencies.[26]

However, new reporting obligations emerged following Hamas's takeover of the Gaza Strip in 2007. These obligations were linked to a new statutory provision on the 'Economic Support Fund' Act that had a special relevance to the oPt, particularly to the work of aid agencies in Gaza. While the provision was of particular relevance to American funds, it still impacted the funding policies of the majority of Western donors due to the fear that it could be used

---

[26] Interview with a USAID-funded project manager in Gaza, 2 February 2017.

indirectly to aid terrorism (Plucknett, 2007: 2). The provision indicates that the secretary of state

> shall take all appropriate steps to ensure that such assistance is not provided to or through any individual, private or government entity, or educational institution that [...] has reason to believe advocates, plans, sponsors, engages in, or has engaged in, terrorist activity; and shall establish procedures specifying the steps to be taken in carrying out this subsection and shall terminate assistance to any individual, entity, or educational institution which he has determined to be involved in or advocating terrorist activity. (Plucknett, 2007: 2–3)

Accordingly, in order to comply with this new provision and be eligible for funding, it became mandatory for NGOs in receipt of US government funding to sign the Anti-Terrorism Certificate (ATC), of which this provision and similar ones were central. Consequently, the amount of information demanded from NGOs had increased significantly.

Reporting became very complicated and was a risky job, a programme officer at a local NGO indicated.[27] In his words, the amount of information

> we have to collect and ask for from our beneficiaries or stakeholders (partner institutions) has become significantly huge. For example, most NGOs who received Western government funding operate under the fear that they would be blacklisted if they failed to accurately identify and verify their aid beneficiaries.[28]

For this purpose, reporting requires local NGOs to obtain and share identity information of their beneficiaries with donors (for security check purposes). This information includes questions that help verify the political affiliation of their own or of their family members. The officer believed that it has become

> quite awkward for the local NGO staff to do this. We work with people to complete eligibility surveys that should normally aim to identify the economic needs of target groups. But in our case, we conduct these surveys to indirectly investigate the political background of beneficiaries and if they could pose any funding risk to us as an organisation or to our donor. For instance, we ask beneficiaries if a member of a family

---

[27] Interview with a programme officer at a local NGO working in the WB and Gaza through USAID funding, WB, 12 February 2017.

[28] Ibid.

died or injured as a result of conflict. Beneficiaries usually think that such questions bring sympathy to their case and improve their eligibility. While in fact they give us a clue if their family members are/were members of military factions.[29]

The peculiar security situation in the Gaza Strip made reporting and information sharing much more complicated. Aid agencies have become fully understanding of the security atmosphere in Gaza, yet this does not stop them from complying with the laws and the criteria set out by donor countries when it comes to obtaining information they believe necessary to approve the dispensing of aid money.[30] Following the 2008 Operation Cast Lead on Gaza, some NGOs began to implement psychological and physical rehabilitation programmes. Some of the surveys designed by international NGOs included questions about the place where some beneficiaries were injured, how they were injured and what they were doing when they got injured. There were different reactions to and interpretations of these questions by the target beneficiaries for these services. Aid workers, whose job is to collect data from the field, found themselves in a sensitive situation where they had to follow the guidelines imposed by their funders. In the meantime, they had to respect and safeguard the privacy and safety of the individuals they aimed to help.

Hence, there is a growing atmosphere of insecurity among NGO workers, on the one hand, because they might be accused of having influence over beneficiaries and because of their ability to access aid assistance. On the other hand, they fear that they may jeopardise the security of specific individuals and thus be accused of collaboration by the local authorities. This, to some extent, was perceived as a justification for Hamas's decision to shut down more than 170 NGOs in Gaza that used to provide services to women, children and other humanitarian organisations. Hamas accused these organisations of posing a threat to national security and for 'plotting internal unrest' in cooperation with external parties, such as donors and international aid agencies (Almeghari, 2008).

The highly securitised reporting system used by NGOs in Gaza, especially following the Hamas takeover of the Strip, had impacted not only the credibility of these NGOs regarding their relations with the Hamas government in Gaza, but also their credibility among their aid beneficiaries.

---

[29] Ibid.

[30] Interview with a social worker at an American NGO to implement a psycho-social support programme for those affected by the 2008–9 Israeli offensive in Gaza, 15 February 2017.

5.5.2 *Aid between Low Efficiency and High Dependency*

The highly securitised aid to Palestinians did not stop or even decrease their dependence on it, but the reverse. As indicated in Chapter 3, donors, when designing their aid programmes, have to follow policies that coincide with the Israeli security standards. In doing so, they implicitly give legitimacy to the latter's economic warfare and de-development of Palestinians in Gaza. The Gaza Strip, compared to other oPt districts, experienced further negative effects of the Oslo Accords' death that have come in the form of serious threats to human and economic security. Regardless of the large amount of aid invested by donors in areas of institutional and public infrastructure since Oslo, these investments failed to sustain a developed and independent economy. This fact may apply to other regions within the oPt, but now the reality indicates that efforts for Gaza to build a self-sustaining and open economy that is linked with the WB and the outside world can no longer be possible.

The gradual deterioration of the security situation in Gaza, and thus the harsh economic conditions, created a tendency among donor agencies and local NGOs to implement short-term relief and humanitarian programmes that lack sustainability. The aims for these programmes have been often to prevent possible humanitarian crises or provide relief services when these crises occur. Consequently, the outcome of this approach failed to achieve any tangible progress at the social and economic levels. Another factor is that donors and NGOs have always found it easier to implement short-term relief programmes due to fewer security restrictions imposed on these programmes than on development ones. In addition, the disbursement of material goods is a way of spending budgets quickly.

There are important consequences for the heightened securitised aid policy imposed by donors, particularly in the period that followed Israel's disengagement from Gaza in 2005. Donors also have varied aid policies, and NGOs had to comply with each individually. This, as a result, made NGOs lose the sense of networking and coordination between them. These policies became the main reference to deciding the kind of activities NGOs can or are willing to implement with an absence of a common agenda that unites their efforts. Consequently, the majority of NGOs' activities and programmes have been repetitive. NGOs in the Gaza Strip were mostly implementing what seemed to be identical programmes. As described by one of the NGO consultants,

> Food parcels, temporary job creation programmes and household income generations became quite popular, and some of these were sometimes

promoted either by NGOs or their partner aid agencies as development programme, yet, in fact, they had no sustainability impact.[31]

The issue here with short-term programmes that have some developmental aspects is that they usually last between three and six months, and, by the law, such programmes do not require the vetting of the individual beneficiaries.[32] However, as we discovered later, these programmes are not implemented according to a comprehensive development agenda or a strategy. This is explained by one of the officers at an American NGO as follows:

We implemented capacity-building programmes for young graduates followed by short-term on-the-job training. However, once the pro-gramme is over, the graduates go home and they miss the opportunity to utilise the skills they gained. What is missing is a comprehensive devel-opment strategy that ensures that money invested in such activities have long-lasting impact on Gaza's economy and those in need.[33]

The absent sustainability of most aid programmes has prompted doubts among aid beneficiaries. Beneficiaries of graduate schemes perceived these programmes, in most cases, as an opportunity to get out of the house and leave the bedroom trap which is caused by lengthy unemployment.[34]

Another important aspect that relates to an absence of sustainability in aid programmes is the repetitive characteristic of many humanitarian projects which were created as a 'race' among individual aid benefi-ciaries. Similarly, beneficiaries developed a habit of registering in as many databases as possible that belong to NGOs through which they can receive assistance. It does not matter to aid beneficiaries whether the services a particular NGO provides are similar to what other NGOs provide. The attitude of aid beneficiaries is that they feel advantaged when they have

---

[31] Interview with an academic and civil society consultant who carries out evaluation con-sultancies for various NGOs in Gaza, 11 December 2016.

[32] Interview with a USAID representative for Gaza Programmes, Ramallah, 20 December 2016.

[33] Interview with a programme officer at an American NGO that received USAID-funded projects, Gaza, 10 March 2017.

[34] A beneficiary of a graduate capacity-building programme implemented by the Palestinian Community Assistance Programme (a USAID-funded project (100 million USD) that aimed to rebuild and improve community infrastructure and housing, develop the economy and provide social assistance in the Gaza Strip. The programme was implemented by Mercy Corps in partnership with a cluster of international and local NGOs (Mercy Corps 2012).

access to assistance from difference sources. Some of the beneficiaries actually resell some of the aid they get, especially food, blankets or other items they do not need.[35]

This again reflects a deficiency embedded in the working mechanisms of local NGOs in Gaza, especially in relation to coordinating their work, identifying their priorities and sharing the database of their actual beneficiaries. Yet, the overall deficiency exists to give more weight to the vetting and security clearance of individual beneficiaries. This comes at the expense of proper planning of aid programmes that take into consideration issues of economic sustainability and actual needs assessments.

5.6 Conclusion

How do we understand the ways the post-Oslo aid agenda influenced the roles civil society and NGOs play in the Gaza Strip? And did the new roles reflect the socio-economic needs of Gaza's population, or are rather guided by donors' expectations and political agendas? In contributing to the development of the 'globalised elite' concept, originally coined by Hanafi and Tabar (2002, 2004, 2005), we saw how the 'NGO' as a concept has become a buzzword. The case of the NGO sector prior to the establishment of the PA illustrated how this sector represented a domain where individuals and professionals could organise in the form of initiatives and institutions to pursue community projects free from the authority of both donors and the nation state. Therefore, to a great extent this sector was able to positively engage with the communities it represented and address their social, economic and political needs. However, when engaging with neoliberal development agendas, represented by the aid industry that was an integral part of the Oslo peace process, the discussion above has shown that the working dynamics of this sector shifted from being based on a national agenda to one based on an international agenda. In this context, we saw that the term 'globalised elite' does not mean that the local elite working in national or international NGOs have an influence on the international development agenda. Instead, they are globalised in the sense that they operate as followers of this agenda and dictate the policies of the organisations they represent. This itself reflects a significant change in the role the civil society sector has played since Oslo.

The idea of civil society in the Gaza Strip has also been reduced to simply implementing donor-funded projects and carrying out humanitarian projects,

---

[35] Ibid.

supposedly for the benefit of society. This, as a result, undermined the role that civil society originally would play in societal reform, political mobilisation, democratisation, good governance and, above all, economic development. The role NGOs had been playing since Oslo, however, indicated the existence of completely new and different paradigms compared to what they traditionally had operated under. These paradigms restricted their work to two agendas. First, the 'aid for peace' donor agenda placed many limitations on how NGOs could carry out and plan their programmes, choose their beneficiaries and, more importantly, reconstruct the dynamics according to which they operate. This includes individuals, bylaws and administrative and financial procedures, and their relations with each other and with the government authorities. These limitations were, most of the times, influenced by a security agenda associated with the 'aid for peace' agenda and consequently made NGOs indirectly part of the control mechanisms that both Israel and donors sought to maintain over the lives of Palestinians in the Gaza Strip. Moreover, they limited their ability to engage in genuine socio-economic development initiatives due to the various type of restrictions that surround their work.

Second, the neoliberal aid agenda imposed by most Western donors has widened the gap between the NGO sector and the population it serves. This was demonstrated in how NGOs shifted from being engaged in programmes that contributed to the socio-economic resilience of the population in Gaza, as well as being part of the resistance against the occupation, to being agents and subjects through which aid agencies sought to undertake their development agenda using the same approach they use globally. In doing so, aid agencies (through NGOs) offered themselves as ideal solutions to society's problems and gradually obtained access in different areas that relate to people's daily lives (education, health, economy) via what they propose as 'development programmes'.

5.6.1 The Biopolitical Powers of NGOs

The emergence of a globalised elite and the role of the NGO sector exemplified aspects of biopolitical powers over the Gaza society. Central to the main theme of this book, this type of power is seen in how the NGO sector had been co-opted by an aid agenda that informed and influenced its relationship with the society it aimed to serve. The absence of NGOs' sovereignty over the type of programmes and activities they desired to implement made this biopolitical power indirect and one that operated through external powers. What happened, however, was not merely that NGOs lost their sovereignty to these external powers, but it created dynamics of control that extended to influence the larger populations these NGOs were meant to serve. Also, the concept of promotion and demotion reflected an embedded biopolitical power that, as Merz (2013: 138) suggests, aims to govern subjects (organisations) and populations together through transforming their general conduct, rationalities and conception of the self. As illustrated throughout the chapter, the deteriorated political and economic situation in Gaza resulted in an increased role of this sector. Its influence extended to almost every vital aspect of Gazans' daily lives following the absence of an internationally recognised government in the Strip. People began to perceive this sector as responsible for managing major services delivery. Yet, the aid policies imposed by donor countries put limitations on how these services were managed and who (organisations and individuals), and under what conditions, could benefit from aid delivered through civil society and NGOs. Consequently, it succeeded to prompt individuals and organisations to transform their norms of conduct based on a reformed ideology and behaviour. Alternatively, if they failed in this self-transformation, they would be banned from achieving any gains or having access to support provided by donors and their counterpart NGOs and aid agencies.

Another aspect of this form of control, reflected in the reformed working dynamics of civil society and NGOs in Gaza, is also seen in the disconnect between biopolitics and liberalism. As indicated in Chapter 2, liberalism, when being associated with development, which dominates the working agenda of most NGOs, 'takes people and their life and freedom as its essential reference point' (Mehta, 1999, quoted in Duffield, 2007: 5). It becomes the form of power that attracts the attention to the diversity of forces and groups (i.e. donors, aid agencies and local NGOs) in a heterogeneous way and for the purpose of regulating the lives of people and the conditions they live within in order to achieve certain goals (Miller and Rose, 1990: 3). In addition to this, the power held by development agencies can be experienced as a territorial illustrations of a 'particular global species-type' where development establishes technologies of control that are 'essential expressions of international bio-power' (Duffield, 2004: 6). According to this and through discourses of development and economic growth, donors and international aid agencies govern people from 'an invisible position through localized institutions' (Merz, 2013: 138). Accordingly, it reconstructed the role of NGOs into that of accomplices to forms of governance and control over the life of Gaza's population. Essentially, neoliberal development discourses and practices attempt to govern 'from a distance', from an almost invisible position through localised institutions for the purpose of transforming individual subjectivities into 'enterprise men and women' (Merz, 2013: 138).

5.6.2 Development–Security Nexus

We tried to make sense of the relationship between the work of NGOs, on the one hand, and development as security, on the other. The security dynamics of NGOs' work reflect the extent to which development became marked by a securitised approach to contain its target groups in their peripheral spaces. The occupied Palestinian territories, particularly the Gaza Strip, have always been vulnerable to donors' securitised practices through the attachment of conditions on aid that prioritise security aspects over development ones. In doing so, donors and international aid agencies were able to influence the organisational behaviour and the structures of local NGOs in Gaza to reflect donors' interests. The securitisation of NGOs' work also detached them from their original national civil resistance platform that once guided their work, to become promoters for the Oslo peace process. This brought the introduction of new modes of civic action, thus containing this sector and enforcing a mechanism of control over the sectors it serves.

This relationship reflects the liberal problematic of security embedded in the work of NGOs as development agencies and partners. By the liberal problematic of security, Duffield (2007) refers to the people and the processes to promote or demote their life in the name of their rights and freedom, yet by practicing different forms of power over their life. Furthermore, the development–security nexus embedded in the work of aid agencies and NGOs (illustrated in this chapter) supports the idea that development as a practice works to govern and control people. Working in the name of people's socio-economic and well-being, development agencies impose mechanisms of control in order to liberate people from their social, political and economic problems. In this sense they claim to control in order to liberate. Additionally, one of the aims of the security–development paradigm is to modulate and change the behaviour of individuals and groups. As Duffield (2001: 308) suggests, this modulation of behaviour is not necessarily done through the use of military power or the reformation of political alliances but rather through penetrating societies using various means under the pretence of developing these societies. In doing so, the liberal technology of security adopted by development agencies, including NGOs, aims to eliminate the risks coming from the underdeveloped people against the developed countries. This is done through establishing management systems through NGOs and other aid agencies. This, consequently, contributes to answering the question of how the securitisation and politicisation of aid delivered through NGOs influence the socio-economic promotion or demotion of both end-user beneficiaries of aid, but also how NGOs reform their agenda and work structures.

One can therefore conclude how the role of NGOs post-Oslo was reconstructed from the emerging aid regime that, first and foremost, was conditioned to a security agenda rather than a development agenda. We have seen an evidence of how the securitisation and politicisation of aid has significant influence on the socio-economic advancement or de-advancement of individuals or groups through re-categorising them against the social and political identities they maintain.

Chapter 6

UNRWA: GREATER BURDENS, TIGHTER FUNDING

6.1 Introduction

Having looked at the aid aspects that relate to funds to the PA and CSOs, it is now time to look at similar aspects peculiar to UNRWA as one of the key organisations responsible for aid delivery to Palestinians in the Gaza Strip. There are two core issues to focus on: first, the ways the post-Oslo aid dynamics have impacted humanitarian operations in Gaza; second, how these dynamics have led to the imposition of further control over the humanitarian spaces in the territory. We have seen in the introductory chapter that the post-aid dynamics are associated with two things: the 'aid for peace' and the set of political and security conditions that influenced this paradigm.

It is important for us to understand the way UNRWA conducts its work and how its operations have changed over past decades, more specifically following the creation of the PA in 1994. The changing working dynamics of the organisation have exposed it to a great deal of criticism from different stakeholders, including refugees, the PA and other humanitarian organisations, especially its service provision in Gaza. There is a need to investigate in depth the challenges the organisation is experiencing in its attempt to continue its operations in Gaza, particularly after the recent significant cut of US funding to the organisation by the Trump administration. Hence, it is essential to this analysis to investigate those elements of control discussed throughout this thesis, and in particular how Western donors impose certain operational agendas on the organisation and how these agendas are influenced by securitised and politicised frameworks.

We will briefly look at the historical role of UNRWA as an organisation, a role that was established solely to assist displaced Palestinian refugees to integrate socially and economically into their new community and to provide the necessary humanitarian relief to facilitate this integration. This will help us demonstrate how the humanitarian operations have changed over time and how UNRWA's roles have changed in accordance with the political and demographic changes on the ground as well as the funding trends of the organisation's main donors. These factors, as will be demonstrated in the following sections, had a significant impact on the level and types of services the organisation could provide and the organisation's autonomy over its operational and financial agendas. The chapter will also show the broad gap between its original humanitarian and developmental role, indicated in its original mandate, and what it does now. In that context, it will discuss the static institutional nature of the organisation against the complex operation and the aspect of its services in Gaza.

There is a need to look at the historical financial dilemma the organisation has experienced in the past two decades and examine the possible causes for this dilemma (e.g. the growth of the refugee population in Gaza and donor reluctance to continue their funding – 'donor fatigue'). Meanwhile, we need to look at the type of funds the organisation depends on to run its operations and how the sustainability of these funds is dependent on the emerging political and security contexts. For instance, how can the increase or decrease in services UNRWA provides to refugees be dependent on the availability of extra funds rather than on fixed need criteria? And how do such mechanisms contribute to raising false expectations among these beneficiaries?

There is a growing gap between the 'relief' and 'work' aspects of UNRWA's operations. 'Relief' represents the humanitarian side of the UNRWA's operations; 'work' reflects the developmental side of its services. Building on the financial dilemma and Western donors' intervention, there has been an imbalance between the humanitarian and developmental roles the organisation has historically played. Accordingly, we will focus more on the programmatic side and the lack of emphasis on services that had a significant impact on refugees' ability to build their own capacities and contribute to their own socio-economic development. We will see how this imbalance, through a discussion of the current reality of the employment and vocational education programme, has affected refugees' developmental prospects.

6.2 Background

Following the Palestinian Nakbeh in 1948, the UN initially established the United Nations Conciliation Commission for Palestine (UNCCP) under Paragraph 2 of the UN General Assembly (UNGA) Resolution 194 (III) in December 1948 (BADIL, 2011: 9). According to this resolution, UNCCP was initially responsible for ensuring that displaced Palestinian refugees return to their home cities, in what is now the state of Israel. Additionally, the organisation was to assist Palestinians resettle in locations they were displaced to. Meanwhile, UNRWA was established according to resolution 302 of the UNGA in the following year (UNRWA, 1949). UNRWA was different from UNCCP in that it has a mandate that states it was to aid approximately 720,000 Palestinian refugees and ensure their social and economic rehabilitation. This included the provision of proper access to food, shelter, education and health services. The United Nations' mandate indicated the responsibilities of the organisation to ensure the protection and safeguarding of the refugees' human rights (BADIL, 2005: 42). This assistance, however, was initially limited to nine months and was meant to reintegrate the Palestinian refugees in their host cities in Palestine and in the neighbouring countries (UNRWA, 1949).

The continuing developments in the Israeli-Palestinian conflict and its prolonged nature, especially the Palestinian refugees' attachment to their 'right of return' as provided by Paragraph 11 of UNGA resolution 194 in 1948, obliged the UNRWA to extend its mandate and keep it active so long as a permanent solution to the Palestinian refugees had not been reached (Alhusseini, 2015: 1). Further to this, the Palestinian refugees do not fall under the 1951 Refugee Convention as UNRWA has been the only UN body responsible for providing them with assistance and protection. Israel, from its side, strongly rejects the refugees' right of return and continuously emphasises this in any future solutions between the two sides, despite this right being asserted in UN resolutions 194 and 237. Meanwhile, the Palestinians are still lacking a fully recognised political body that could defend the rights of these refugees and provide them with the protection they need.

The number of Palestinian refugees has now exceeded 5 million, one-third of which live in the 58 UNRWA refugee camps in the oPt, Jordan, Syria and Lebanon and are actively in receipt of UNRWA's services (UNRWA, 2016d). Today, UNRWA has more than 30,000 employees working in the above duty stations, the majority of whom are Palestinian refugees except for a small number of international staff (UNRWA, 2016d). Seen as a 'quasi-government' organisation (Alhusseini, 2015: 1), UNRWA provides basic public services in different crucial fields: education, health, relief and social services, infrastructure and camp development, and microfinance and microenterprise (UNRWA, 2016d). The organisation has also played a significant role in protecting Palestinian refugees during armed conflict. This was more obvious during Israel's most recent offensive on Gaza in 2014, where some 270,000 refugees became internally displaced and sought shelter in UNRWA schools as a result (UNRWA, 2014a).

6.2.1 A Static Organisation

Regardless of the big role UNRWA plays (in terms of the size of its operations and the population it serves), the organisation has remained static and has shown little institutional development that would correspond to its growing role. The organisation continues to operate according to a limited mandate that ranges between three and five years. The main reason behind this is that the organisation serves Palestinian refugees whose issue is directly associated with the Israeli-Palestinian conflict. Consequently, the UNRWA's attempts to extend its mandate to a longer period (or make it semi-permanent) failed due to objections from key members of the Security Council (Bartholomeusz, 2009: 468–69). Although the council recognises the importance of the role this organisation plays to maintain stability in the region, according to Bartholomeusz (2009: 469), it demonstrated a preference to limit the organisation's ability to grow and expand.

   This, as a result, constrains the organisation when it comes to carrying out long-term planning that would assist in achieving its goals beyond that under which it was founded (i.e. contribute to refugees' socio-economic integration and development). IN CONTRAST, THE UNGA REMAINS HESITANT TO EXPAND UNRWA's STRUCTURE AND FUNDING MECHANISM AS A SEMI-PERMANENT ORGANISATION (ALHUSSEINI, 2015: 2). AT THE MOMENT, ONLY 5 PER CENT OF UNRWA's BUDGET IS REGULAR AND IS COVERED BY THE UN GENERAL BUDGet, while the rest comes from voluntary contributions of member states. Furthermore, the organisation operates under no guaranteed budget and there is no provision that ensures this. Plus, the organisation has a legal duty to ensure sustainable service provision for the registered 5 million refugees (ibid.: 2). This became more evident when UNRWA decided to reduce its service as a result of severe financial difficulties. Accordingly, the organisation faced harsh criticism, to which the UN's legal counsel responded as follows:

> At no time has the General Assembly laid down a mandate for UNRWA which is precise either to the nature and level of services to be rendered by the Agency. [...] From the legal point of view, it is therefore to be concluded that the Commissioner-General has the authority to establish the level of UNRWA services within the resources available to him to carry out those services. (quoted in Alhusseini, 2015: 2).

Accordingly, the lack of legal and financial guarantees, in principle, impacted how the organisation designs its operational agenda. This is despite the fact it continues the provision of key services. Yet, it is believed that the organisation could have far more potential if it were to act more freely in terms of an open mandate (Bartholomeusz, 2009: 468).

6.2.2 *Complex Operations in Gaza*

UNRWA's operations in the Gaza Strip appear to be very complicated considering the political, economic and social environment, especially since Israel's withdrawal from Gaza in the summer of 2005. The Gaza Strip is home to almost 1.26 million Palestinian refugees, 73 per cent of its total population until 2014 (UNRWA, 2014b). The majority of this refugee population continues to live in the eight highly crowded camps which are geographically spread across the Strip. These camps lack sufficient infrastructural and economic development and suffer from severe congestion.

The agency provides education to nearly 80 per cent of Gaza's elementary school pupils (240,000 students) in 247 school structures, not including students and trainees enrolled in UNRWA's vocational and technical training centres, with classroom capacity exceeding 55 students per classroom. Ninety-four per cent of these schools operate on a double-shift basis, hosting a school in the morning and one in the afternoon with teaching staff estimated to be 8,500 (UNRWA, 2016b). In the heath sector, UNRWA runs 22 primary health care facilities with medical staff estimated at 4,250 members dealing with approximately 4.5 million annual outpatient general consultation visits (UNRWA, 2016c). The health and education sectors reflect the extraordinary pressure the organisation faces in order to meet daily demands on service by the refugees in Gaza. Currently, the organisation lacks an independent plan to increase the number of schools, since such a plan is fully dependent on funding specific for this reason. Additionally, most donors who contribute to UNRWA's budget have been far more interested in funding humanitarian projects, except for reconstructing schools that were destroyed by Israel (ibid.).

Another crucial sector within UNRWA, much needed in the Gaza Strip, is the relief and social services sector. The main goal of this sector is to provide the impoverished refugees with a social safety net through the provision of multiple services that include food supplies, cash and other forms of assistance. As of 2013, more than 700,000 refugees were registered as regular beneficiaries of this programme (UNRWA, 2016e). This number increased dramatically during and after Israeli aggression upon the Strip (2008 and 2014), as more refugees lost their homes and employment and became in need for food assistance and sheltering. The services provided by this sector also include community rehabilitation and individual support programmes for young people, women and other vulnerable groups on the basis of specific needs for each group. Funding for this section, as will be discussed in the following section, has witnessed a short-term increase by individual donors to meet some periodic demands caused by any Israeli offensive (i.e. to cover urgent short-term humanitarian need (food and temporary shelter)).

Regardless of the financial difficulties and the conditions imposed by some Western donors on its programmatic and operational agenda,[1] what these figures indicate is that UNRWA works as a parallel service provider in Gaza. Moreover, as Bocco (2009: 234) suggests, it is considered a 'non-territorial administration without a coercive power, which has to achieve objectives mainly through mediation'. Meanwhile, the size of UNRWA's operations and the scope of its services have prompted refugees as well as other stakeholders to call the organisation the 'blue state'. Denying the organisation's autonomy is jeopardised by these conditions, and thus cannot meet refugees' expectations in an environment surrounded with continuing political and economic uncertainty.

6.2.3 The Aspects of UNRWA's Assistance in Gaza

The number of households that depend on UNRWA's assistance, especially food assistance and cash, has been increasing over the past decade. As discussed in Chapter 3, the beginning of the Second Intifada in September 2000 witnessed a severe drop in the living conditions of Palestinians in the Strip due to Gazan labourers' gradual loss of access to the Israeli labour market. Following the Israeli withdrawal from Gaza in 2005, no Gaza labourers were permitted to work inside Israel. During this period, Israel had also increased the restrictions on the freedom of movement of both goods and traders, leading to a worsening of the economic conditions. As a result, UNRWA, as is usual, had to face new changing socio-economic realities which made it necessary for it to respond. The organisation's assistance to the refugee sector is necessary to fill the slim margin between relative poverty and abject poverty in the absence of necessary income among ordinary Gazan refugees who seek to secure sustainable paid work. By emphasising the relief aspect of its work, UNRWA again has undermined the economic integration aspect that the organisation had adopted in the past during more complicated circumstances (i.e. the early years of the refugee crisis).

Today, UNRWA's Food and Cash Assistance programme is the biggest among other programmes mentioned earlier. This is due to the overwhelming dependence on emergency food assistance, which for the organisation attests to the depth of the 'human dignity crisis' (UNRWA, 2013). The organisation claims that the increasing pressure to meet the ever-growing economic hardship in the Strip, amidst decreasing financial resources and strict

---

[1] Funding conditions that usually relate to the type of programmes to implement, category of beneficiaries, cutting overhead expenses and those relating to adopting the anti-terrorism act.

conditions imposed by some Western donors, forced it to introduce new, more restrictive eligibility criteria, thus enabling it to work with the 'poorest of the poor' only. According to these criteria, UNRWA divides this category into two sub-categories: the abject poor and the absolute poor; each is afforded different entitlements and assistance packages. The current criteria used by UNRWA are based on the caloric need of each category taking into consideration the number of people living in a single household. For instance, the abject poor receive specific amounts of flour, rice, sugar, sunflower oil, milk and canned meat that would cover 76 per cent of their caloric need. Meanwhile, the absolute poor receive 40 per cent of their daily needs (UNRWA, 2013).

At the same time, a very small proportion of families living in the 'unbearable circumstances of abject poverty', as referred to by the organisation, are eligible to receive a small cash grant that aims to complement the food assistance these families receive (UNRWA, 2013). Each family can be entitled at approximately 780 USD at the most to help it buy food supplies that UNRWA does not cover in its quarterly food ration. This can also be used to buy other non-food basic utilities and cover costs such as transport, emergency

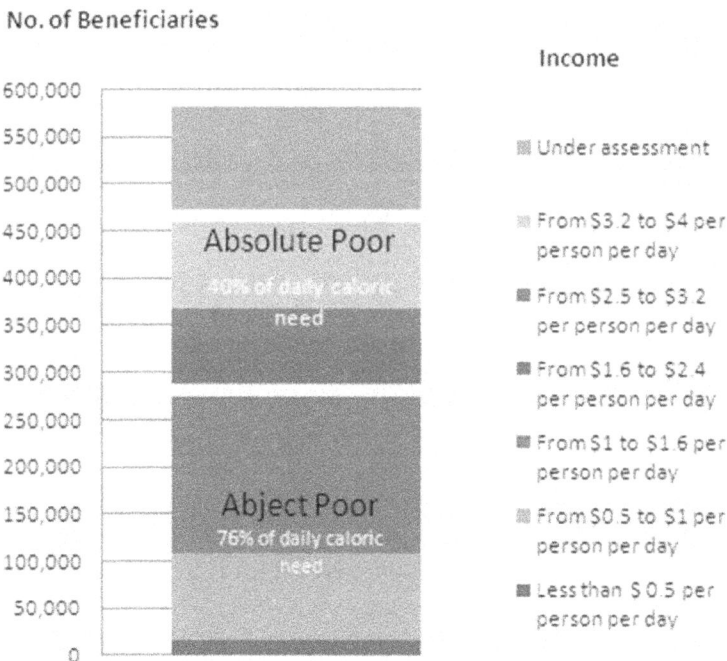

Figure 6.1 Beneficiaries of UNRWA's food Programme
(*Source:* UNRWA, 2013).

Table 6.1 UNRWA requirements for food and cash assistance

UNRWA Requirements Snapshot			
Intervention	Annual cost per refugee	Refugees assisted needs	Funding
Food assistance	$123	564,964	$56.6 million
Cash assistance	$135	273,200	$36.9 million

Source: UNRWA (2013).

house maintenance and medicine that patients, for example, cannot receive as part of the primary health care services the organisation provides.

A significant implication of these figures is that food coupons and other forms of emergency assistance are now crucial in the lives of families in Gaza, especially those coming from a refugee background. With high unemployment, securing food coupons reinforced by routine humanitarian assistance, provided by either UNRWA or other humanitarian organisations, have become an everyday duty for the heads of the households. It is referred to as a 'job' among the unemployed, where, instead of searching for skill-based jobs, heads of households bear the responsibility of securing these coupons every month.

The following section will discuss the funding dilemma the organisation experiences with regard to how it impacts the overall service delivery, its impact on refugees' livelihoods and the role of UNRWA's donors in exacerbating this dilemma by intervening in the organisation's plans and how it implements its programmes and activities.

6.3 Funding Dilemmas

Funding for UNRWA has always been controversial and a dilemma the organisation has experienced for decades. In principle, the organisation has a semi-permanent status, which requires it to have regular funding to continue its operations. Its voluntary contributions, mainly coming from the United States and the European Union, saw a slight increase over the years. This increase, however, has not been enough to cover the annual budget increase estimated at 5 per cent. Moreover, a set of conditions have been attached to these contributions that limited the organisation's ability to use these funds in areas where it was necessary (i.e. activities, programmes and beneficiaries). For UNRWA's financial officer, the increase in donor contributions has always been met with a similar increase in the refugee population, yet in a context that is characterised with continuing economic deterioration and uncertainty. Meanwhile, UNRWA is facing constant pressure from its primary donors to adopt strategies that would lead to a decline in the rate at which the budgetary costs of its services rise. For instance, the organisation would need to tighten its criteria for selecting its beneficiaries and to restructure its health and education services. As shown in Table 6.2, Gaza hosts the highest number of Palestinian refugees compared with the overall population living in the territory. Accordingly, the impact of this financial deficit is mostly felt in UNRWA's field office in Gaza, and it has impacted the level and quality of services sectors, such as education, health and camps' infrastructure development.[2] This also indirectly contributed to weakening the refugees' ability to advance socially and economically within the communities they live in.

Obviously, despite the organisation having a general budget, each field office has its own sub-budget that is decided and designed according to the local needs of the refugees in this particular area. In the words of a UNRWA governor in Gaza, the budget for Gaza's field office depends on three main budgetary items: a general fund, a project fund and an emergency fund.

> While the general fund is characterised as 'fixed' and 'permanent', and is used to cover the organisational day-to-day operations, both other funds are temporary and are dependent on donors' choice to provide funding for particular projects on the basis of their own agenda and for short-term purposes. For example, some donors provide limited funding following a major humanitarian crisis and other donors choose to provide special project funding to focus on issues of gender and women empowerment.[3]

What can be understood from this is that UNRWA can only operate with full autonomy within its fixed budget that only represents 5 per cent of its overall budget,[4] and the rest of its programmatic operation is decided and influenced by the big donors (European Union and United States). According to this, UNRWA has been unable to develop or upgrade its

---

[2] Ibid.

[3] Interview with a UNRWA governor in the Gaza Strip, Gaza, 1 April 2017 (UNRWA has divided its areas of services into five governorates, each represented with a governor, who represents UNRWA's chief director and supervises the day-to-day service in a particular governorate).

[4] UNRWA is still one of the United Nations' largest programmes and its commissioner-general is assigned directly by the UN secretary general after consultation with the UNRWA Advisory Commission. The organisation's accountability to serving the Palestinian refugee population is guided by the Accountability to Affected Populations (AAP) framework, as defined by the Inter-Agency Standing Committee. According

Table 6.2 Distribution of Palestinian refugees worldwide

Inside (mid-2013)		Outside	
		Jordan	2,797,674
WB	906,369	Lebanon, Syria, Egypt	415,066
		Saudi Arabia	436,157
Gaza Strip	1,285,033	Kuwait and other Gulf countries	61,917
		Libya and Iraq	309,582
		Other Arab countries	163,632
		The Americas	115,542
		Other countries	6,523
			236,357 (only USA)
			300,977
Total inside	4,642,385	Total outside	4,843,427

Source: PASSIA (2014).

essential services since the core funding that comes under the general fund has remained unchanged. These core services cover health, education and some aspects of social services. The organisation has carried out these services in almost the same manner for decades. Any expansion in UNRWA's services in Gaza, however, such as building new schools or opening new clinics, usually comes under emergency projects only. Against this background, the governor indicated that for those not familiar with the mechanisms of how UNRWA runs its operations, what usually appears to happen is that the organisation

systematically and gradually cuts its funding for the main services. However, we need to bear in mind that UNRWA operates under unsustainable financial resources that are usually determined by donors. During the past ten years, we probably witnessed an increased level of support to some sectors such as cash and food subsistence, but this was mainly coming from additional irregular funding that the organisation has received during times of emergency. This type of funding usually aims to prevent things from falling apart. So what

---

to the AAP, UNRWA has to 'take account of, give account to and be held to account by the populations they seek to assist' (i.e. the Palestinian refugees themselves, and not the funding countries that contribute to sustaining the organisation's operations). See UNRWA. 2017. 'UNRWA framework for Accountability to Affected Populations'. https://www.unrwa.org/resources/strategy-policy/unrwa-framework-accountability-affected-populations. Accessed 19 March 2018.

happens in fact is that developmental plans, either on the level of services and programmes or the institution's capacities can only occur if major donors allow it by providing additional funds for this purpose or through releasing the conditions attached to what they already provide. I do agree that such funding mechanisms aim to keep poverty or abject poverty at its very thin line, but in the longer term we see that the percentage of the refugee population that fails to progress, or maybe experience a deterioration in their economic conditions, continues to grow.[5]

UNRWA's leadership admits that the organisation has had a deficit for almost 20 years, yet it has been working hard to cope with this deficit and has provided the same type of services over this period.[6] The organisation's strategy to deal with this deficit, however, was to decrease the amount of services provided rather than stopping one or more types of services completely. For instance, the organisation had to tighten its procurement of new equipment and furniture to schools and clinics and stop recruiting new permanent staff on all sectors. It also worked on lowering the quality of some of its food and health supplies under the guiding principle that 'providing a lower quality service is better than stopping it altogether'.[7] So far, such a strategy has had a serious impact on the organisation's ability to develop the education and health sectors and to ensure that the organisation will be able to maintain proper service provision over a longer period (if work continued according to the same funding mechanism imposed by the major donors).[8]

6.3.1 High Expectations, Lost Autonomy

Besides the rising level of poverty and unemployment in the Gaza strip, there were three major Israeli offensives in 2008, 2001 and 2014. Consequently, UNRWA in Gaza witnessed a significant increase in donor support following Hamas's victory in the Palestinian parliamentary elections in 2006. There are two main reasons for this increase. First, according to the majority of Western donors, mainly the United States and the European Union, there was no legitimate government through which aid and humanitarian support could be coordinated and delivered in Gaza. Second, UNRWA is the biggest humanitarian organisation that works in the field and one that has sufficient institutional and operational infrastructure that donors could rely upon to channel

---

[5] Interview with a UNRWA governor in the Gaza Strip, Gaza, 1 April 2017.
[6] Interview with a senior financial officer in UNRWA's field office, Gaza, 5 April 2017.
[7] Ibid.
[8] Ibid.

their emergency support through. Accordingly, an Emergency Programme officer in UNRWA's Gaza field office referred that the organisation benefited from a sudden and huge rise in donor support, one reflected by the scope of humanitarian assistance provided to the needy and affected refugees in the Gaza Strip.[9] This increase, however, came with further complications in terms of how the big donors emphasise their control over the organisation by influencing how the organisation determines the pool of its beneficiaries and aid recipients. As mentioned earlier, the organisation was pushed toward a narrowing of its selection criteria for beneficiaries in various ways, for instance, by tightening the socio-economic factors and adding a security background check.

This expansion has also had impacts at different levels. First, at the organisation's structural level, UNRWA had to create emergency employment programmes. This meant it had to recruit several thousands of temporary staff members and aid workers to assist in the day-to-day service delivery and address the new procedural requirement pertaining to background checks as proposed, principally by US donors.[10] Although these temporary employment programmes did occasionally have some, albeit limited, impact on alleviating the level of unemployment (and was a source of income for many of the unemployed labourers and their families) it severely impacted refugees' autonomy. The reduced autonomy is caused by the way these temporary programmes are designed to increase the level control over refugees' means of living by both UNRWA and its contributing donors. This also pushed UNRWA to lose the status it traditionally held as a provider of permanent employment, a factor that enabled many refugee households to focus on developing the capacities of their children rather than merely ensuring their daily living.

Second, UNRWA failed to follow a systematic approach to determine how it should expand its services during emergencies. For instance, the content and proportion of its food and cash assistance were quite generous during emergencies. This generosity was not based on need vis-á-vis emergencies, but rather the availability of extra funds. According to a clerk working at a UNRWA distribution centre, UNRWA's food stores would be full of unusual food and non-food items that UNRWA would not normally distribute during a quarterly ration.[11] This, of course, is usually of acute relief to families who suffer from poverty or had been affected somehow by the Israeli offensives.

---

[9] Interview with a programme officer working in UNRWA's emergency programme in Gaza, Gaza, 10 April 2017.
[10] Ibid.
[11] Interview with a clerk working at a UNRWA distribution centre in Gaza, 6 April 2017.

This approach again, however, creates false expectations among refugees, and it negatively impacts their self-autonomy over food and other means of living in the long term.[12]

On three occasions mentioned earlier (Israeli offensives), the trend of UNRWA's assistance did not last. Refugees and other aid recipients usually suffered from a sudden drop in the amount of assistance they would receive from the organisation, leaving refugee households with a serious aid assistance gap. The problem, as seen by UNRWA's beneficiaries, is that UNRWA increased its assistance to eligible households in the event of extraordinary economic conditions caused by an environment of security instability. However, as indicated by one of UNRWA's aid beneficiaries:

> The economic conditions and the political instability that prompted UNRWA to increase its assistance to refugees still remains. What UNRWA's strategy has done, in fact, was to create a bubble for those living under severe economic hardship, either caused by the Israel war or have been going on for some time. For us, it feels like a nightmare when the social worker tells me that my food assistance would be reduced. Some of these refugees would find it easier to tell them that one of their children was killed during the war rather than telling them that UNRWA would cut or reduce its assistance. It is not logical for an organisation the size of UNRWA to plan its assistance on the basis of extra funds it receives from donors and then reduce it after a couple of weeks.[13]

Another beneficiary described the way UNRWA designs its emergency programme, done on the basis of funding criteria, as a contradictory one as it related to the ultimate purpose under which the organisation was originally founded.

> It is not about the continuity of food coupons, food parcels, or maybe a couple of hundred dollars, it is about the size of the crises a lot of refugees are currently living under. This organisation was originally created to provide relief and support for Palestinian refugees in a situation that was no worse than the current situation in the Gaza Strip for refugees. If UNRWA jumps to help refugees in the first few weeks of any offensives, then stops or decreases its assistance while the humanitarian

---

[12] Ibid.

[13] Interview with a beneficiary of the UNRWA food programme.

situation remains the same, then it is legitimate for us to start questioning the reasons and the motives of such assistance.[14]

6.3.2 Donor Fatigue

UNRWA's governor addressed the issues expressed by these participants to what he called funding fatigue caused by donor unwillingness to continue funding a never-ending refugee problem. He also indicated that some other donors were not happy with the way UNRWA's humanitarian operations in the Gaza Strip were carried out. They propose that the organisation should take sustainability into consideration as part of any funding it is entitled to receive.[15] Both assumptions are, however, problematic. Although some would describe UNRWA as an obsolete organisation, due to the fact that the context within which it was created no longer exists, it is still expected to deliver the same services it did six decades ago. Accordingly, one can describe the current strategy UNRWA follows in carrying out many of its programmes in Gaza as one that is emergency-dependent. The organisation ties the sustainability of many of its programmes to additional funds that are themselves hugely dependent on and tied to some of the donors' decisions (i.e. the United States and the European Union); these programmes are usually implemented during crises times. What this means is that these programmes, in theory, continue to exist, but in practice, their content is hugely reduced, which means many of the basic services are cut down.

This funding fatigue gives the general impression within the organisation that donors' reluctance, or more precisely resistance, to continue with their financial support through the current mechanism was one way to end its mission. Within this background, many donors believe that UNRWA has fulfilled its role in helping the Palestinian refugees settle in their host countries and what was expected from it: assist them to economically and socially integrate into their new communities. This type of donor attitude towards both the organisation and refugees alike raised one assumption, as described by UNRWA's senior poverty advisor:

> UNRWA should not do what it is doing now forever. Refugees should be prepared for a new reality where UNRWA will, sooner or later, no longer be there, and the broader reality is that the issue of refugees is soon to be dead and forgotten and the first step toward this is to end UNRWA's

---

[14] Ibid.
[15] Interview with a UNRWA governor in the Gaza Strip, Gaza, 1 April 2017.

operations. This might not be politically sound but if we are to look at the current trends of donors' behaviour compared to the political discourses surrounding the issue of refugees and right of return, then we will begin to realise that this assumption is possible and closer to reality than ever.[16]

The following, however, according to the poverty advisor, is important to note:

> The current situation is complicated, especially the condition of refugees in Syria, and probably the situation in Lebanon will be more sensitive over the time. However, if we zoom out and look at the bigger picture, we would begin to see that the situation of the refugee in Gaza is no less complicated. We have to take into consideration that Gaza is a locked-in geographical area that has lost all prospects of economic development. The territories' demographic reality of which refugees represent the overwhelming majority of the population, the significantly rising poverty and destroyed economic infrastructure are beyond the organisation's capacity and the scope of its operation. Of significance here, we are no longer talking about economic integration or settlement but rather the organisation is heavily pushed to get involved in a situation that has to do with new political realities.[17]

In relation to this, the structural changes that the organisation was urged to make have also impacted its employees. For instance, many of the personnel rights and benefits have been reduced, including their annual increments, administrative promotions, end-of-service benefits and other benefits.[18] This prompted UNRWA employees' union in Gaza to organise several strikes across 2013–15 to deny donor-led intervention into how the organisation runs its administrative and operational agendas, both necessary to ensure refugees' socio-economic integration and advancement.

> The organisation has been following a systematic plan to reduce its staff numbers. For instance, those who retire or leave are not being equally replaced, and in the event they are replaced, they will not be hired on a similar salary scale and are not entitled to the same benefits that the organisation historically guaranteed for its staff. Nowadays, there is a shortage of staff in almost every sector. This puts us as employees at odds with the refugees as they feel we are conspiring with the organisation against them.[19]

---

[16] Interview with a senior poverty advisor in UNRWA's headquarters in Amman, 21 August 2016.

[17] Ibid.

[18] Interview with administrative staff at UNRWA's field office in Gaza, 5 May 2017.

[19] Ibid.

Again, it can be understood that the organisation realises its increasing financial challenges, especially as these challenges are coupled with even more complicated humanitarian challenges in the region. In this context, Alhusseini (2015: 6) states that UNRWA's headquarters are seriously engaged in discussions to explore ways to enlarge the organisation's donor base. One way to do this is to bring in new primary contributors to the organisation in order to reduce the burden placed on existing contributors (i.e. the United States and the European Union). Currently, Saudi Arabia occasionally covers some of the budgetary deficits in the organisation's operations in the oPt in general and more specifically in Gaza due to the peculiar situation in this territory. This happened on different occasions when there were strikes by the UNRWA's staff as well as by beneficiaries that obstructed the organisation's operations.[20] The potential new donors of significance include countries like China, Russia, India and Brazil (Alhusseini, 2015: 6). For these countries, however, the absence of any prospects for progress on issues like Palestinian reconciliation, ending economic sanctions and the blockade of Gaza and, more generally, progress on the peace process with the Palestinians remains problematic.

6.4 Between Work and Relief

In discussing 'relief' and 'work', the two pillars of the humanitarian and development work of the UNRWA, this section will first look at the strategies the organisation has historically relied upon in facilitating refugees' socio-economic reintegration. It will discuss the different elements of the work programmes that UNRWA currently runs. This includes short-term employment schemes, graduate employment schemes and vocational training programmes. The second part of this section will look at the organisation's current humanitarian practices, the factors influencing these practices and the way these practices encourage further control over humanitarian spaces in Gaza. It will show how the funding trends UNRWA was forced to work under have rather led to refugees' de-development in the sense that it focused only on providing the very basic food and cash support to refugees while neglecting the impact education and capacity-building programmes have on the refugees' continued socio-economic advancement and integration.

When the organisation was first founded, the assumption was that it would work to provide both relief services for the Palestinian refugees as well as development services that would empower them to integrate within their new societies. The latter was first faced with resistance by both the refugees themselves

---

[20] Interview with a UNRWA governor in the Gaza Strip, Gaza, 1 April 2017.

and the Arab states that hosted them. The reason for this was that the economic prioritisation represented in the work programmes implied that there was no assumption that the refugees would return to their homes (in what was now Israel); this was essentially an indirect means of accepting the status quo. This did not stop UNRWA, however, from continuing its mission to 'strengthen the economy of the host countries while providing employment to refugees, thus make them self-sufficient' (UNRWA, 1982: 59), to a point where refugees would become self-sufficient.

Over 60 years, UNRWA has adopted several development approaches, and each approach was influenced by different development debates within the mother organisation (i.e. the United Nations). The 'top-down' modernist approach followed in the 1950s came in the form of the agricultural development programme and took into consideration the fact that many of the refugees came from an agrarian background. UNRWA worked, therefore, to empower these agrarian communities. With more refugees believing education was a way to enhance their status and address their needs in their host societies, the organisation adopted the basic needs approach between the 1960s and the 1970s and had expanded this to include the participatory approach in the 1980s (human rights approach) following the First Intifada in 1987 as this period witnessed serious violations of human rights by Israel (Bocco, 2009: 247). Most recently, the organisation incorporated microfinance and microenterprise programmes as an approach for self-empowerment of individual refugees and small groups.

This, in brief, summarises the organisation's ideology that economic development was conducive to social and political stability in the communities where the refugees had lived. It also shows the pro-active role the organisation played in managing the Israeli-Palestinian conflict through the use of different development approaches that addressed the various socio-economic needs of the Palestinian refugees. However, in examining this aspect of UNRWA's work in Gaza in the past two decades, it can be demonstrated that the organisation has lacked the ability to apply particular development strategies or ideologies independent of Western donors' intervention in the name of developing the underdeveloped. This reflects how the entire Palestinian population's autonomy, particularly those living in the Gaza Strip, is jeopardised by a global economic agenda that demands that surplus populations must submit fully to their developer.

The work/employment sector was gradually being abolished since the PA took control over the Gaza Strip. The reason for this is that UNRWA was the biggest employer in Gaza and people tended to see the employment the organisation provided as possessing the highest job security compared to other employers. This was no longer the case, however, when the PA provided thousands of employment opportunities in the first few years of its establish-ment in 1994, with even greater financial benefits and the same level of job security. Of significance, however, is that employment within the PA provided opportunities to advance someone politically, especially in a community where a high proportion was politically affiliated. Accordingly, the PA became the biggest employment provider in Gaza followed by a private sector that flourished for a limited period following the political and security stability that characterised the 1994–2000 period. This, in turn, lifted some of the burden off UNRWA, especially with more investment by the PA in the primary service sectors (i.e. education, health and general infrastructure).

6.4.1 Short-Term Work Programmes

As indicated in Chapter 3, the stability that characterised the early years of the PA (1994–2000) did not last as the political and security atmosphere deteriorated quickly after the Second Intifada (2000). This, therefore, had a significant impact on the economic situation in Gaza. Accordingly, Israel began to gradually end Gazan labourers' access to its employment market, until it was completely banned before its withdrawal from Gaza in 2005. Several thousands of Gaza's skilled labourers became unemployed and the majority of them began to depend on UNRWA's food assistance. Although some of these labourers succeeded in investing their savings in starting up small enterprises, the majority felt the high risk of such investment in an unstable environment or lacked the business skills necessary to succeed.

The size of the economic burden brought by the sharp increase in unemploy-ment was far too great for UNRWA to handle. The organisation had lacked the institutional or employment capacity to provide employment opportunities for such a large number of skilled labours or even suggest a share-taking mech-anism with the PA in order to economically reintegrate them.[21] Alternatively, UNRWA found it much more feasible to continue supporting refugees who were undergoing economic hardship, as a result of their unemployment via its existing relief programme, than to engage in a costly economic reintegration process. UNRWA's approach in this context obviously indicated that it nei-ther has the institutional capacity to run economic reintegration programmes similar to long-established previous practice, nor does it possess the backing of international donors to do so. In the words of a specialist academic from Gaza, for four decades (1950–90) the organisation

---

[21] Interview with a senior poverty advisor in UNRWA's field office in Gaza, Gaza, 5 May 2017.

had the willingness to invest in building new infrastructure for education, health, camp development and other vital areas. Now the organisation is struggling to keep these existing structures running, given the decreasing financial resources coming from donors for core and fixed programmes, in addition to the pressure Western donors put on UNRWA to review its pool of beneficiaries in such a way that would reduce the services enjoyed by them, thus reduce the overall budget.[22]

This did not mean that UNRWA completely stopped its recruitment of new staff for its field offices in Gaza. The work programme, however, never again existed in the same format it did in the past. Instead, the European Union, as the biggest sponsor for temporary work schemes, suggested these schemes could be an alternative to the food and cash assistance. According to UNRWA's poverty advisor:

These programmes provide rotating employment for several thousands of unemployed skills workers in Gaza; especially, they were implemented in partnership with other vital sectors, such as the agricultural sector and the public sanitation and infrastructure sectors. The employment schemes ranged between three and nine months of employment and did not require any special skills on the side of workers. It was basically cash for work that served two goals.[23]

To UNRWA, the nature of these programmes did not intend to rebuild the professional capacity of beneficiaries so they could later facilitate their integration in the already weak labour market in Gaza.[24] On the contrary, it again influenced their self-reliance and autonomy. UNRWA's policy adviser described this as

a huge responsibility that should be undertaken by the government only. The continuous deterioration of the economic situation of refugees in Gaza pushes people to see UNRWA as their legitimate government [...] this cannot be true. UNRWA continues to meet its responsibilities

---

[22] Interview with an academic at the Faculty of Commerce and Political Science at the Islamic University of Gaza who researches the work of international organisations and NGOs working in the oPt, Gaza, 10 December 2016.

[23] Interview with a senior poverty advisor in UNRWA's field office in Gaza, Gaza, 5 May 2017.

[24] Interview with a former policy advisor for UNRWA and consultant for international organisations in Gaza, Gaza, 21 December 2016.

towards these refugees but the organisation cannot operate on the same scope or manner it used to do 50 or 60 years ago […] it cannot meet those responsibilities of a government.[25]

6.4.2 Graduate Employment Schemes

An additional aspect that shows how UNRWA's work programme has been profoundly reshaped is the graduate employment scheme. This scheme is also dependent on providing temporary employment for fresh university graduates for periods that range between three and six months. This scheme is not run on a permanent basis but rather is dependent on available funds from particular donors sourced specifically for this purpose. The organisation's former policy advisor indicated that, in the past, UNRWA used to assist educated Palestinians with university degrees to obtain work in the neighbouring Arab countries.[26] It did so through cooperation with the government of these countries under the belief that the remittances of those foreign workers were quite necessary for the economic well-being of refugees living in the oPt. This became gradually impossible, however, following the Gulf War in 1991. Today, these employment programmes have humanitarian perspectives rather than developmental ones in the sense that beneficiaries of these programmes are assessed on the basis of need rather than qualifications and skills. What this means, according to UNRWA's poverty advisory, is that the EU donor has proposed this concept of employment to lower the unemployment rate and to soften the anger felt among Gaza's population this issue causes. Accordingly, beneficiaries selected for these programmes are determined according to the need criteria that take into consideration both their individual economic needs and also those of the entire household.

This mechanism of employment indicates structural deficiencies between how UNRWA contributed to the professional development of refugees in the past and how these programmes have been reconstructed and adapted to serve humanitarian purposes, and it reflects the level of influence some donors have on the organisation, its plans and how it carries out its services.

6.4.3 Vocational Training Programmes

Vocational training programmes in Gaza are another aspect that indicate the level to which both UNRWA's financial dilemma and Western donors' intervention in the organisation's operations have pushed it to neglect the

---

[25] Ibid.
[26] Ibid.

development aspect of its services. UNRWA's vocational training centre, located next to its main field office in Gaza, was for years perceived as a prestigious centre. Moreover, those who graduated from it, for many years, were among the most highly qualified vocational degree holders. Until the early 1980s, Gaza lacked any postgraduate colleges or institutes apart from another vocational training centre that was run under the Israeli Civil Administration's Education Directorate. The latter's lack of quality and specialisation thus made UNRWA's centre a pioneer in this field.[27] Enrolment in this centre was only restricted to refugees from the Gaza Strip and was highly competitive due to the employment prospects it guaranteed to its graduates following their obtaining of what was at the time unique vocational training. According to UNRWA's public information officer, the majority of Gazan labourers used to join the Israeli labour market as young as 13 years old without any practical experience. As a result, they were taken advantage of by their Israeli employers in various ways, for instance, by being given low wages and benefits.

The centre provided opportunities for local labourers to train in various fields, including blacksmithing, carpentry, electronics, vehicle maintenance, agriculture and other applied specialisms that the local markets needed at the time.[28] This was despite many of these highly trained labourers also joining the Israeli labour market due to relatively high daily wage rates. The current reality of UNRWA's vocational training is completely different. UNRWA's former policy adviser suggested that UNRWA made little effort in developing its vocational centre in Gaza due to the fact it would require the organisation to invest a large amount of donors' funding to expand its vocational facilities, recruiting highly qualified trainers and providing more job opportunities for its graduates.[29] This investment would not occur unless it is driven by proposals of particular donors since the organisation cannot carry out such plans from its fixed budget (core budget).

With many colleges and universities providing a large number of advanced vocational training programmes, some of which are four-year postgraduate programmes, the centre's graduates lost their competitive advantage in a tight labour market which already sought the best of the best. UNRWA's strategy to develop its vocational training centres is not consistent in that the organisation has not followed a similar strategy with its centres in the WB and Jordan in particular. For example, UNRWA provides a four-year university degree education in some of its colleges in the WB, and it also provides university education

---

[27] Interview with a public information officer at UNRWA, Gaza, 14 December 2016.
[28] Ibid.
[29] Interview with a former policy advisor for UNRWA and consultant for international organisations in Gaza, Gaza, 21 December 2016.

in various subjects in Amman/Jordan. However, as the organisation's policy advisor explained:

> This is not to suggest that UNRWA purposefully wants to restrict such services in the Gaza Strip but maybe the changing dynamics in the work of the organisation in the territory have impacted the way it prioritises particular services or programmes over others. The development of humanitarian situation in Gaza over the past 15 years pushed UNRWA's donors to channel their money towards immediate relief services and to neglect long-term poverty alleviation programmes.[30]

6.4.4 The Control of Humanitarian Spaces

The first part of this section examines how UNRWA is performing at the developmental level in Gaza. This includes an analysis of its work and how this lacks development aspects that the organisation vowed to have, as indicated in its founding constitution. It is important at this point to assess the humanitarian aspects and examine the dynamics according to which UNRWA is carrying out its operations in the Gaza Strip. Also, it is important to examine how UNRWA's work directly lifted many of the burdens that Israel as an occupying power should bear according to the Geneva Refugee Convention (1951). Generally, spanning these 65 years, UNRWA has maintained a position of political neutrality when pursuing its activities and delivering its services while coping with multiple needs of the Palestinian refugees. The promotion of self-reliance, economic integration and resettlement have been the core principles for its relief and work programmes. These principles, however, were necessary and relevant in order to alleviate the refugee crisis at a time when hundreds of thousands of refugees were ending up in a number of countries across the world. With the absence of any prospects for peace between Israel and Palestine, we realise that principles of resettlement and economic reintegration, to a great extent, have been achieved (excluding the recent crisis of Palestinian refugees in Syria). This is reinforced when viewing the current situation (at the time of writing) where the right of return of these refugees has become far less realistic.

Against this background, UNRWA is criticised mainly in that it sets out strategies and plans its operations that, in most times, are too general and do not reflect the peculiarities of the geographical areas it operates in. For instance, UNRWA has one set of policies that are designed, as placed under the general principle that they are refugees, to guide its working relationship

---

[30] Ibid.

with the Palestinian refugees wherever they are. Accordingly, as Alhusseini (2010: 9) suggests, to administer its relief services, UNRWA designed a punitive type of 'regime' that applies to all. This regime consists of norms and regulations that allow the organisation to structure its relationship with these refugees in areas such as 'registration', 'eligibility' (Alhusseini, 2010: 9), or need criteria and ration cards. The intensity of such a regime depends on the level of humanitarian intervention by UNRWA and the level of need of a particular group of refugees. It is the type of intervention that facilitates how much UNRWA can govern the life of the refugee population and how many humanitarian spaces it can control. This assumption is described by a specialist Gaza academic figure:

> Governing the refugee population and their controlling humanitarian spaces mean that UNRWA's operations are not limited to service provision and relief but rather extends to intervening in people's lives; that is, how much they eat, what houses they own, what furniture they have, what type of transport they use and, sometimes, how many children they should decide to have.[31]

Unlike six decades ago, humanitarian support for refugees is not a general case and it does not target every refugee or every family. It targets those groups that meet the criteria set out by UNRWA, and the more people who meet poverty criteria, the further humanitarian spaces are controlled. Put another way, controlling the refugee population occurs when poverty becomes an overwhelming characteristic of a particular refugee group. As will be shown in the paragraphs below, UNRWA's governor indicated that these criteria guide how the organisation carries out its operations and identifies its target group from within the Palestinian registered refugees. The application of these criteria, however, varies hugely where Gaza, due to more than 75 per cent of its registered refugees living in abject poverty, tends to be subject to the toughest criteria when it comes to identifying or categorising its poverty groups.[32]

The UNRWA official described the poverty assessment process as one that is too complicated as it 'uses nearly 60 variables that leaves both UNRWA staff and beneficiaries, alike, confused. At the end, when comparing the results as determined by the "system" with the reality that we see here in Gaza, we know that these results are inaccurate and unrealistic'.[33] The UNRWA governor

---

[31] Interview with an academic at the Faculty of Commerce and Political Science at the Islamic University of Gaza who researches the work of international organisations and NGOs working in the oPt, Gaza, 10 December 2016.

[32] Interview with a UNRWA governor in the Gaza Strip, Gaza, 1 April 2017.

[33] Ibid.

indicated that one cause of this inaccuracy in determining the level of poverty, and how Gaza gets most affected by it, is that the poverty questionnaire designed by the UNRWA headquarters in Jordan (and all its field offices) depends principally on these variables:

> The questionnaire uses fixed criteria using international standards of defining poverty without looking at the context-specific issues that include issues that are far beyond measuring poverty alone such as the historical background of the Palestinian refugee issue, the ongoing conflict, and the changing political and economic atmosphere. Furthermore, it does not determine poverty according to its original context taking into consideration average income per household, average prices and context-specific main household supplies other than food.[34]

Moreover, the senior poverty advisor indicated that the variables used to measure poverty, and later determine the eligibility of a particular group of individuals or families, include the type of accommodation (i.e. flat or house), the condition of accommodation, number of rooms, number of children, level of education of head of household, age and type of furniture.[35] All these variables are applied in a correlation using an 'international criteria such as looking at a male refugee whose weight is 50+ kg and height is 150+ cm. This person is estimated to consume 2200 calories a day, if he can get it given his or her economic conditions, he will then be eligible for UNRWA's assistance, if not then UNRWA provides him with 70% of his calorie need'.[36] According to these criteria, individual households are given quarterly (every three months) flour, sugar, sunflower oil and, sometimes, canned meat.

A UNRWA social worker pointed out that UNRWA's existing poverty evaluation system is problematic and has various deficiencies that social workers themselves continuously relay to the organisation.[37] The inability, however, to use individual family factors, with relevant socio-economic factors, creates further complications that lead to worsening abject poverty among Gaza's refugees as well as creating other types of problems. There are now more issues that poverty-poor families face. These, in the longer term, will end any prospects for improving the economic conditions of refugees. Among the issues are child labour, school absence by refugee children, poor educational

---

[34] Ibid.

[35] Interview with a senior poverty advisor in UNRWA's field office in Gaza, Gaza, 5 May 2017.

[36] Ibid.

[37] Interview with a social worker at UNRWA, Gaza, 15 April 2017.

attainment for those attending schools, health issues resulting from poor sheltering conditions and other psychosocial issues resulting either from individual economic hardship or more generally from the deteriorating living conditions in refugee camps.[38]

What this indicates again is a wider issue with how UNRWA deals with poverty issues. The organisation's former policy advisor referred to this as a 'disconnect between the overall UNRWA poverty policy and the demographic and economic conditions of refugees in Gaza'.[39] He relayed this disconnect to the fact that UNRWA continues to perceive the refugee camps in the same manner it did 60 years ago, indicating that

> camps were like any other neighbourhood in Gaza, they even had better services and infrastructure than other neighbourhoods. Now camps are highly condensed [...] houses are attached to each other and roads are too tight as a result of unorganised expansion. People cannot walk side by side in some roads. More than 15 people living in a two- or a three-bedroom house [...] some family members are forced to sleep in the kitchen or in the toilet. The food substance families get every three months can only sustain these families for three or four weeks, and many are forced to sell this food substance in order to buy other essentials.[40]

Accordingly, the current format of UNRWA's assistance in Gaza illustrates that poverty is managed to a certain level rather than tackled towards finding relative long-term solutions. According to UNRWA's poverty advisor, this format is influenced by EU and the US donors' humanitarian vision. This suggests that the large scope of the humanitarian crisis requires the organisation to tighten its eligibility criteria in such a way that would limit the number of beneficiaries and to tighten the scope of its services.

6.5 Compromised Humanitarianism

This section will discuss some of the additional challenges that surround the work of UNRWA. This sets aside the financial challenges and emerging challenges that relate to its overall humanitarian or developmental roles in the past two decades, particularly following the PA's establishment in 1994. These challenges still relate, in one way or another, to UNRWA's funding

---

[38] Interview with a female social worker at UNRWA in Khan Yunis, Gaza, 15 April 2017.
[39] Interview with a former policy advisor for UNRWA and consultant for international organisations in Gaza, Gaza, 21 December 2016.
[40] Ibid.

dynamics, thus how UNRWA constructs and formats its operational agenda in the Palestinian territories, particularly in the Gaza Strip. An important factor is the rise of Hamas and its seizure of power in the Gaza Strip in 2007 and how this resulted in adding additional humanitarian burdens on the organisation and created new political and technical complexities that affected how the organisation operates. These can be summarised in two major challenges as discussed in the following paragraphs: the American donors' intervention and UNRWA's relationship with the divided Palestinian governments.

6.5.1 *The US Donor Intervention*

Historically, UNRWA's work with the Palestinian refugees has been carried out on an eligibility basis determined by two major factors. First, to be a registered Palestinian refugee and, second, to meet need-based criteria as determined by the organisation. This does not, however, mean that donors have given full consent for the organisation to use their money and deliver its services according to these two primary factors. For instance, the United States, according to UNRWA's records, has historically maintained a status as a top-ranking donor to the organisation's budget (UNRWA, 2016a), in its 1961 Foreign Assistance Act (Section 301 c), which mentions the following:

> No contributions by the United States shall be made to the United Nations Relief and Works Agency for Palestine Refugees in the Near East except on the condition that the United Nations Relief and Works Agency take all possible measures to assure that no part of the United States contribution shall be used to furnish assistance to any refugee who is receiving military training as a member of the so-called Palestine Liberation Army or any other guerrilla type organization or who has engaged in any act of terrorism. (US Department of States, 2014)

UNRWA's information officers interpreted this Act and other similar Acts as a traditional procedure that had no impact whatsoever on the flexibility the organisation always enjoyed in dealing with donors' funding.[41] During the first two decades of UNRWA's operation, the focus was principally on delivering humanitarian support for the refugees in the camps and UNRWA worked entirely independently from any donor's intervention. The reasons for this are, first, there was not much involvement by the Palestinian political parties on how humanitarian work was conducted or how foreign assistance for the Palestinians was managed. Second, partisanship among Palestinians

---

[41] Interview with a public information officer at UNRWA, Gaza, 14 December 2016.

was very weak and it was mostly seen among Palestinians and their political parties that were operating in the diaspora. Put in different terms,
Palestinian political parties' involvement in CSOs and party-affiliated
NGOs began late in the 1970s and more intensively after the First Intifada
in 1987.

UNRWA's relations with the US and European donors became complex
over the years, especially with the political and security developments within
the oPt. For instance, the adoption of bombing attacks inside Israel following
the establishment of the PA, and the progress the Palestinian factions made on
developing their military capabilities, had prompted Western donors to exert
more pressure on UNRWA to monitor its spending criteria. What concerned
donors was that some of these parties had strong connections with pioneering
CSOs that UNRWA and donors alike had depended upon in implementing
some of their programmes. Therefore, monitoring the application of Act
301(c) became more serious as the United States began to regularly urge
UNRWA to take more counter-terrorism measures when delivering its services
to groups and individuals, mainly in the Gaza Strip.

The financial executive at UNRWA indicated that the US government
began to tighten its funding conditions on UNRWA to ensure proper and full
application of the Act.[42] Among the procedures the US government wanted
UNWRA to follow was to expand its reporting mechanism in such a way that
would allow the former to have access to the organisation's database, review
its beneficiaries' lists and audit its local partner organisations that UNRWA
relies on/subcontracts with in implementing some of its activities. In addition
to that, UNRWA is obliged to train its relevant staff member and registry
clerks who potentially deal with information that would lead to identifying
ineligible individuals or groups according to the anti-terrorism criteria. The
organisation also has been facing unprecedented pressure by the US government to undertake background checks on its local staff in Gaza who are occupying managerial positions at different levels. This came following accusations
that the UNRWA staff union in Gaza included members of Hamas and other
organisations the US consider to be terrorist organisations. The organisation,
therefore, on several occasions, was officially requested to take further actions
that would ensure UNRWA staff have no direct political affiliation with any
of the classified groups and to take disciplinary measures against those who
violate UNRWA's principles of impartiality when carrying out humanitarian
and relief services.[43] Although UNRWA has usually given its assurances to

---

[42] Interview with UNRWA's chief financial executive, UNRWA Field Office, Gaza, 7
May 2017.
[43] Ibid.

its donors that no donor money would reach ineligible people or be used for purposes other than that agreed, this level of criticism by major donors has always been perceived as direct intervention. In the words of the financial executive, this intervention is

> very unusual, as local UNRWA's officials know more about the sensitivity of UNRWA's work in the Gaza Strip given the present political atmosphere and the socio-economic conditions. We realise that some of the donors' measures or requirements have a serious impact on the organisation's sovereignty, and this indeed puts restrictions and limitations on the overall operational strategy, according to which the UNRWA delivers its humanitarian support and some of its development programmes.[44]

In effect UNRWA had to terminate partnership agreements it previously had with local CSOs and NGOs in Gaza. It also had to cancel the implementation of community programmes (mainly youth, gender and microfinance programmes) that these organisations were subcontracted to oversee.[45] UNRWA could not follow the same implementation mechanisms imposed by the US government and USAID projects in particular (i.e. carrying out a background check for every individual beneficiary). The reasons for this are threefold. First, it would contravene the existing system used by UNRWA to determine the level of eligibility for its beneficiaries, particularly as UNRWA mainly uses poverty as its primary criteria. Second, as the biggest humanitarian aid provider in Gaza that serves a sector representing the overwhelming majority of the population (i.e. refugees), conducting background checks on individual beneficiaries would cause lengthy delays in delivering relief service, especially during times of conflict when relief aid is much needed.[46] Third, it would be very difficult for UNRWA to justify the reasons to its beneficiaries as to why it decided to end its assistance to them, especially if the factors beyond this decision related to their political affiliation or securitised background check the organisation conducted on their behalf. This would be perceived with great anger by the beneficiary as the organisation itself would be contradicting the principle of neutrality if the eligibility criteria are politicised in such a way.

---

[44] Ibid.
[45] Interview with a UNRWA governor in the Gaza Strip, Gaza, 1 April 2017.
[46] Ibid.

6.5.2 The Palestinian Internal Political Division Dividing UNRWA

Some of the challenges caused by internal Palestinian politics may not directly relate to the internal Palestinian dispute, but instead, and to some extent, are indirectly related to it. To begin with, the UNRWA governor indicated how the Palestinian political split continues to be problematic for the work of UNRWA in the Gaza Strip. First, at the donor level, as indicated in the previous chapter, UNRWA has to comply, as do all international organisations, with the no-contact policy (with the Hamas government) in the Gaza Strip as imposed by the Quartet, of which the United Nations is a member. This is practically more complicated, however, when it comes to actual application. In fact, the interpretation of the no-contact policy for UNRWA, whose existence precedes the existence of all the Palestinian political parties, is twofold: (1) UNRWA must ensure that no funds are used for military purposes, as indicated previously; (2) it is not possible for the organisation to carry out its activities or services without a minimum level of coordination with the relevant government institutions in the Gaza Strip. Yet by doing so, UNRWA becomes liable to be sanctioned by it donors, particularly the US government. For instance, UNRWA must coordinate with Palestinian ministries, such as the Ministry of Health, the Ministry of Education and other vital government institutions that UNRWA relies heavily on to obtain necessary information for it to plan and implement some of its activities. However, according to UNRWA's financial executive in Gaza, UNRWA fell into the trap of Palestinian political division, where it has been forced to coordinate its work with two governments, each claiming the legitimacy over the other.

> These issues extend further than satisfying a particular government. UNRWA, most of the times, finds itself obliged to follow the agendas of two separate governments, the one in Gaza who is actually on the ground and is better connected to the socio-economic reality of the Strip and the other in Ramallah who is better connected with the international community and can facilitate and coordinate funding with donors, which in turn is necessary for the work of UNRWA.[47]

A second effect of Palestinian divisions on the work of UNRWA seems more indirect, but it has a clear and serious impact on the organisation's work in Gaza. The ongoing blockade of Gaza, which Israel justifies as inevitable so long as the territory is ruled by a terrorist organisation (Krieger and Horn,

---

[47] Interview with UNRWA's chief financial executive, UNRWA Field Office, Gaza, 7 May 2017.

2011), has impacted the work of UNRWA in various ways. First, according to UNRWA's poverty advisor, the cost of food and medical supplies has become three times more expensive than before the blockade.[48] This, as a result, had exhausted UNRWA's budgets and pushed the organisation to take certain measures to overcome this, such as lowering its procurement policies to be able to buy cheaper items rather than reducing the amounts of food assistance for its refugees. Second, and despite being a UN organisation, UNRWA still had to experience the consequences of the blockade on Gaza. On many occasions, the organisation lacked the ability to ensure smooth access of food and medical supplies through the Israeli crossings, especially during the Israeli offenses on Gaza in 2008 and 2014.[49] The UNRWA's governor indicated that there have been moments of dispute between the organisation and the coordinator of the government activities in the territories (a unit in the Israeli Ministry of Defence that coordinates civilian issues in the WB and Gaza).[50] The reason for this dispute is that the latter accused UNRWA on several occasions of allowing Hamas and other terrorist organisations for using the organisation's facilities for military purposes, such as storing military equipment and using these facilities as bases to launch rockets against Israel. Israel had used these allegations as an excuse to target UNRWA's facilities. This included the bombing of schools that were used as shelter for displaced families during the offences in 2008 and 2014 and bombing UNRWA's main food warehouse in 2014.

6.6 Summary and Discussion

We examined the ways the post-Oslo aid dynamics impacted the humanitarian operations in Gaza and principally the work of UNRWA as the biggest humanitarian organisation that serves the refugee population in the Gaza Strip. We also looked at the ways these dynamics led to the imposition of further control over the humanitarian spaces in the territory. To understand the dynamics that surrounded UNRWA's work before and after the Oslo era, as indicated in both questions, it was important to see how its operations changed over the period since the beginning of the Palestinian refugee crisis in 1948 up to the current day. Accordingly, the first section began with describing the role the organisation played so as to facilitate the economic and social integration of the Palestinian refugees registered with the organisation (mainly in the Palestinian territories, Jordan, Lebanon and Syria). It demonstrated how

---

[48] Interview with a senior poverty advisor in UNRWA's field office in Gaza, Gaza, 5 May 2017.

[49] Ibid.

[50] Interview with a UNRWA governor in the Gaza Strip, Gaza, 1 April 2017.

UNRWA, as a quasi-governmental organisation, has continued to work within a limited mandate until the present time. This limited mandate, as a result, puts limitations on the organisation's autonomy and its ability to develop and expand so it can meet the growing needs of the refugee population. Moreover, the limited mandate is also an indirect factor among other factors discussed in the remaining sections. Importantly, here is how donors' influence over UNRWA's mandate and structural operations have had negative impacts on the autonomy of refugees and weakened their socio-economic integration in Gaza.

We have seen the complex reality of UNRWA's work in Gaza, highlighting some of the emerging challenges related to the doubling of the refugee population in the territory. This briefly detailed the type and scope of services UNRWA provides in areas of health, education and relief and social services. The aspect of UNRWA's assistance was also discussed, principally in relation to the political and economic changes that followed the Second Intifada in 2000 and the Israeli withdrawal from Gaza in 2005, and how these major events seriously impacted UNRWA's food and cash assistance as a result of the increased level of poverty. These aspects of UNRWAs work in the Gaza Strip demonstrated how UNRWA's donors indirectly imposed mechanisms of control over the refugee population via influencing its operational frameworks. Consequently, these frameworks lacked elements of socio-economic integration or aspects of development as UNRWA's mandates initially proposed.

The chapter has demonstrated that the reconstruction of UNRWA's role and operations in the Gaza Strip was significantly impacted by this funding dilemma. By exploring the budgetary issues that relate to how UNRWA plans and structures its core services and programmes, it again demonstrated how UNRWA's financial and administrative sovereignty has been negatively influenced by Western donor's willingness to continue or increase their funding. As a result, the organisation's limited ability to expand and develop its core services (i.e. health and education) so that these services meet the needs of the refugee population was severely affected. This increasing level of Western donor intervention in UNRWA's operations contributed to what seems to be 'sanctioned humanitarianism', where the refugee population, or surplus population as referred to in Chapter 2, becomes victim to certain political or financial agendas of particular donors. Accordingly, both the organisation and the population it serves either become victims of a global development or economic agenda or a political agenda that specifically relates to Western donors' aid agenda.

The chapter also addressed how unusual funding trends have resulted in creating false expectations among refugees in an environment characterised by severe economic hardship. This in many cases made the entire refugee population captivated by a politicised donors' agenda or a temporary emergency agenda. Both types of agenda again weaken the socio-economic freedom and autonomy of this refugee population. Moreover, the predictions upon signing the Oslo Accords (1993) was that the PA would alleviate much of the pressure experienced by UNRWA through providing services and acting more or less like a government body. The PA's poor institutional and economic performance, however, all surrounded by political and economic uncertainty, resulted in increasing the pressure on UNRWA. The following is of notable importance: the major cause of UNRWA's current financial deficit is what was described as 'donor fatigue'. This fatigue reflects a sense of hopelessness and a potential unwillingness among donors to continue supporting the organisation in the same way or to the same extent they did in the past. The impact of this is mostly felt in UNRWA's field office in Gaza and is represented in the structural changes the organisations had to make in order to satisfy donors, on the one hand, and to minimise its expenses, on the other. Another serious impact of this fatigue is the absence of sustainability in UNRWA's programme, at both humanitarian and developmental levels. This is caused by the loss of sovereign decision-making and planning on issues that relate to the use of extra funds from donors and advance emergency preparedness other than increasing food and cash assistance when a crisis occurs.

Choosing between humanitarian work and development work has been hugely imbalanced. The emphasis on a temporary humanitarian agenda, which operates during times of crisis and one that manages/controls abject poverty, made the sovereignty of the entire refugee population vulnerable to these agendas. UNRWA's original vision for social and economic integration of refugees was at the core of their long-term socio-economic development, especially its work and education programmes. On the contrary, the current reality of temporary humanitarianism adopted by the organisation supports discussion surrounding the creation and control of surplus people (wasted lives).

Accordingly, the refugee population is no longer a development priority, but rather must be contained and controlled so that they would have no negative impact on developed peoples. It is containment that occurs when the ultimate purpose of temporary humanitarianism is to manage abject poverty from exceeding a certain limit, but not to seek solutions that would eradicate it. Furthermore, it also demonstrated how neglecting the developmental aspects played a role in reconstructing how humanitarianism operates among the refugee population in Gaza. It is assessing individuals and groups against a need criterion that is not ultimately based on socio-economic factors that take into consideration the economic and political realities that exist but rather on criteria that mainly depend on Western donors' funding trends.

The changing political dynamics in the Gaza Strip (i.e. rise of Hamas, the Palestinian division and the Israeli offensives) also created new funding dynamics to UNRWA. These dynamics are represented mainly in the greater level of Western donors' interventions (mainly the US donors) and the tightening of financial and administrative conditions on how the organisation carries out its operations and delivers its services to the refugee population. The new aspects of UNRWA's work in Gaza imposed by its Western donors, especially those that relate to forcing the organisation to investigate the political background of its beneficiaries (both individuals and organisations) and to tighten its eligibility criteria to issues that relate to home ownership, type and quality of furniture and other fixed assets, contributed to fostering control over humanitarian spaces of the refugee population in the Gaza Strip. Furthermore, UNRWA's humanitarian efforts seem to have been affected by Palestinian political divisions, which is indirectly influenced by external factors pertaining to Palestinian parties' position on peace with Israel and the adoption of military resistance. The organisation is forced to comply with the Quartet's no-contact policy with Hamas and to respect the internationally recognised Palestinian government in Ramallah. Accordingly, UNRWA and its beneficiaries are caught in the middle of different political agendas that put limitations on the humanitarian practices in the Gaza Strip.

To conclude, for more than six decades, UNRWA has played a vital role in serving the Palestinian population, particularly in the Gaza Strip, where more than 75 per cent of the overall population is refugees. The discussions in the chapter, however, demonstrated that the post-Oslo foreign aid dynamics exposed UNRWA to wider interventions by donors in how the organisation serves refugees in the Gaza Strip. UNRWA's original mandate combines humanitarian and developmental services, and both are central to refugees' socio-economic integration and development and continue to be today. Yet, the element of control and de-development, demonstrated throughout this book, is shown again in how changing funding dynamics have impacted the organisation's ability to work with refugees according to the traditional framework of socio-economic integration. The funding dilemma the organisation has experienced for more than two decades exposed the organisation and its refugee population to control measures imposed, in the main, by Western donors. UNRWA, on the one hand, can no longer expand and develop its services to include the in-need refugee population and is forced to operate most of the time according to an emergency humanitarian agenda. On the other hand, these control dynamics by donors illustrated the concept of surplus people creation (i.e. refugees), discussed in Chapter 2, where aid works as a regulatory control technique. Donors' intervention in determining the level and scope of humanitarian assistance refugees are eligible to receive and determining the level of eligibility is central to the concept of development as a liberal problematic of security where aid operates as a power design that has the ability to create new social sectors and separate, isolate and redefine others according to socio-economic measures.

Chapter 7

CONCLUSION: FOREIGN AID, DE-DEVELOPMENT AND THE OBJECTIFICATION OF 'SURPLUS PEOPLE'

7.1 Introduction

For more than seven decades, Palestinians in the Gaza Strip have lived under various and multi-layered forms of control. This control extended from the Ottoman era over the Levant region, including Palestine in the 1830s, followed by the British Mandate (1920–48) and Egyptian administration (1948–67). Shortly after the 1948 *Nakbeh*, and under the Egyptian administration and the newly formed UNRWA administration, the Palestinian population in Gaza was isolated from the rest of Palestine. However, the 1967 Israeli military occupation of the remainder of historical Palestine, particularly the Gaza Strip, has had the most significant effect by reshaping the socio-economic and political realities on the ground (up to the present day). Control over the territory has not only impacted every aspect of people's lives, but has systematically restricted their abilities and potential to progress, politically, economically and socially. The occupation's socio-economic warfare and control have applied Sara Roy's 'de-development' concept. Discussions in this book have therefore acknowledged that the Israeli occupation has been, and continues to be, the main factor of control over the Palestinian population in the Gaza Strip.

However, in this book we aimed to go beyond the Israeli occupation as the main instrument of control and de-development and to examine how foreign aid has facilitated the emergence of new forms of control over the Palestinians living in the Gaza Strip in the period that followed the signing of the 1993 Oslo Accords. By the emergence of new forms of control, we explored the aspects of life that have been influenced by the working dynamics of foreign aid delivery and the work of aid agencies in Gaza, and to see the ways in which Palestinians living in the Gaza Strip are controlled and have evolved since the Oslo Accords and continue to evolve in such a way that affects their daily lives.

This book has provided empirical evidence with some examples that support the analysis presented in this conclusion. In brief, the book has relied on the post-development theory as a framework that guided the analysis of the relationship between the 'developed' and the 'underdeveloped' worlds. The framework emphasised that the emergence of 'underdeveloped' people or nations was originally a social construct determined by the 'developed' on the basis of the latter's economic growth and modernisation. Accordingly, the framework suggested that development, as a practice, facilitated the creation of 'surplus people', perceived as a threat to the developed world and one that requires the intervention through development or development aid to prevent it from harming the modernised world. As an extension of this intervention, the framework suggests that development is a power design that works to control and govern people in all aspects of their social, economic and political life, assuming that, by doing so, it secures their biological and social interest. Additionally, the means of control embedded in development practice emphasises the further creation of surplus people and its tightening control over them.

7.2 Socio-economic Division, Control and De-development

Discussions in this book have attributed the systematic process of de-development and economic control to Israel's role as an occupying military power. Chapter 3, for instance, clearly demonstrated the different approaches and policies the occupation utilised as part of its economic warfare on Gaza. The chapter detailed Israel's economic measures as represented in the form of curfews, closures and restricted mobility of people and goods in and out of the Gaza Strip, all of which summarised Israel's economic warfare since the First Intifada throughout the establishment of the PA and Hamas's taking control of the Gaza Strip. These control and de-development dynamics continued to exist after the Oslo Accords (1993) and the establishment of the PA (1994). Therefore, the core theme of investigation in this book was to look at the role foreign aid has played in intensifying the socio-economic divisions among the Palestinian population in Gaza and, with this, how aid also operated as an additional dynamic of control and de-development.

The establishment of a self-autonomous PA within the framework of the Oslo peace agreement is found to have extended a mechanism of control over the Palestinian population, especially those living in the Gaza Strip (Chapter 3). This is due to the peculiarities of its geographical location, the deteriorated economic conditions and the internal political division that has always characterised the territory. The core of the extension of control over the Palestinians was a direct result of the 'partner for peace' paradigm. This paradigm defined what a credible Palestinian peace partner is and the type of role and duties such a partner should fulfil so as to maintain its credibility in the eyes of both Israel and the international community. Meanwhile, the PA's role, in pursuing the continued flow of aid necessary to reinforce its role as a government body and popular Palestinian support for it, has directly become one of a security agent that caters to Israeli security. This was evident in the security vetting process of public service employees that was aimed at ensuring their full allegiance to the Palestinian leadership's choice of a peace agreement with Israel. It was also important to gain more public popularity for Fatah as the Palestinian party capable of ensuring international funds necessary to pay public sector employees. It was also necessary, finally, to weaken the political opposition (i.e. Hamas, Islamic Jihad and some members of secular parties with a clear opposition to Oslo Accords) by limiting their access to employment and representation in public institutions.

The process of ensuring and enforcing the peace process paradigm has significantly contributed to a new legacy of institutional and political corruption. At the political level, the Fatah-led PA punished its opponents through political imprisonment and the political de-legitimisation of those opposing peace agreements with Israel. Meanwhile, the impact at the socio-economic level was much larger as the PA's political favouritism widened the socio-economic gaps between Gaza's socio-economic groups. This was especially clear in the emergence of a new political elite that managed to infiltrate and mix with the traditional economic elite that existed before the establishment of the PA in 1994. This process occurred again when Hamas came to power in 2006 through the emergence of a tunnel economy. In the first case, the economic advantages enjoyed by the PA political elite contributed to worsening the socio-economic injustices in terms of ordinary people's access to public services and employment. Secondly, Hamas managed to deepen its economic control over the Gaza Strip by weakening formal trade.

The issue of political and social division expanded beyond looking at the exacerbating impact of the securitisation and politicisation of foreign aid upon these divisions both within Gaza and between Gaza and the WB (Chapter 4). We can see that the existing political division among Palestinians can be attributed largely to the intervention of some Western countries (particularly the American donors) in Palestinian internal politics, especially following Hamas's electoral victory in 2006. Clearly, in some tangible example, foreign aid was used as a tool to put pressure on the PA to reject the outcome of the Palestinian elections that brought Hamas to power. By threatening to halt or cut off aid, the PA was directly forced to adopt the same preconditions put by the

Quartet on the Middle East and Israel (i.e. denouncing terrorism, recognising Israel and disarming Hamas) in order to reconsider Hamas's participation in political life. This consequently led to the political division between the WB and Gaza and to the establishment of two separate Palestinian governments. The governing of public services, the level of poverty and dependence on humanitarian aid continued to deteriorate because of the Palestinian political division. The poor flow of international (non-humanitarian) aid to the territory, from (almost) all donors, including Arab countries except Qatar, continued to be delivered but at a much complicated process.

Meanwhile, it was important to also look at how the post-Oslo aid agenda contributed to the reconstructing of the role of the NGO sector in the Gaza Strip (Chapter 5). Evidently, this sector has gone through a systematic process of change both in structure and in identity. Prior to the Oslo Accords, this sector represented a key pillar of national resistance in the Gaza Strip against the occupier's practices against the Palestinian population. This was seen in the sector's ability to reach out to the communities it aimed to serve at different levels and how much this contributed to enhancing the population's resilience. The change in the role of most NGOs can be attributed to the fact that they gradually became guided, first, by an international development agenda, and second, by an individual donor agenda that tends to offer aid money as part of the aid-for-peace agenda (i.e. the US government and the European Union). Accordingly, although the NGO sector continued to be informed and aware of the developmental and humanitarian needs of the population, their ability to develop plans and agendas that would address these needs became severely limited. They had to either accept what was being offered by donors (in terms of projects or activities) or be deprived of receiving any funding at all.

At the same time, many of their projects were not implemented according to a comprehensive national strategic plan/agenda (which the PA failed to develop over the past two decades, 1994–2013) and were characterised by redundancy in the nature or type of projects. This was caused either by the absence of coordination and communication between organisations themselves, to set up and define development or humanitarian priorities, or by the 'take it or leave it' policy followed mainly by the US donors. These American donors insisted on implementing projects and activities that do not take into consideration social and cultural values or the more pressing needs of some communities in the Gaza Strip. Examples include the implementation of youth programmes in some rural areas in the Gaza Strip that called for religious freedoms and normalisation programmes under the umbrella of cultural exchange programmes that involved the participation of Israeli groups, issues that are highly sensitive in Palestinian society. These projects also included the implementation of programmes that obviously could have no sustainability prospects given the nature of these programmes, for instance, spending millions on so-called environmental projects by employing thousands of unemployed skills workers to manually clean streets in Gaza. This type of programme can only suggest that the United States and European Union decided to take the simple route rather than to challenge Israel to facilitate the implementation of more strategic projects that involve allowing necessary equipment and machinery to the Gaza Strip for the implementation of such projects.

It is also important to understand the impact of politicisation and securitisation of foreign aid on creating socio-economic division among NGOs and aid beneficiaries. We found that securitising and politicising foreign aid first led to a fragmentation of the civil society sector. Organisations were categorised according to how donors perceived them. These perceptions were based on the political background of directors and senior staff, their affiliation with Palestinian political parties and finally their ability to implement programmes as suggested by individual donors and their willingness to accept vetting procedures that targeted their partner organisations and individual aid recipients. Second, the wider role that NGOs began to play in the Gaza Strip, partly due to corruption allegations against the PA or the fear that a donor's funding was used to support military organisations, led to the facilitation of preferential ties between leaders of these sectors and Western donors and aid agencies. The book demonstrated how these preferential ties contributed to the growth and expansion of a social sector within the Gaza Strip, which I referred to as a 'globalised elite'. By examining this group of globalised elites, we found that despite them representing a group of aid practitioners that ostensibly had no political agenda at the institutional level, the politicisation and securitisation is nonetheless highly embedded in the donors' aid agenda. What this meant was that these aid practitioners, most of whom are from Gaza and represent the population in Gaza, have little influence most of the time on what their institutions plan in terms of programmes and the way these institutions affect their beneficiaries. Furthermore, this group developed into a closed homogenous group that represents a 'well-off middle class' that also have good connections with the PA's political elite. The preferential ties with donors and PA elites maintained by the larger NGOs contributed, on occasion, to weakening smaller NGOs. This is due to aspects of bias towards organisations that share the same socio-cultural values (sometimes religious values) and due to the political affiliations of the smaller organisations. This, therefore, impacted the level of access to services and programmes of smaller or marginalised communities smaller NGOs serve and represent.

Meanwhile, these aspects of control and development have also been reflected at the level of humanitarian operations, especially since humanitarian aid increased substantially since Israel's withdrawal from Gaza in 2005 (Chapter 6). There was a need to examine the ways new aid dynamics led to the imposition of further control over humanitarian spaces in Gaza. UNRWA, as a key agency that has been servicing Palestinian refugees in the Gaza Strip (who represent approximately seventy per cent of the overall population), has experienced funding dilemmas over the past 20 years. This dilemma is related either directly related to new funding priorities of donors post the 1993 Oslo Accords, who expanded their work with the PA and the NGO sector in areas other than relief, or indirectly to funding fatigue for an ongoing refugee crisis spanning almost seven decades. Over time, this funding fatigue facilitated a gradual intervention by donors in how the UNRWA plans and runs its services and programmes that serve the refugee population. This was particularly damaging to the Gaza Strip's refugees due to the consistent and continuous growth in the level of poverty and the political instability the Strip suffered since Israel's withdrawal in 2005. What exacerbated the situation and made it more complex is that Israel considered its withdrawal from the Strip as ending its occupation and that it had no legal obligation[1] to provide the services the territory needs. In fact, this occupation continues in many aspects and spans land, sea and aid areas. Instead, the donor community provided limited and conditioned humanitarian relief, while Israel denies its responsibility to provide services to the occupied population living in the Strip.

The Western donors' interventions, particularly American donors, had a significant impact on UNRWA's institutional sovereignty and its ability to maintain its traditional relief and work programmes that, over the years, contributed to Gazan refugees' welfare in areas of education, health, employment and capacity building. At the same time, the organisations were prompted to redefine their need criteria to cope with the shortage of aid funding, which exacerbated the abject poverty of refugees. Nevertheless, refugees are risking continued access to services as a result of the imposition of stricter need criteria that UNRWA has historically guaranteed for them. Yet, such measures are influenced by key donors (i.e. the United States and European Union) as a condition to maintain their funding to UNRWA. It was a sovereignty guaranteed by UNRWA's ability to act independently of donors when it came to address the needs of the refugee population. The gradual weakening of the organisation's sovereignty resulted in intervention and determining how much needy people should eat over a particular period of time, what they should eat and how often they should eat. The background for the current economic hardship of refugees is connected to the fact that the population is instead

---

[1] 'Legal obligation' is defined as an occupying power since its control over Gaza's airspace, land and sea is continuing.

assessed according to general criteria set by UNRWA and donors rather than taking into consideration socio-economic factors, the needs of individuals and families, and the political instability in the Gaza Strip.

7.3 Interchangeable Approaches, Identical Outcomes

Control and de-development, in the case of Gaza, have been mutually reinforcing each other. Control, as represented in the Israeli occupation, not only paralysed Gaza's ability to maintain agricultural, industrial and trade infrastructures, but also worked systematically to weaken these, either directly through destroying them or indirectly through restrictions that prevented these structures from operating normally (i.e. restrictions on freedom of mobility and of goods). Consequently, Gaza's economic problems were not caused by the lack of resources, potentials or workforce – altogether necessary to achieve economic advancement. On the contrary, at the centre of Israeli military control over the Gaza Strip was the economic colonialism through which it aimed to emphasise as well as deepen the Strip's total economic dependence on the occupier. This would happen either by making Gaza's labour force entirely dependent on having access to the Israel labour market or through weakening the absorptive capacity of Gaza's local labour market.

The international aid regime that emerged after the 1993 Oslo Accords, however, indirectly accelerated the dynamics of control and de-development that were already in place. What is meant by this is an additional layer of control over the Palestinians, particularly in the Gaza Strip (due to its geopolitics and socio-economic realities). The elements of control and de-development have not been necessarily asymmetrical to those associated with the Israeli occupation, but in many cases yielded to and corresponded with, rather than confronted or defied, the facts and conditions created by Israel on the ground. For instance, the discussion of foreign aid to the PA revealed the political tension underpinned by the principle that aid has been given to the PA per the framework of a peace agreement of which Israel (the occupier) is a primary partner. What this later meant was that foreign aid delivery to the PA has been conditional on addressing the interests (security or otherwise) of Israel. This comes at the expense of proper implementation of programmes that would facilitate the development of economic infrastructure within the Gaza Strip. This would gradually weaken, or end, the historical economic dependence of the territory on Israel and/or independently address the humanitarian interests of the population in the Gaza Strip without relying on Israel. Instead, the security framework that guided the PA–donor(s) relationship, especially the American peace sponsor, empowered the security establishment within the

PA and contributed to the rise of a political and economic elite that benefited from the security–peace framework.

There has been a consistent failure on behalf of the PA to build the sustainable economic foundations necessary to create positive socio-economic results on the lives of the population in Gaza. The PA's political and security leadership (during both Arafat and Abbas eras), however, utilised funding to the PA from donor funds to enhance their political position and foster their popularity among supporters from within their parties and strengthen their relationship with allies from other Palestinian factions and build affiliations with the private sector. Therefore, there were issues of favouritism in public sector employment which benefited supporters of the peace process paradigm and Fatah supporters in general. This type of favouritism paved the way for a broader financial and administrative corruption at different managerial levels that, over a short period, contributed to the emergence and growth of a new socio-economic elite. Furthermore, it enabled the Palestinian political elite within the PA to use a 'carrot and stick' approach to control employees within the security establishment and the public sector. This was done by directly threatening to suspend them or cut their salaries once if they did not show full support of the political leadership.

Consequently, it is important to emphasise that control embedded in the security-driven 'peace for aid' paradigm adopted by donors prompted the establishment of a PA, whose ongoing existence is conditioned by fulfilling a political and economic manifesto that failed to appeal to all Palestinians. Indeed, the PA was an unelected body from its very establishment. The PA leadership, meanwhile, underestimated the socio-economic, as well as political, consequences of accepting a security-driven aid agenda that was meant to serve Israel's interests in the first place. Nevertheless, the PA leadership exploited aid to suppress its opposition and expanded socio-economic gains at the individual level. Although donors expressed their dissatisfaction with the PA performance at the financial level or administrative and democratic freedoms, they took rare measures to encourage serious reform. On the contrary, Western donors (particularly the United States) maintained unconditional support for the PA's security establishment to be able to maintain security coordination with Israel.

The security paradigm was very problematic for Gaza. First, it was obvious even before the establishment of the PA that Israel wished to disengage from Gaza and end its economic and humanitarian responsibility for the territory. This saw Israel's approach to the territory reduced to a mere security-based perspective. This was clear in the various measures described in Chapter 4. Second, Israel succeeded to promote this perspective among most donors. As a result, we saw variations in the aid agenda between the Gaza Strip and the

WB. Third, high securitisation of the Gaza Strip by both Israel and Western donors also influenced how the PA security leadership deals with Gaza in terms of its relationship with the Palestinian political parties, especially those advocating armed resistance against Israel, and the general population's political affiliation and political views. Therefore, the current political division and the growing socio-economic gap in Gaza are not merely attributed to internal Palestinian factors. Rather, they are strongly associated with a broader framework that governs the PA's relationship with the Strip and the relationship between the key Palestinian political parties (i.e. the peace-for-aid framework).

Another aspect of this control has been demonstrated in the biopolitical governmentality embedded in the working dynamics of Gaza's civil society sector following the post-Oslo foreign aid agenda. Biopolitics, as explained in Chapter 2, is the ability to govern mass populations through interventions by influencing the way they live, starting from what they eat and how they reproduce. Hence, the importance of the civil society to biopolitical governmentality is demonstrated in its ability to govern from within as a sector that has historically represented the communities it served. Yet this time, it is proxy governmentality that served an external donor's agenda.

We have seen that the aid agenda to civil society witnessed a similar level of securitisation to that of the aid to the PA. This was first evidenced by how this securitisation managed to reform this sector and how it prevented it from maintaining the role it had played for more than five decades (prior to the establishment of the PA) as a national resilience actor. Second, this sector became driven by predominantly the Western donors' aid agenda that over time contributed to isolating the sector from the status quo of where it operates. Instead, a focus on fulfilling terms and conditions of individual donors or their affiliate funding agencies was emphasised when it came to planning and carrying out developmental or humanitarian activities. Again, this was evidenced in the security vetting procedures that bound the work of most of the NGOs when it came to their interaction with aid beneficiaries and recipients. According to these procedures, NGOs had to categorise aid recipients based on security data and political affiliation rather than their actual socio-economic needs.

Western donors, mainly from the United States, imposed a multi-layered security governance regime upon the CSO sector, one that works according to the post-9/11 war on terror framework as well as the security conditions of the state of Israel. Consequently, the NGO sector lost autonomy over 'how' and 'what' they can deliver to the population in Gaza based on a local or national agenda. We have also seen a social aspect of this detachment underpinned by the emergence of a 'globalised elite' who enjoy a partnership that extends to implementing the securitised agenda of the Western donor or serving the political and economic interest of its local associates. The evidence for this is demonstrated in socio-economic advantages the NGO elite began to enjoy as part of their relationship with the political elite at both the level of the PA and the Hamas government in the Gaza Strip, for example, the partnership in profitable businesses in real estate and general trade of basic supplies. This elite also benefited from its preferential ties with donors, especially as it guaranteed better freedom of movement and connections with the outside world, which play a positive role in its social and economic growth.

Additionally, the intervention in the work of the UNRWA by some Western donors not only impacted the traditional notion of humanitarianism, according to which the organisation has operated since its inauguration in 1949, but it was also evident how this intervention gradually led to the abolition of development concepts which were previously embedded in the relief programmes. These included professional capacity building, vocational programmes, permanent employment and post-secondary school education. Control and de-development were also evident in the funding fatigue claim, especially in the period that followed the establishment of the PA that has continuously influenced how the UNRWA defines and redefines its 'relief' and 'work' objectives as compared to how it originally did since its establishment. Importantly, however, under Gaza's current political reality, humanitarianism became one aspect of managing a refugee regime in a similar way to assessments of refugee crises that exist elsewhere (for instance, the Iraqi and Syrian refugee crises). In the case of the Gaza Strip, the humanitarian operations are highly influenced by the political dilemma that surrounds Palestinian political divisions, the Israeli-Palestinian conflict and the Palestinian factions' relationship with neighbouring countries, particularly Egypt. This was clear in the way terms such as 'abject poverty' and 'extreme poverty' became two fundamental characteristics of the refugee communities in Gaza. Meanwhile, the organisation is gradually losing its historical legacy of being an empowering agent for these communities.

7.4 Foreign Aid and Control over Gaza's 'Surplus People'

In situating the Gaza Strip within the security–development nexus as a control framework, Gaza represents a unique case under which heterogeneous control mechanisms and structures are produced and materialised by some Western donors, in particularly sponsors of the peace-for-aid paradigm (i.e. the American donors and some EU donors). Yet, regardless of the heterogeneity of these mechanisms and structures, over time, they become complementary to the original control mechanism represented by the Israeli occupation. Therefore, discussions in this book contributed to broadening the existing understanding of the control dynamics embedded in development practices and their impact on the target societies. They did so by examining how these control dynamics can be reinforced when attached to and guided by add-itional security dynamics (i.e. those of Israel) other than those imposed by parties who are seeking to do development.

For instance, this book implied Duffield's 'liberal problematic of develop-ment', a problematic that is embedded in the relationship between develop-ment and security in which the former is concerned with people and the latter with a group of processes that work to promote or demote the life of these people (2007: 4). We suggested that development establishes forms of power over people through a group of social and economic processes, under the framework of ensuring people's rights, freedoms, security and other develop-ment slogans. These forms of power are seen in how particular development or humanitarian programmes are implemented in accordance with security acts that belong to individual donor countries (i.e. post 9/11 anti-terrorism acts). These acts influenced the delivery of various aid programmes and the work and structures of local organisations that delivered these programmes. Yet, the link that is missing here with regard to the Gaza case is that this aid is delivered, supposedly, according to a post-conflict development agenda, while the actual conflict is ongoing. This continues to directly impact the aid agenda by imposing additional conditions on both the aid provider and aid recipients, or indirectly through creating conditions on the ground that weaken the effectiveness of aid programmes and further complicate their implementation. Examples include restricting the freedom of mobility of both individuals and goods and promoting additional security conditions to some donors when applying for their programmes. This is done in such a way so that these conditions aid the mutual interest of both Israel and Western donors.

Extending the lessons of Duffield's liberal problematic of development, we analysed the relevance of Foucault's concept of biopolitical govern-ance (1979) in strategizing control over the population in Gaza. Chapter 2 explains that biopolitical power extends its impact to establish power over the basic living of human beings. Accordingly, we saw that we attach cer-tain political, security or programmatic conditions that relate to defining poverty and needs and that do not focus on achieving mere developmental or humanitarian objectives, or that relate to achieving certain economic or infrastructural advancement. Rather, they expand the power they enjoy infiltrating socio-economic as well as political spaces through which people and structures operate and interact. At the structural level, biopolitical power is demonstrated in how foreign aid turned these structures into sur-veillance tools through salaries, employment, food coupons and other forms of aid, to either influence the population's political attitude and views or to at least ensure their political neutrality. At the agency level (i.e. agency versus structure), it consequently influenced how individuals that belong to these structures perceive and interact with each other according to the overall interest of organisations they belong to or to the interest of the socio-economic level they are affiliated to. For example, we saw how the PA political elite used political and financial incentives and measures to ensure the support for the peace paradigm among its affiliates. Similarly, we saw how NGOs shifted from being a key element in the national resistance that ensured Gaza's resilience to being politically neutral, which ensured compliance with donors' policies. In doing so, foreign aid has successfully facilitated the occupier's strategic aid of surveillance. Therefore, Foucault's concept of biopolitical power is seen to be relevant in explaining the nature of the power pyramid that governs the relationship between Israel and Western donors, between donors and PA/NGOs and finally between PA/NGOs and the people in Gaza.

Having established the presence of biopolitical power, we showed how the security paradigm embedded in development, as suggested by Duffield (2001: 310), can modulate, reform and influence the behaviour of surplus people, who are an underdeveloped population perceived as a security threat to modernisation and to the developed world. The security paradigm of the occupation, according to this notion of control, cannot be separated from the security paradigm of development, as both have a common goal and share the same characteristics, yet through a different set of approaches. Although Duffield (2001) suggested that the security paradigm of aid is not based on 'arms and external political alliance between states', we have witnessed a totally different scenario in the Palestinian case, particularly when it comes to coordinating aid and development activities in the Gaza Strip after Hamas's victory in 2006 and even before. This was evident in, first, how development aid to the PA was in the form of direct military and security capacity building of the PA's security forces to confront the opposition (i.e. Hamas). This was clear before and after Hamas came to power in the Gaza Strip. Second, the entire vetting procedure that aid beneficiaries undergo is based on collecting intelligence data via the PA, for which the PA intelligence capacity building is ongoing and has not been affected by forms of sanctions the United States decided to take against the PA as a result of seeking recognition within the United Nations. Therefore, the securitisation and politicisation of development in the Palestinian case, and most particularly in the Gaza case, have involved, unlike what Duffield suggests (2001, 2004), arming and building alliances, sometimes in the name of those foreign aid seeks to benefit.

7.5 Objectifying 'Surplus People'

We also emphasised that the foreign aid provision to the PA was based on the peace-for-aid paradigm according to which international donors would assist the Palestinians to establish their state. Upon signing the Oslo Accords, it was taken for granted that peace had been achieved and accordingly foreign aid was delivered according to a post-conflict development/reconstruction framework. In fact, the conflict is evolving, and its settlement has become further complicated. The early consequence of such an escalation of conflict was that the development aid framework was never independent of political and security concerns that initially guided the peace-for-aid paradigm. The role, therefore, of the aid agenda that influenced Western donors and PA, or more specifically Western donors and the Palestinians, was to infiltrate Palestinian society through aid for the sake of changing their attitude, allegiance and ideology from within in such a way that it would make peace with Israel, or the entire peace-for-aid paradigm, more successful. This was demonstrated by the emphasis placed on the political identity and the political affiliations of any parties that could be involved in the aid provision process, essentially a determination as to whether they are aid workers or aid recipients. Accordingly, non-alliance, or declared support for the peace paradigm, has always been an essential part of the aid delivery.

This is all combined under the name of 'development', which happens to be appealing as a term, yet it brings with it a wider process of social control and transformation that operates to change society's conduct and makes it compatible with the original paradigm of aid for peace.

The book has expanded the understanding of 'surplus people' and 'wasted lives', introduced by Bauman (2004) and Duffield (2007), as a social category and a design. This was done by providing a reflection on a living example and a significant case study, that is, the population in Gaza, which adds more importance to these terms. While Bauman (2004: 6) suggests that the production of such categories reflects an alternative meaning to colonization and imperialism reproduced by the power differential embedded in 'development' as an industry, Duffield (2007: 9) indicates how 'development', as a postcolonial industry, portrays this social category as a problematic population that requires remedial attention through intervention. The core purpose of this intervention is not only to control this social category and to limit the risk it poses, but also to ensure the stability and the security of other developed societies. Building forth on their work, discussions in this book provide empirical descriptions of the processes that lead to the production of Gaza's surplus people. For instance, I referred to the different sets of securitised and politicised foreign aid eligibility criteria delivered through the PA, or by CSOs and UNRWA, and how the use of such an eligibility system leads to a significant objectification of certain individuals or groups. Patients in Gaza are allowed access to medical care in the WB or Israel based on their security background. Students, businessmen or even aid workers are also treated according to these rules. This is very similar to what Foucault illustrated in the surveillance system used in schools and educational institutions in general. Students are judged based on predefined criteria that aim at individualizing and objectifying them; then they are categorised and judged according to these criteria (Foucault, 1979: 184). Accordingly, we provide empirical evidence of such production and have contributed to providing factual characteristics of both the processes through which this production occurs and the characteristics of the surplus people themselves, according to how foreign aid providers perceive them. We have also contributed to further our understanding of the power relations and dynamics between donors and beneficiaries and the implications unbalanced power relations have upon the overall idea and purpose of foreign aid or development aid in general.

Moreover, existing debates, in discussing 'surplus people' production, focus on aid providers as the main actors that influence that dynamics through which this production occurs. Yet, while this holds to be true, these actors (foreign aid providers) influence how local social sectors interact with and perceive each other, which is influenced by their preferential ties with donors and their own socio-economic and political interests. For instance, we saw how the PA political elite and the CSOs' leaders seek to achieve socio-economic advantages as part of their relationship with American and EU donors. Hamas as well built its own alliances with non-US and non-EU donors, such as Qatar, Turkey and Iran, which in many cases enabled the movement to achieve political gains at both local and international levels.

7.6 Why Foreign Aid Then?

Discussing foreign aid in the context of Gaza and Palestine, in general, should go beyond talking about the routine issues of aid dependency, aid effectiveness or development cooperation because, in doing so, donors or aid providers neglect the reality within which foreign aid is delivered and the environment within which development agencies operate. Accordingly, we should seriously analyse the feasibility and effectiveness of the current frameworks that guide aid delivery to the Palestinians. This is particularly important in the Gaza Strip due to the existing political reality of Hamas control and how aid delivery during this period deteriorated aspects of sovereignty over people's own living and the sovereignty of the institutions that serve them.

Investing aid in peace as a paradigm is no longer valid or doable since failure in achieving peace between Israel and the Palestinians has become more evident than ever. Plus, the current political realities both inside Israel and among Palestinians suggest it is impossible to achieve any progress in that regard. Meanwhile, there is a noticeable failure, or perhaps even negligence, in the purpose of maintaining aid delivery to the Palestinians under a failed peace paradigm. There is also a need to evaluate the actual contribution and impact of foreign aid on the Palestinian socio-economic development against the various limitations and conditionality that are associated with aid delivery. More importantly, there is a need to define the real and main beneficiary of foreign aid given to the Palestinians: Is it the Palestinians? Is it Israel? Or is it to support political stability in the region? It is important to find answers to these questions before we engage ourselves in investigating the impact of aid on either promoting peace between Israel and Palestine or contributing to Palestinians' socio-economic development. Otherwise, the only approach to evaluate any development initiatives that are directed towards the Palestinians, and of which foreign aid is the primary tool, is to situate it within a neo-colonialist framework. Because the only success foreign aid has achieved since the 1993 Oslo Accords is establishing the following: an unelected Palestinian national governing body that is now divided between Fatah and Hamas, a PA that is held accountable before the international community, Israel, the dis-satisfied Palestinian people and the anti-Oslo Palestinian parties for its own political failures and for the failures of both Israel and donors in this regard.

BIBLIOGRAPHY

Abdelnabi, N. 2012. *Economic and Social Implications of Palestinian Authority Budgets 2000–2010*. Gaza: Al-Azhar University.

Agamben, G. 1998. *Homo Sacer: Sovereign Power and Bare Life*. Stanford: Stanford University Press.

Alashqar, Y. 2015. 'Civil society in Gaza: Critical challenges to secular and nationalist civil society organizations'. *McGill Journal of Middle East Studies Blog*. Accessed April 2018. https://mjmes.wordpress.com/2014/05/06/article-7-2/.

Alhusseini, J. 2010. 'UNRWA and the refugees: A difficult but lasting marriage'. *Journal of Palestine Studies* 40(1): 6–26.

———. 2015. 'UNRWA's funding and the Palestine refugees' future'. Institute for Palestine Studies; Arabic version accessed June 2016. http://www.palestine-studies.org/sites/default/files/uploads/files/Jalal%20Husseini_0.pdf.

Alijla, A. 2014. 'The epic failure of Palestinian civil society'. Your Middle East. Accessed January 2016. http://www.yourmiddleeast.com/opinion/the-epic-failure-of-palestinian-civil-society_28094.

Almeghari, R. 2008. 'Gaza organizations caught in the crossfire'. Gaza: Electronic Intifada. Accessed May 2016. https://electronicintifada.net/content/gaza-organizations-caught-crossfire/7650.

Arnon, A., and Spivak, A. 1998. 'Economic aspects of the Oslo process'. *Palestine-Israel Journal* 5(3). Accessed December 2017. https://pij.org/articles/388.

Arnon, A., and Weinblatt, J. 2001. 'Sovereignty and economic development: The case of Israel and Palestine'. *The Economic Journal* 111(472): 291–308.

BADIL. 2005. Closing Protection Gaps: Handbook on Protection of Palestinian Refugees in States Signatories to the 1951 Refugee Convention: Badil Resource Center.

———. 2011. *Closing Protection Gaps: A Handbook on Protection of Palestinian Refugees in States Signatories to the 1951 Refugee Convention*. Bethlehem, Palestine: BADIL Resource Center for Palestinian Residency and Refugee Rights.

Balzacq, T. 2005. 'The three faces of securitization: Political agency, audience and context'. *European Journal of International Relations* 11(2): 171–201.

Barsalou, J. 2003. 'Missing the mark: Foreign aid to the Palestinians'. *Middle East Policy* 10(4): 48–56.

Bartholomeusz, L. 2009. 'The mandate of UNRWA at sixty'. *Refugee Survey Quarterly* 28(2–3): 452–74.

Bauman, Z. 2004. *Wasted Lives: Modernity and Its Outcasts*. Cambridge: Polity.

Bennis, P., and Cassidy, N. 1990. *From Stones to Statehood: The Palestinian Uprising*. London: Zed.

Bhungalia, L. 2010. 'A liminal territory: Gaza, executive discretion, and sanctions turned humanitarian'. *GeoJournal* 75(4): 347–57.

Biggs, S. D., and Neame, A. 1994. 'NGOs negotiating room for manoeuvre: Reflections concerning autonomy and accountability within the New Policy Agenda', 31–41. In Edwards, M., and Hulme, D. (eds), *Beyond the Magic Bullet: NGO Performance and Accountability in the Post-Cold War World*. Connecticut: Kumarian Press.

Bocco, R. 2009. 'UNRWA and the Palestinian refugees: a history within history'. *Refugee Survey Quarterly* 28(2–3): 229–52.

Brislin, R. W. 1970. 'Back-translation for cross-cultural research'. *Journal of Cross-Cultural Psychology* 1(3): 185–216.

Brown, N. J. 2003. *Palestinian Politics after the Oslo Accords: Resuming Arab Palestine*. London: University of California Press.

Brynen, R. 1996. 'Buying peace? A critical assessment of international aid to the West Bank and Gaza'. *Journal of Palestine Studies* 25(3):79–92.

———. 2000. *A Very Political Economy: Peacebuilding and Foreign Aid in the West Bank and Gaza*. Washington DC: US Institute of Peace Press.

———. 2005. 'Donor aid to Palestine: Attitudes, incentives, patronage and peace', 129–42. In Keating, M., Le More, A., and Lowe, R. (eds), *Aid, Diplomacy, and Facts on the Ground: The Case of Palestine*. London, UK: Chatham House.

B'Tselem. 2012. 'The Paris Protocol'. Jerusalem: B'Tselem. Accessed January 2014. http://www.btselem.org/freedom_of_movement/paris_protocol.

Buzan, B., and Wæver, O. 2009. 'Macrosecuritisation and security constellations: Reconsidering scale in securitisation theory'. Review of International Studies 35(2): 253–76.

Byman, D. 2010. 'How to handle Hamas: The perils of ignoring Gaza's leadership'. *Foreign Affairs* 89: 45–62.

Carmi, N. A. 1999. *OSLO: Before and After: The Status of Human Rights in the Occupied Territories*. Jerusalem: B'Tselem.

Challand, B. 2008. *Palestinian Civil Society: Foreign Donors and the Power to Promote and Exclude*. New York: Routledge.

Chinnery, H., Thompson, S. B., Noroozi, S., Dyer, B., and Rees, K. 2016. 'Questionnaire study to gain an insight into the manufacturing and fitting process of artificial eyes in children: An ocularist perspective'. *International Ophthalmology* 1(2):1–9.

Cohen, L., Manion, L., and Morrison, K. 2000. *Research Methods in Education*. London: RoutledgeFalmer.

Cowen, M., and Shenton, R. 1995. 'The invention of development', 27–43. In Crush, J. (ed), *Power of Development*. London: Routledge.

Cowen, M. P., and Shenton, R. W. 1996. *Doctrines of Development*. London and New York: Routledge.

Crush, J. (ed). 2006. *Power of Development*. London: Routledge.

Danewid, I. 2017. 'White innocence in the Black Mediterranean: Hospitality and the erasure of history'. *Third World Quarterly* 38(7): 1674–89.

Dean, M. 1999. *Governmentality: Power and Rule in Modern Society*. London: Sage.

Diwan, I., and Shaban R. 1999. *Development Under Adversity: The Palestinian Economy in Transition*. Washington DC: World Bank.

Duffield, M. 2001. 'Governing the borderlands: Decoding the power of aid'. *Disasters* 25(4): 308–20.

———. 2004. 'Carry on killing: Global governance, humanitarianism and terror'. *Danish Institute for International Studies Working Paper No. 23*. Copenhagen: Danish Institute of International Studies. Accessed 23 August 2018. http://www.diis.dk/sw8141.asp.

———. 2005. 'Social reconstruction: The reuniting of aid and politics'. *Development* 48(3): 16–24.

———. 2007. *Development, Security and Unending War: Governing the World of Peoples*. Cambridge: Polity.

———. 2011. *Human (In)security, Liberal Interventionism and Fortified Aid Compounds*. Theory Talks. Accessed March 2014.http://www.theory-talks.org/2011/07/theory-talk-41.html.

The Economist. 2005. 'Palestinians in Gaza: Will they sink or swim?' Accessed November 2014. http://www.economist.com/node/4423784.

Edwards, M. 1994. 'International non-governmental organizations, "good government" and the "new policy agenda": Lessons of experience at the programme level'. *Democratization* 1(2): 504–15.

Escobar, A. 1997. 'The making and unmaking of the Third World through development', 85–93. In Rahnema, M., and Bawtree, V. (eds), *The Post-Development Reader*. London: Zed Books.

Esteva, G. 1992. 'Development'. In Sachs, W. (ed.), *The Development Dictionary: A Guide to Knowledge as Power*. London: Zed Books.

Evans, B. 2010. 'Foucault's legacy: Security, war and violence in the 21st century'. *Security Dialogue* 41(4): 413–33.

Farsakh, L. 2000. 'The Palestinian economy and the Oslo "Peace Process"'. Accessed 3 November 2018. http://tari.org/index.php?option=com_content&view=article&id=9:the-palestinian-economy-and-the-oslo-peace-processq&catid=1:fact-sheets&Itemid=11.

De Feyter, S. (2011). 'Impact of international donors' new policy agenda on project collaboration between community-based women organizations and NGOs in the Kibera slums of Nairobi, Kenya'. *Afrika Focus* 24(1): 33–50.

Ferguson, J. 1994. *The Anti-Politics Machine: 'Development', Depoliticization, and Bureaucratic Power in Lesotho*. Minneapolis: University of Minnesota Press

———. 1997. 'Development bureaucratic power in Lesotho'. In Rahnema, M., and Bawtree, V. (eds), *The Post-Development Reader*. London: Zed Books.

Ferraro, V. 2008. 'Dependency theory: An introduction'. In Secondi, G. (ed.), *The Development Economics*. London: Routledge.

Fischer, S., Alonso-Gamo, P., and Von Allmen, U. E. 2001. 'Economic developments in the West Bank and Gaza since Oslo'. *The Economic Journal* 111(472): 254–75.

Foucault, M. 1972. *The Archaeology of Knowledge and the Discourse on Language*. New York: Pantheons Books.

———. 1972. *The Archaeology of Knowledge*. London: Routledge.

———. 1976. *The Will to Knowledge: The History of Sexuality Vol. I*. London: Penguin.

———. 1979. *Discipline and Punish*. New York: Vintage.

———. 1984. 'Right of death and power over life', 264. *The Foucault Reader*. New York: Pantheon Books.

Fowler, A. 1998. 'Authentic NGDO partnerships in the new policy agenda for international aid: dead end or light ahead?', *Development and Change* 29: 137–59.

Frank, A. G. 1966. *The Development of Underdevelopment*. Boston, MA: New England Free Press.

Gisha. 2010. *Three Years of Gaza Closure – By the Numbers*. Tel Aviv: Gisha. Accessed November 2014. http://gisha.org/press/702.

Goldenberg, S. 2008. *US Plotted to Overthrow Hamas after Election Victory*. *The Guardian*. Accessed November 2015. http://www.theguardian.com/world/2008/mar/04/usa.israelandthepalestinians .

Greig, A., Hulme, D., and Turner, M. 2007. *Challenging Global Inequality: Development Theory and Practice in the 21st Century*. Basingstoke: Palgrave Macmillan.

Gronemeyer, M. 1992. 'Helping'. In Sachs, W. (ed.), *The Development Dictionary: A Guide to Knowledge as Power*. London: Zed Books.

Haddad, T. 2016. *Palestine Ltd.: Neoliberalism and Nationalism in the Occupied Territory*. London: IB Tauris.

Hamdan, A. 2011. *Foreign Aid and the Molding of the Palestinian Space*. Ramallah: Bisan Center for Research and Development.

Hammami, R. 2000. 'Palestinian NGOs since Oslo: From NGO politics to social movements?' *Middle East Report* 214: 16–19, 27, 48.

Hanafi, S., and Tabar, L. 2002. *NGOs, Elite Formation and the Second Intifada*. Beirut: American University of Beirut. Accessed 27 September 2016. http://www.ism-italia.org/wp-content/uploads/ngos-elite-formation-and-the-second-intifada.pdf.

———. 2004. *Palestinian NGOs and the Second Intifada*. London: Human Practical Network. Accessed April 2016 http://odihpn.org/magazine/palestinian-ngos-and-the-second-intifada/.

———. 2005. 'The new Palestinian globalized elite'. *Jerusalem Quarterly* 24: 13–32.

Harvard. 2006. 'Population projections for socioeconomic development in the Gaza Strip'. *Program on Humanitarian Policy and Conflict Research*. Working Paper No. 1.

Hettne, B. 1995. *Development Theory and the Three Worlds: Towards an International Political Economy of Development*. Essex: Longman.

Howell, J. 2014. 'The securitisation of NGOs post-9/11'. *Conflict, Security & Development* 14(2): 151–79.

Howell, J., and Lind, J. 2009. *Counter-Terrorism, Aid and Civil Society: Before and After the War on Terror*. UK: Palgrave-Macmillan.

Hulme, D., and Edwards, M. (eds), 1995. *NGOs Performance and Accountability: Beyond the Magic Bullet*. Connecticut: Kumarian.

Hunter, F. R. 1993. *The Palestinian Uprising: A War by Other Means*. London: I.B. Tauris.

International Crisis Group 2006. 'Enter Hamas: The challenges of political integration' *Middle East Report* 49 (January): 1–41.

Kessler, V. 1999. 'Palestine's external trade performance under the Paris Protocol: Hopes and disillusions'. In Philippe, B., and Pissarides, C. (eds), *Evaluating the Paris Protocol: Economic Relations Between Israel and the Palestinian Territories*. Brussels: European Commission.

Khalidi, R. 2012. 'After the Arab Spring in Palestine: Contesting the Neoliberal Narrative of Palestinian National Liberation'. *Jadaliyya*. Accessed September 2015. http://www.jadaliyya.com/pages/index/4789/after-the-arab-spring-in-palestine_contesting-the-.

Khalidi, R., and Samour, S. 2011. 'Neoliberalism as liberation: The statehood program and the remaking of the Palestinian national movement'. *Journal of Palestine Studies* 40(2): 6–25

Khalidi, R., and Taghdisi-Rad, S. 2009. 'The economic dimensions of prolonged occupation: Continuity and change in Israeli policy towards the Palestinian economy'. *United Nations Conference on Trade and Development*. New York and Geneva: United Nations.

Kothari, U. 2005. 'Authority and expertise: The professionalisation of international development and the ordering of dissent'. *Antipode* 37(3): 425–46.

Krieger, H. L., and Horn, J. 2011. 'Israel's envoys to US, UN justify Gaza blockade'. *Jerusalem Post*. Accessed September 2016. http://www.jpost.com/Diplomacy-and-Politics/Israels-envoys-to-US-UN-justify-Gaza-blockade.

De Larrinaga, M., and Doucet, M. G. 2008. 'Sovereign power and the biopolitics of human security'. *Security Dialogue* 39(5): 517–37.

Lasensky, S. 2005. 'Chequebook diplomacy: The US, the Oslo process and the role of foreign aid', 41–58. In Keating, M., Le More, A., and Lowe, R. (eds), *Aid, Diplomacy, and Facts on the Ground: The Case of Palestine*. London: Chatham House.

Lasensky, S., and Grace, R. 2009. Dollars and Diplomacy: Foreign Aid and the Palestinian Question. Washington D.C.: United States Institute of Peace. Accessed 16 April 2018. https://www.usip.org/sites/default/files/palestinian_aid.pdf.

Lloyd, V., Gatherer, A., and Kalsy, S. 2006. 'Conducting qualitative interview research with people with expressive language difficulties'. *Qualitative Health Research* 16: 1386–1404.

Lozano-Neira, N., and Marchbank, J. 2016. 'Is she one of us? Intersecting identities and social research'. *Gender Identity and Research Relationships*. Bingley, UK: Emerald Group.

Lummis, D. 1992. 'Equality'. In Sachs, W. (ed.), *The Development Dictionary: A Guide to Knowledge as Power*. London: Zed Books.

Manheim, J., Rich, R., and Willnat, L. 2001. *Empirical Political Analysis: Research Methods in Political Science*. New York: Longman.

Manzo, K. 1991. 'Modernist discourse and the crisis of development theory'. *Studies in Comparative International Development* 26(2): 3–36.

Marsh, D., and Furlong, P. 2010. 'A skin not a sweater: Ontology and epistemology in political science'. In Marsh, D., and Stoker, G. (eds), *Theory and Methods in Political Science*. 3rd ed. Hampshire: Palgrave Macmillan.

McDowall, D. 1989. *Palestine and Israel: The Uprising and Beyond*. London: I.B. Tauris.

McMichael, P. 2011. *Development and Social Change: A Global Perspective*. London: Sage.

Mehmet, O. 1999. *Westernizing the Third World: The Eurocentricity of Economic Development Theories*. London: Routledge.

Mercy Corps. 2012. Performance Evaluation TOR. West Bank and Gaza. Accessed 3 January 2018. http://www.mercycorps.org/sites/default/files/pcap-performance_evalution_tor.pdf.

Merz, S. 2013. 'Reforming resistance: Neoliberalism and the co-option of civil society organisations in Palestine'. In Fisher, R. (ed.), *Managing Democracy, Managing Dissent*. London: Corporate Watch.

Miller, P., and Rose, N. 1990. 'Governing economic life'. *Economy and Society* 19(1): 1–31.

Milton-Edwards, B. 2008. 'The ascendance of political Islam: Hamas and consolidation in the Gaza Strip'. *Third World Quarterly* 29(8): 1585–99.

Moore, M. 2006. 'Good government: Introduction'. *IDS Bulletin* 37(4): 50–56.

Le More, A. 2005. 'Killing with kindness: Funding the demise of a Palestinian state'. *International Affairs* 81: 981–99.

———. 2008. *International Assistance to the Palestinians after Oslo: Political Guilt, Wasted Money*. Oxon: Routledge.

Morgenthau, H. 1962. 'A political theory of foreign aid'. *American Political Science Review* 56(2): 301–9.

Murad, N. L. 2007. 'Aid to Palestinians that would really help'. *HiPiC Conference*. Hiroshima: Hiroshima University

Nabulsi, K. 2005. 'The state-building project: What went wrong?' In Keating, M., Le More, A., and Lowe, R. (eds), *Aid, Diplomacy and Facts on the Ground: The Case of Palestine*. London, UK: Chatham House.

OCHA. 2017. 'Gaza Strip: Access and movement in 2016'. *Jerusalem OCHA*. https://www.ochaopt.org/content/gaza-strip-access-and-movement-2016.

Oppenheim, A. N. 2000. *Questionnaire Design, Interviewing and Attitude Measurement*. London, UK: Bloomsbury.

PASSIA. 2014. *Endless Injustice: Palestinian Refugees 66 Year On*. Jersusalem: PASSIA. Accessed August 2016. http://passia.org/media/filer_public/cc/b7/ccb7bc3c-d86e-416b-8fef-fa632aed67d1/refugees_2014.pdf.

PCBS. 2014. *Indicators*. Ramallah: Palestinian Central Bureau of Statistics. Accessed November 2014. http://www.pcbs.gov.ps/site/881/default.aspx.

———. 2015. 'Press Release of the Results of the Labour Force Survey'. http://www.pcbs.gov.ps/post.aspx?lang=en&ItemID=1397.

———. 2016. *Palestine Book for Annual Statistics*. Ramallah: PCBS. http://www.pcbs.gov.ps/Downloads/book2238.pdf.

Peabody, R. L., Hammond, S. W., Torcom, J., Brown, L. P., Thompson, C., and Kolodny, R. 1990. 'Interviewing political elites'. *PS: Political Science & Politics* 23(3): 451–55.

Pelham, N. 2011. 'Gaza's tunnel complex'. *Middle East Report*. http://www.merip.org/mer/mer261/gazas-tunnel-complex.

———. 2012. 'Gaza's tunnel phenomenon: The unintended dynamics of Israel's siege'. *Journal of Palestine Studies* 41(4), 6–31.

Peretz, D. 1977. 'Palestinian social stratification: The political implications'. *Journal of Palestine Studies* 7(1), 48–74.

Pieterse, J. N. 2010. *Development Theory*. London: Sage.

Plucknett, R. 2007. 'Updated anti-terrorism procedures: USAID/West Bank and Gaza'. https://www.usaid.gov/sites/default/files/documents/1883/2007-WBG-26.pdf.

PMA. 2015. *PMA Annual Reports*. Ramallah: Palestinian Monetary Authority. http://www.pma.ps/Default.aspx?tabid=509&language=en-US.

Portland Trust. 2010. *The Private Sector in Gaza*. Ramallah: The Portland Trust.

———. (ed.). 2012. *The Private Sector in the Gaza Strip*. Ramallah: Portland Trust. http://www.portlandtrust.org/sites/default/files/peb/feature_gaza_feb_2012.pdf.

———. 2013. 'Palestinian economic bulletin'. http://www.portlandtrust.org/sites/default/files/peb/issue84_september_2013_0.pdf.

Prusher, I. 1997. 'US doubts its role as main donor to Palestinians'. *The Christian Science Monitor*. Accessed November 2014. http://www.csmonitor.com/1997/0618/061897.intl.intl.3.html.

Pulu, T. B. 2013. 'Modern colonialism: Dialogues with Sefita Hao'uli, Kalafi Moala, and Melino Maka;. *Te Kaharoa* 6(1): 345–90.

Qarmout, T., and Beland, D. 2012. 'The politics of international aid to the Gaza Strip'. *Journal of Palestine Studies* 41(4): 32–47.

Quartet. 2006. *Quartet Statement*. Accessed March 2010. http://www.un.org/news/dh/infocus/middle_east/quartet-9may2006.htm.

Rabinow, P. 1984. *The Foucault Reader: An Introduction to Foucault's Thought*. London: Penguin Books.

Reuters. 2015. 'Palestinians want world pressure on Israel after Netanyahu win'. Accessed 27 September 2020. http://ara.reuters.com/article/topNews/idARACAE78K01K20110921.

Roberts, N. 2005. 'Hard lessons from Oslo: Foreign aid and the mistakes of the 1990s'. In Keating, M., Le More, A., and Lowe, R. (eds), *Aid Diplomacy and Facts on the Ground*. London: Chatham House.

Robinson, M. 1993. 'Governance, democracy and conditionality: NGOs and the new policy agenda'. In Klayton, A. (ed.), *Governance, Democracy and Conditionality: What Role for NGOs?* Oxford: INTRAC.

Rosen, S. 2012. 'Kuwait expels thousands of Palestinians'. *Middle East Quarterly* 19. http://www.meforum.org/3391/kuwait-expels-palestinians.

Roy, S. 1987. 'The Gaza Strip: A case of economic de-development'. *Journal of Palestine Studies* 17(1): 56–88.

———. 1994. '"The seed of chaos, and of night"': The Gaza Strip after the Oslo agreement'. *Journal of Palestine Studies* 23(3): 85–98.

———. 1995. *The Gaza Strip: The Political Economy of De-development*. Washington, DC: Institute for Palestine Studies.

———. 1999. 'De-development revisited: Palestinian economy and society since Oslo'. *Journal of Palestine Studies* 28(3): 64–82.

———. 2001a. 'Civil society in the Gaza Strip: Obstacles to social reconstruction'. In Norton, A. (ed.) , *Civil Society in the Middle East*. New York: Brill.

———. 2001b. 'Palestinian society and economy: The continued denial of possibility'. *Journal of Palestine Studies* 30(4), 5–20.

———. 2002. 'Ending the Palestinian economy'. *Middle East Policy* 9(4): 122–65.

———. 2005. 'Praying with Their Eyes Closed: Reflections on the Disengagement from Gaza'. *Journal of Palestine Studies* 64: 70.

———. 2011. *Hamas and Civil Society in Gaza: Engaging the Islamist Social Sector*. Oxford, Princeton University Press.

———. 2012. 'A deliberate cruelty: Rendering Gaza unviable'. *Edward Said Memorial Lecture – Video*. Washington, DC: The Palestine Center.

———. 2013. *Hamas and Civil Society in Gaza: Engaging the Islamist Social Sector*. Princeton, NJ: Princeton University Press.

———. 2007. *Failing Peace: Gaza and the Palestinian-Israeli Conflict*. London: Pluto Press.

Sachs, W. 1992. *The Development Dictionary: A Guide to Knowledge as Power*. London: Zed Books.

Sadiq, N. 2012. 'Civil society organizations: Oslo as a turning point in their work among the masses'. *Palestine-Israel Journal of Politics, Economics, and Culture* 18(2/3): 42–45.

Said, E. 1979. *Orientalism*. New York: Vintage.

Samhouri, H. 2006. 'Gaza economic predicament one year after disengagement: What went wrong'. *Crown Centre for Middle East Studies*.

Sayigh, Y. 2010. 'Hamas rule in Gaza: Three years on'. *Middle East Brief No. 41, Crown Center for Middle East Studies*. Accessed 2 February 2017. https://www.brandeis.edu/crown/publications/middle-east-briefs/pdfs/1-100/meb41.pdf.

Schulz, M. 2013. 'Palestinian civil society'. In Peters, J., and Newman, D. (eds), *The Routledge Handbook on the Israeli-Palestinian Conflict*. London: Routledge.

Schumacher, E. F. 1989. *Small Is beautiful: A Study of Economics as if People Mattered*. London: Penguin.

Selby, J. 2011. 'The political economy of peace processes'. *Whose Peace: Critical Perspectives on the Political Economy of Peacebuilding*. Basingstoke: Palgrave Macmillan.

Sen, A. 1999. *Development as freedom*. Oxford, UK: Oxford University Press.

Shaban, O. 2013. *Palestinian Authority Faces Crisis Over Salaries*. Accessed December 2015. http://www.al-monitor.com/pulse/originals/2013/02/palestinian-authority-economic-crisis.html.

Shanin, T. 1997. 'The idea of progress'. In Rahnema, M., and Bawtree, V. (eds), *The Post-development Reader*. London: Zed Books.

Shaoul, J. 2010. 'WikiLeaks confirms Fatah sought Israeli-US support for attack on Hamas'. Accessed November 2015. https://www.wsws.org/en/articles/2010/12/gaza-d29.html.

Sharon, A. 2005. *Sharon's Speech on Gaza Pullout.* London: BBC. Accessed January 2014. http://news.bbc.co.uk/1/hi/world/middle_east/4154798.stm.

Shiqaqi, K. 2006. 'The Palestinian elections: Sweeping victory, uncertain mandate'. *Journal of Democracy* 17(3): 116–30.

Sperber, A. D. 2004. 'Translation and validation of study instruments for cross-cultural research'. *Gastroenterology* 126(1): S124–28.

Stephens, N. 2007. 'Collecting data from elites and ultra elites: Telephone and face-to-face interviews with macroeconomists'. *Qualitative Research* 7(2), 203–16.

Strand, T. 2014. 'Tightening the noose: The institutionalized impoverishment of Gaza, 2005–2010'. *Journal of Palestine Studies* 43(2), 6–23.

Sultana, F. 2007. 'Reflexivity, positionality and participatory ethics: Negotiating fieldwork dilemmas in international research'. *ACME* 6(3), 374–85.

Tabar, L., Hanafi, S. 2005. 'The Intifada and the aid industry: The impact of the new liberal agenda on the Palestinian NGOs'. *Comparative Studies of South Asia, Africa and the Middle East* 23(1–2), 205–14.

Tartir, A. 2012. 'Aid and development in Palestine: Anything, but linear relationship. Can aid contribute to development?' *Conferences & Public Events Module.* Ibrahim Abu-Lughd Institute of International Studies, Birzeit University

Tongco, M. D. C. 2007. 'Purposive sampling as a tool for informant selection'. *Ethnobotany Research & Applications* 5: 147–58.

Truman, H. 1949. 'Inaugural address'. Accessed 20 December 2013. http://www.presidency.ucsb.edu/ws/?pid=13282.

Turner, M. 2009. 'The power of "shock and awe": The Palestinian Authority and the road to reform'. *International Peacekeeping* 16(4), 562–77.

———. 2011. 'Creating "partners for peace": The Palestinian Authority and the International Statebuilding Agenda'. *Journal of Intervention and Statebuilding* 5 (1): 1–21.

———. 2012. 'Completing the circle: Peacebuilding as colonial practice in the occupied Palestinian territory'. *International Peacekeeping* 19(4): 492–507.

———. 2014. 'The political economy of Western aid in the occupied Palestinian territory since 1993'. In Turner, M., and Shweiki, O. (eds), *Decolonizing Palestinian Political Economy: De-development and Beyond.* London: Palgrave Macmillan.

UNCTAD. 1988. *Recent Economic Developments in the Occupied Palestinian Territories, with Special Reference to the External Trade Sector.* Geneva: UNCTAD Secretariat.

———. 1989. *Recent Economic Developments in the Occupied Palestinian Territory.* Geneva: UNCTAD Secretariat.

———. 1991. *Recent Economic Developments in the Occupied Palestinian Territory. Assistance to the Palestinian People.* Geneva: UNCTAD Secretariat.

———. 1993. *Developments in the Economy of the Occupied Palestinian Territory.* Geneva: UNCTAD Secretariat.

———. 2001. *Report on UNCTAD's Assistance to the Palestinian People.* Geneva: UNCTAD Secretariat.

UNDP. 2010. *One Year After: Gaza Early Recovery and Reconstruction Needs Assessment.* Jerusalem: UNDP.

UNISPAL. 2009. 'The humanitarian impact of two years of blockade on the Gaza Strip'. https://unispal.un.org/DPA/DPR/unispal.nsf/0/0DFF75BB11E69292852576120 04B4859.

United Nations. 2012. *Gaza in 2020: A liveable Place?* Palestinian Occupied Territory. United Nations.

UNRWA. 1949. *General Assembly Resolution 302*. New York: UNRWA. Accessed July 2016. http://www.unrwa.org/content/general-assembly-resolution-302.

———. 1982. *Brief History 1950–1982*. Vienna, UNRWA.

———. 2013. 'Food and cash assistance in Gaza'. http://www.unrwa.org/userfiles/file/publications/gaza/Food%20and%20Cash%20Assistance%20in%20Gaza.pdf.

———. 2014a. 'UNRWA situation report'. https://www.unrwa.org/newsroom/emergency-reports/gaza-situation-report-27: UNRWA.

———. 2014b. 'Where we work'. Accessed July 2016. http://www.unrwa.org/where-we-work/gaza-strip.

———. 2016a. *Donor Charts*. New York: UNRWA. Accessed August 2016. http://www.unrwa.org/how-you-can-help/government-partners/funding-trends/donor-charts.

———. 2016b. 'Gaza situation report 159'. Accessed September 2016. http://www.unrwa.org/newsroom/emergency-reports/gaza-situation-report-159.

———. 2016c. 'Health in the Gaza Strip'. Accessed September 2016.http://www.unrwa.org/activity/health-gaza-strip.

———. 2016d. 'Palestine refugees'. Accessed July 2016. http://www.unrwa.org/palestine-refugees.

———. 2016e. 'RSS in the Gaza Strip'. Accessed July 2016. http://www.unrwa.org/activity/rss-gaza-strip.

———. 2016f. 'Working at UNRWA'. Accessed July 2016. http://www.unrwa.org/careers/working-unrwa.

USAID. 2012. 'Foreign assistance fast facts: FY2011'. Accessed 19 February 2013. http://gbk.eads.usaidallnet.gov/data/fast-facts.html.

US Department of States. 2014. *Framework for Cooperation Between the United Nations Relief and Works Agency for Palestine Refugees in the Near East and the Government of the United States of America for 2015*. Washington: US Department of States. http://www.state.gov/j/prm/releases/frameworknew/234468.htm.

Vromen, A. 2010. 'Debating methods: Rediscovering qualitative approaches', 249–66. In Marsh, D., and Stoker, G. (eds), *Theory and Methods in Political Science*. 2nd ed. Hampshire: Palgrave Macmillan.

Watt, N., and Sherwood, H. 2010. 'David Cameron: Israeli blockade has turned Gaza into a "prison camp"'. *The Guardian*, 17.

Weissglass, D. 2007. 'An embargo on Gaza'. *Jerusalem Yedi'ot Aharonot*. Accessed November 2014. http://www.ynetnews.com/articles/0,7340,L-3446557,00.html.

Weisman, S. 2006. 'Rice admits U.S. underestimated Hamas strength'. *New York Times*. Accessed November 2014. http://www.nytimes.com/2006/01/30/international/middleeast/30diplo.html?pagewanted=print&_r=0.

WFP, FAO & PCBS. 2010. *Socio-Economic and Food Security Survey: West Bank and Gaza Strip*. Occupied Palestinian Territory: WFP.

WikiLeaks. 2011a. 'FM Livni seeks new mechanism for delivering aid to Palestinians. Accessed November 2014. http://wikileaks.redfoxcenter.org/cable/2006/04/06TELAVIV1318.html.

———. 2011b. 'Israeli MOD's Amos Giladon Gaza–West Bank crossings, Suleiman visit and Iran'. Accessed November 2014. http://wikileaks.org/cable/2006/03/06TELAVIV991.html#.

Wildeman, J., and Tartir, A. 2013. 'Can Oslo's failed aid model be laid to rest?'. Accessed January 2014. http://al-shabaka.org/sites/default/files/TartirWildeman_PolicyBrief_En_Sep_2013.pdf.

Willis, K. 2011. *Theories and Practices of Development*. London, Routledge.

Wilson, N., and McClean, S. I. 1994. *Questionnaire Design: A Practical Introduction*. Lincoln, UK: University of Ulster Coleraine.

World Bank. 2004. *Stagnation of Revival? Israeli Disengagement and Palestinian Economic Prospects*. Washington, DC: World Bank.

———. 2015. 'Economic monitoring report to the ad hoc Liaison Committee'. http://documents.worldbank.org/curated/en/563181468182960504/pdf/96601-REVISED-WP-Box391464B-AHLC-May-21-Book-fix-footnotes.pdf.

World Bank and PCBS. 2003. *Poverty in the West Bank and Gaza after Three Years of Economic Crisis*. Washington, DC: World Bank.

Zagha, A., and Zomlot, H. 2004. 'Israel and the Palestinian economy: Integration or containment?', 130–50. In Amundsen, I., Giacaman, G., and Khan, M. H. (eds), *State Formation in Palestine: Viability and Governance during a Social Transformation*. London: Routledge.

Zanotti, J. 2013. *U.S. Foreign Aid to the Palestinians*. Washington: Congressional Research Service.

———. 2016. 'U.S. foreign aid to the Palestinians'. Congressional Research Service. https://fas.org/sgp/crs/mideast/RS22967.pdf.

Ziai, A. 2011. 'Some reflections on the concept of "development"', ZEF Working Paper Series 81, Centre for Development Research, University of Bonn.

INDEX

www.ingramcontent.com/pod-product-compliance
Lightning Source LLC
Chambersburg PA
CBHW022356280326
41935CB00007B/207